# THE

# HARVARD MEDICAL

# SCHOOL GUIDE TO

# OVERCOMING

# THYROID PROBLEMS

## JEFFREY R. GARBER, M.D.

### WITH SANDRA SARDELLA WHITE

**McGraw·Hill**

New York   Chicago   San Francisco   Lisbon   London   Madrid   Mexico City
Milan   New Delhi   San Juan   Seoul   Singapore   Sydney   Toronto

**Library of Congress Cataloging-in-Publication Data**

Garber, Jeffrey R.
    The Harvard Medical School guide to overcoming thyroid problems / Jeffrey R. Garber
with Sandra Sardella White.
       p.    cm.
    ISBN 0-07-144471-8
    1. Thyroid gland—Diseases—Popular works.    I. Title: Guide to overcoming thyroid
problems.    II. Sardella White, Sandra.    III. Title.

    RC655.G26    2005
    616.4'4—dc22                                   2005000902

*For those seeking information about thyroid disorders.*
*In memory of Aaron, Mae, and Judah.*
*—Jeffrey R. Garber*

*In memory of Carlo M. Sardella, a gifted writer and newsman*
*whose colorful presence is greatly missed.*
*—Sandra Sardella White*

1 2 3 4 5 6 7 8 9 0   DOC/DOC   0 9 8 7 6 5

ISBN 0-07-144471-8

Interior design by Think Design Group, LLC
Artwork on pages 2, 86, 101, 190 by Scott Leighton; pages 4, 22, 23, 52, 53 by Joel Harris; pages
8, 80, 100 from Custom Medical Stock Photography; page 143 courtesy of Colin McArdle; pages
144–146 provided by Helen H. Wang, M.D., Dr.P.H., Associate Professor of Pathology, Harvard
Medical School, and Director of Cytopathology, Beth Israel Deaconess Medical Center

McGraw-Hill books are available at special quantity discounts to use as premiums and sales
promotions, or for use in corporate training programs. For more information, please write to
the Director of Special Sales, Professional Publishing, McGraw-Hill, Two Penn Plaza, New York,
NY 10121-2298. Or contact your local bookstore.

The information contained in this book is intended to provide helpful and informative material
on the subject addressed. It is not intended to serve as a replacement for professional medical
advice. Any use of the information in this book is at the reader's discretion. The author, the
publisher, and the President and Fellows of Harvard College specifically disclaim any and all
liability arising directly or indirectly from the use or application of any information contained in
this book. A health-care professional should be consulted regarding your specific situation.

This book is printed on acid-free paper.

# Contents

# Acknowledgments

Throughout the creation of this book, from its inception through its many drafts, production, and publication, many people helped to enrich its pages.

I would like to especially thank Sandy White for her extraordinary focus, timeliness, and wonderful writing. I am particularly grateful for Sandy's journalistic skill, which was the key to capturing the experiences of patients and the views of experts that contributed immensely to the value of our collaborative effort. I would also like to thank editors Nancy Ferrari and Kathleen Cahill Allison of Harvard Health Publications and Judith McCarthy of McGraw-Hill for their invaluable assistance.

I also want to thank the many patients I have had the privilege to participate in the care of, for the lessons they have taught me about overcoming thyroid conditions. Special thanks to those who graciously agreed to be interviewed for this book so that others could also learn from their experiences.

I am in debt to many specialists who offered their expertise without hesitation. Many thanks to Rebecca S. Bahn, M.D., of the Mayo Clinic Endocrinology Division; Brian M. Casey, M.D., of the University of Texas Southwestern Medical Center Obstetrics and Gynecology Division; James Connolly, M.D., Kevin Donohoe, M.D., Colin McArdle, M.D., J. Anthony Parker, M.D., Ph.D., and Helen H. Wang, M.D., Dr.P.H., colleagues in the Beth Israel Deaconess Medical Center departments of anatomic pathology, cytopathology, radiology, and nuclear medicine; John Kukora, M.D., President of the American Association of Endocrine Surgeons; Stephanie Lee, M.D., Ph.D., and Elizabeth N.

Pearce, M.D., M.Sc., colleagues in the endocrine divisions of Harvard Vanguard Medical Associates and Boston Medical Center; Marvin Mitchell, M.D., Emeritus Director of the New England Newborn Screening Program; Yolanda Oertel, M.D., of the Washington Hospital Center Washington Cancer Institute; Steven I. Sherman, M.D., of the Department of Endocrine Neoplasia and Hormonal Disorders, M. D. Anderson Cancer Center.

I would like to thank William Kang and Jill Susarrey of Harvard Vanguard Medical Associates Endocrine Division for their help with the countless tasks that led to the timely completion of this book.

Thanks to my mother-in-law, Lillian, for her interest, and my wife, Sheri, and sons, Ben and Solly, for their enthusiasm and encouragement.

—JRG

I would like to thank Kay Cahill Allison, my mentor, and Jeff Garber, for this incredible learning experience. It was a privilege to work with a physician who is so well regarded by so many patients. For her insights, I want to thank my close friend Carmen Kenrich, who beat thyroid cancer. Thanks also to my daughters, Samantha, Allyson, and Jessica, for their patience and to my husband, Rob, for always encouraging me to go for it.

—SSW

# Introduction

Your thyroid gland is like one of those auto parts you never heard of until your car breaks down. It gets little attention until it wreaks havoc on all aspects of your life.

Your thyroid is so undervalued that you are in good company if you don't understand its basic function or how important it is to your health. You wouldn't be alone to learn that your most vital organs rely on it to function properly. Instead, a malfunctioning thyroid has garnered a reputation for being responsible for obesity. What most people do not know is that weight changes, a symptom of thyroid disease, are typically minimal and pale in comparison to the serious medical consequences of an underlying thyroid condition, such as a racing heart, high blood pressure, congestive heart failure, dementia, and severe depression. Untreated thyroid problems may also lead to infertility. In babies, thyroid problems can cause mental retardation.

If you never knew your thyroid was so important, it's probably because its work is done behind the scenes. It discreetly influences every bodily function without taking much credit. It does this by producing hormones that oversee your metabolism and set the pace of how efficiently every cell in your body functions, so its grasp engulfs your entire being. That is why if something is wrong with your thyroid, it can affect almost everything you do. If your thyroid is underactive you can become exhausted, cold all of the time, and depressed as well as develop dry skin, hair loss, constipation, a low pulse, and more—all at the same time. An underactive thyroid, known as hypothyroidism, affects more than 9.5 million people, mostly women.

If your thyroid is overproducing hormone, you may experience a range of different problems. You might feel anxious and out of breath, sweat intolerably, and feel your heart flutter. All the while, you may be questioning what, if anything, is wrong with you.

Most people learn about their hypothyroidism in the same manner as Marie, a forty-year-old travel editor, did. She thought her problems were all in her head, even though her mood and outlook on life had never been so low. She became so exhausted all the time that she continually had to will herself to get up from the couch. She began crying periodically for no apparent reason. She gained some weight, but she hardly ever felt hungry. And oddly enough, her hair was coming out in clumps every day—in the shower, on her hairbrush, and on her pillow. It was the hair loss that raised the red flag and prompted her to see a doctor. The first doctor she visited suggested that she try the popular hair-loss treatment Rogaine. It wasn't until she got a second opinion that she was diagnosed with hypothyroidism and successfully treated.

Jerry, a fifty-year-old experienced mountain climber and runner, had always been in excellent shape for his age. His first indication that something was wrong was when his pulse seemed abnormally high after exercising, but he let it go. Then slowly, over the course of the year, he started piecing together symptoms that didn't concern him until a routine mountain climb left him gasping for air. It turns out he is one of 2.6 million people in the United States with hyperthyroidism: a condition that, like hypothyroidism, can have life-threatening consequences if left untreated.

Thyroid diseases are easily diagnosed with a simple blood test and easily treated. The advent of more sensitive blood tests in recent years has lead to more and more diagnoses of these conditions. Yet failure to recognize the vague symptoms of thyroid problems is to blame for why many people are believed to be suffering needlessly.

Thyroid disease is too often missed in primary care doctors' offices throughout the country. While some doctors check thyroid function periodically, there is widespread debate over the cost-effectiveness of routine screening for thyroid disease. Thus, many doctors do not check it, even when certain vague signs and symptoms in their patients suggest that they should. In fact, it is not uncommon for someone to be treated for depression or for high cholesterol when an underlying thyroid disease is causing the problem. Pregnancy is a common trigger for thyroid disease, and yet many women who may be at risk are not tested for it.

In addition to more than twelve million people who suffer from hypothyroidism and hyperthyroidism, more than twenty thousand people are diagnosed annually with thyroid cancer in the United States. While most causes of thyroid cancer are not well understood, development of cancerous thyroid lumps, called nodules, has been linked to exposure to certain forms of radiation during childhood through a type of X-ray used as treatment during the 1940s and 1950s.

A National Cancer Institute study shows that some Americans who were children during the 1950s may be at an increased risk for thyroid cancer due to exposure to fallout from atomic weapons testing done in the United States around this time. Luckily, most common forms of thyroid cancer are slow growing and easily treated. Sometimes, however, more aggressive types can spread to vital organs and become difficult to control.

Information is power. The purpose of this book is to arm you with the most up-to-date, medically accurate information on a range of thyroid topics, enabling you to overcome your thyroid condition. It will help you to recognize the confounding symptoms of thyroid diseases and their risk factors, including thyroid cancer.

This book can also be used as a guide to help explain some misconceptions about your condition that you may be confused about. It offers the latest information on the treatments and insights to controversial topics, such as whether mild hypothyroidism ought to be treated and whether alternative therapies, such as desiccated animal thyroid glands or drugs that combine T3 and T4, are right for you.

If you have a thyroid problem and plan to become pregnant, the section on pregnancy is a guide to help ensure your optimal health during this special time in your life. This section will also help you identify signs and symptoms of thyroid diseases that may emerge during and after pregnancy and, if you have a healthy thyroid gland, offers you guidelines on how to protect you and your baby from hypothyroidism. If you are already a parent, the section on childhood thyroid disease will help you recognize thyroid conditions and offer insights on special treatment concerns for children.

Overcoming a thyroid disease is very attainable. Treatment typically involves a lifetime commitment that, over the long haul, may seem effortless. If you follow a few simple guidelines, outlined in this book, you can live a highly active, completely normal life.

# CHAPTER 1

# Your Thyroid Gland

For a small gland, your thyroid has a lot of responsibility. Behind every beat that your heart makes, every breath that you take, and every surge of energy that you feel, your thyroid plays a role. Yet, unless you've ever been diagnosed with a thyroid problem, chances are you're not entirely sure what your thyroid is, what it does, and where exactly it is.

The thyroid is tiny, weighing less than an ounce, and it is shaped like a butterfly. When functioning normally, it perches unobtrusively with its wings wrapped around the front of your windpipe, below your voice box, or larynx (see Figure 1.1). Its slight size could easily fool you into underestimating its importance to your health. Yet this gland controls the pace at which every cell, tissue, and organ in your body functions, from your muscles, bones, and skin to your digestive tract, brain, heart, and more. It does this primarily by secreting hormones that control how fast and efficiently cells convert nutrients into energy—a chemical activity known as metabolism—which enables the cells that make up all of your body tissues to perform their functions.

## How Your Thyroid Gland Works

Think of your thyroid as a car engine that sets the pace at which your body operates. An engine produces the required amount of

**FIGURE 1.1** Anatomy of Your Thyroid

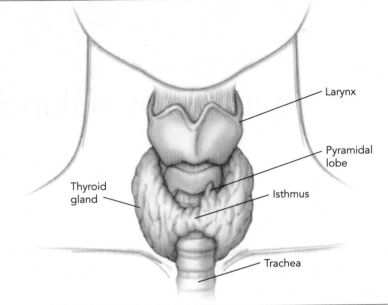

*Your small thyroid gland sits just below your larynx.*

energy for a car to move at a certain speed. In the same way, your thyroid gland manufactures enough thyroid hormone to prompt your cells to perform a function at a certain rate.

Just as a car can't produce energy without gas, your thyroid needs fuel to produce thyroid hormone. This fuel is iodine. Iodine comes from your diet and is found in iodized table salt, seafood, bread, and milk. Your thyroid extracts this necessary ingredient from your bloodstream and uses it to make two kinds of thyroid hormone: *thyroxine*, also called T4 because it contains four iodine atoms, and *triiodothyronine*, or T3, which contains three iodine atoms. T3 is made from T4 when one atom is removed, a conversion that occurs mostly outside the thyroid in organs and tissues where T3 is used the most, such as the liver, the kidneys, and the brain.

Once T4 is produced, it is stored within the thyroid's vast number of microscopic follicles. Some T3 is also produced and stored in the thyroid. When your body needs thyroid hormone,

## Fast Fact: What Is Metabolism?

Metabolism is the chemical activity by which cells convert nutrients into energy. Thyroid hormone sets the pace of metabolism. During metabolism, energy is released from the carbohydrates, proteins, fats, and other nutrients that you eat. The metabolic process generates heat, carbon dioxide, water, and waste products. The energy created is used to carry out essential chemical transformations that empower your body tissues to function properly. Metabolism affects your body temperature, body weight, energy level, muscle strength, psychological health, fertility, and more.

it is secreted into your bloodstream in quantities set to meet the metabolic needs of your cells. The hormone easily slips into the cells in need and attaches to special receptors located in the cells' nuclei.

Your car engine produces energy, but you tell it how fast to go by stepping on the accelerator. The thyroid also needs some direction; it gets this from your pituitary gland, which is located at the base of your brain. No larger than a pea, the pituitary gland is sometimes known as the "master gland" because it controls the functions of the thyroid and the other glands that make up the endocrine system. Your pituitary gland sends messages to your thyroid gland, telling it how much thyroid hormone to make. These messages come in the form of *thyroid-stimulating hormone* (TSH). TSH levels in your bloodstream rise or fall depending on whether enough thyroid hormone is produced to meet your body's needs. Higher levels of TSH prompt the thyroid to produce more thyroid hormone. Conversely, low TSH levels signal the thyroid to slow down production (see Figure 1.2).

The pituitary gland gets its information in several ways. It is able to read and respond directly to the amounts of T4 circulating in the blood, but it also responds to the hypothalamus, which is a section of the brain that releases its own hormone, *thyrotropin-*

**FIGURE 1.2** Normal Thyroid

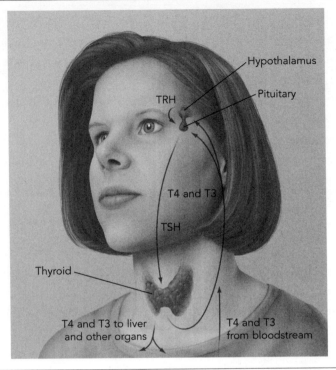

*Normally, the hypothalamus sends a signal in the form of thyrotropin-releasing hormone (TRH) that enables the pituitary gland to secrete thyroid-stimulating hormone (TSH). In response, the thyroid gland releases T4 and a small amount of T3, which travel to the liver and other organs, where T4 is converted to T3 and enters the bloodstream. Like a heating system with a thermostat at a constant temperature, a normally functioning thyroid operates at a steady pace without much variation in hormone levels.*

*releasing hormone* (TRH). TRH stimulates TSH production in the pituitary gland. This network of communication between the hypothalamus, the pituitary gland, and the thyroid gland is referred to as the hypothalamic–pituitary–thyroid axis (HPT axis).

## When Things Go Wrong

The HPT axis is a highly efficient network of communication. Normally, the thyroid doles out just the right amount of hormone to keep your body running smoothly. TSH levels remain fairly constant, yet they respond to the slightest changes in T4 levels and vice versa. But even the best networks are subject to interference.

When such outside influences as disease, damage to the thyroid, or certain medicines break down communication, your thyroid might not produce enough hormone. This would slow down all of your body's functions, a condition known as *hypothyroidism*, or underactive thyroid. Your thyroid could also produce too much hormone, sending your systems into overdrive, a condition known as *hyperthyroidism*, or overactive thyroid. These two conditions are most often features of an underlying thyroid disease.

When considering thyroid disease, doctors ask two main questions: First, is the thyroid gland inappropriately producing an abnormal amount of thyroid hormone? And second, is there a structural change in the thyroid, such as a lump—known as a nodule—or an enlargement—known as a goiter? (See Table 1.1.) Though one of these characteristics does not necessarily imply that the other is present, many thyroid disorders display both.

## Out of Gas

Sometimes the thyroid can't meet your body's demands for thyroid hormone, even though TSH levels increase. As your body slows down, you may feel cold, tired, and even depressed. You may gain weight, even though you're eating less.

There could be a number of reasons why your thyroid is not performing well. For example, if your body isn't getting enough iodine, your thyroid can't make enough thyroid hormone, but it will try to respond to rising TSH levels by working harder and harder anyway. This can cause your thyroid to become enlarged and develop into a goiter that looks like a protrusion or large swelling in your neck. Goiters used to be common, but they have become much less common in developed countries because of iodine-fortified foods.

In other cases, your thyroid comes under attack by your body's own immune system. Normally, substances called antibodies protect you from dangerous bacteria and viruses. But in this condition, known as *Hashimoto's thyroiditis*, your antibodies mistake

**TABLE 1.1** Thyroid Disorders at a Glance

| Disorder | Goiter | Nodules | Hypo-thyroidism | Hyper-thyroidism | Comment |
|---|---|---|---|---|---|
| Hashimoto's Thyroiditis | Sometimes | No; may be difficult to distinguish from nodular thyroid disease | Yes | No | Most common cause of hypo-thyroidism in the United States |
| Graves' Disease | Usually | No | No | Yes | Most common cause of hyper-thyroidism in the United States |
| Thyroiditis (silent, postpartum, subacute) | Often | No | Yes | Yes | Progression from hyperthy-roidism to hypothyroidism to resolution is typical |
| Iodine Deficiency | Yes | No, but may develop over a long period of time | Yes | No | Leading cause of hypothyroid-ism worldwide but uncommon in nonimmigrant U.S. population |
| Solitary Toxic Adenoma | Yes | Yes | No | Yes | The goiter (enlargement) is due to the adenoma (a benign tumor) |
| Simple Goiter | Yes | No | No | No | Thyroid enlarge-ment with no known cause; thyroid function is normal |
| Multinodular Goiter | Yes | Yes | No | No | May evolve into a toxic multi-nodular goiter (see below) |
| Toxic Multinodular Goiter | Yes | Yes | No | Yes | A frequent cause of hyper-thyroidism in older people |

your thyroid for a foreign invader. Hashimoto's thyroiditis involves the presence of two types of antibodies called *antithyroid peroxidase* (anti-TPO) and *antithyroglobulin* (anti-Tg) antibodies. These antibodies play a role in the destruction of the thyroid by the immune system. Over time, your defenseless thyroid, inflamed and scarred, surrenders and fails. Ailments like Hashimoto's thy-

## Fast Fact: Thyroiditis

Thyroiditis is a term for any condition involving thyroid inflammation and malfunction. Hashimoto's thyroiditis, the most common cause of hypothyroidism in the United States, is caused by abnormal antibodies. Other forms of thyroiditis are usually temporary and cause the thyroid to leak excessive amounts of hormone before it crashes into a state of hypothyroidism.

roiditis that result from an abnormal immune response are called autoimmune diseases. Hashimoto's thyroiditis is but one form of thyroiditis—an inflammation of the thyroid—that causes hypothyroidism. Other forms of thyroiditis are discussed below.

### Revved Up

Sometimes your thyroid keeps churning out more thyroid hormone, even when your pituitary gland completely shuts down TSH production, a clear signal that your body has had enough. Yet the thyroid appears oblivious to the lack of signals and continues to produce too much, pushing your metabolism into overdrive and speeding up your body's processes. This is hyperthyroidism. If you're hyperthyroid, your pulse may be racing, you feel irritable and overheated, and you have trouble sleeping. You may lose weight in spite of a good appetite and experience anxiety and nervousness. As with hypothyroidism, you may develop a goiter; in this case, your thyroid enlarges because your thyroid is working so hard overproducing thyroid hormone (see Figure 1.3).

A *toxic multinodular goiter* is to blame for hyperthyroidism in many people over sixty years old. This occurs when the thyroid enlarges and develops nodules, which are essentially lumps of thyroid cells that form as part of the thyroid. Nodules may develop on the outer surface of the gland where the doctor can feel them during an examination. If they develop inside the gland, however, they may not be apparent to the touch. Nodules throw off communication between the thyroid and the pituitary gland because

**FIGURE 1.3** A Goiter

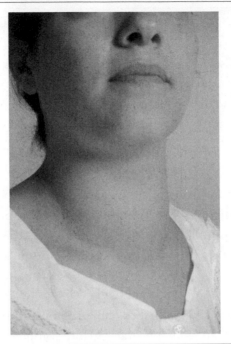

*When a diseased thyroid enlarges, it's known as a goiter.*

they independently produce thyroid hormone and do not depend on TSH to produce hormone.

A type of single nodule, called a *solitary toxic adenoma*, causes hyperthyroidism in the same way—by producing thyroid hormone at its own whim, regardless of the messages from the pituitary gland.

Not all nodules cause thyroid imbalance. There are different kinds of single nodules that can range from the size of a pea, or even smaller, to the size of a plum, or even bigger. Most are completely harmless and don't affect thyroid function in the least. These include fluid-containing nodules called cysts and adenomas, which are solid but equally harmless. A very small percentage of nodules are cancerous. Cancerous nodules do not directly affect thyroid function and therefore do not cause an overactive or underactive thyroid.

Another cause of a revved-up thyroid is *Graves' disease*, an autoimmune disease that is the most common cause of hyperthyroidism in the United States. As with Hashimoto's thyroiditis, antibodies attack the thyroid, but in this case, they stimulate the thyroid to overproduce thyroid hormone. The kinds of antibodies present in Graves' disease are known as *thyrotropin receptor antibodies* (TRAb), including one kind known as *thyroid-stimulating immunoglobulins* (TSIs). They work by mimicking TSH, attaching to the TSH receptor on the thyroid gland and confusing the thyroid into producing too much hormone.

In addition to symptoms of hyperthyroidism, some people with Graves' disease develop *thyroid eye disease*. Its features vary from case to case and may be characterized by swollen, bulging, red eyes; widely open eyelids; and double vision. In its most severe form, diminished visual acuity may be present.

## Racing and Burning Out

A third category of thyroid diseases, sometimes called *resolving thyroiditis*, includes conditions that cause your inflamed thyroid to leak thyroid hormone into your bloodstream, causing you to experience the symptoms of hyperthyroidism. Once your thyroid's supply of the hormone is depleted, your thyroid hormone levels fall below normal and you then become hypothyroid. Eventually, in about six to eight months, the thyroid spontaneously recovers and normal function is restored in most people. However, a small percentage of those affected develop permanent hypothyroidism.

These temporary forms of thyroiditis often occur in people with a family history of autoimmune disease. They sometimes go undetected because the inflammation is mild and painless. This is the case with *postpartum thyroiditis*, the most common form of resolving thyroiditis, which occurs in 4–9 percent of women during the months after they have delivered a baby. During this period, the immune system goes from being partially suppressed as a result of hormonal changes in pregnancy to active, a transition that can trigger the disease. *Silent thyroiditis* is essentially the same as postpartum thyroiditis. The only difference is that it is unrelated to pregnancy and can occur in men and women, although it does occur primarily in women.

*Subacute thyroiditis* is a painful version of the above-mentioned conditions that may be caused by a group of viruses. Also known as de Quervain's thyroiditis, subacute viral thyroiditis ranges in severity. If you have this disease and it's on the severe side, you may feel like you're suffering from the flu. You'll have a fever, muscle aches and pains, and a painful swollen thyroid that feels like a terrible sore throat. You may also experience detectable signs of having too much thyroid hormone. (These signs are discussed in Chapter 5.)

## Who Is at Risk for Thyroid Disease?

More than 5 percent of all Americans have thyroid disorders. Most people who are diagnosed with thyroid disease find that they are part of a group considered more at risk than others. The following have been identified as risk factors for thyroid diseases.

### Gender

Numerous population studies conducted over the years have reported that both hypothyroidism and hyperthyroidism are far more prevalent in women than in men. The American Association of Clinical Endocrinologists reports that women may be as much as five to eight times more likely than men to suffer from thyroid disease. Researchers do not fully understand why women are more likely than men to have a thyroid problem, but it may have something to do with estrogen. Some evidence suggests that estrogen affects the immune system—particularly white blood cells that produce antibodies, known as B cells—which may have implications for the development of autoimmune diseases, including thyroid disease. One explanation for the development of postpartum thyroiditis is that during pregnancy function of both B cells and other white blood cells that help combat infection, called T cells, are believed to be suppressed by high levels of circulating estrogen. The rebound of the B and T cells from this suppression after delivery is thought to trigger the disease.

Evidence also points to estrogen's involvement in the development of Graves' disease. Since Graves' disease is uncommon before puberty, when estrogen levels are low, estrogen—in combination with genes on the X and Y chromosomes, rather than the genes alone—is believed to be responsible for more women developing Graves' disease because of its effect on the immune system. Estrogen's impact on the immune system is also believed to play a role in the development of other autoimmune diseases, and women are at a higher risk for autoimmune disease. Graves' disease and Hashimoto's thyroiditis, both autoimmune conditions, are to blame for the majority of people with recognized thyroid disease, particularly in women.

Moreover, changes in estrogen levels may contribute to the development of thyroid disease after menopause, when estrogen levels drop.

## Age

Hypothyroidism is common in people over age sixty, and the risk of hypothyroidism increases steadily with age, especially among women (see Figure 1.4). More than 17 percent of women and 8 percent of men show signs of hypothyroidism after the age of sixty-five. These rate increases are believed to be mostly due to an increase in the presence of antibodies that cause Hashimoto's thyroiditis. The reason older people are at risk is unclear. Researchers once believed that hypothyroidism is a normal part of aging because of the many age-related physiological changes that occur in a normal thyroid gland. As you get older, the rate at which your body tissues absorb oxygen declines slightly, your thyroid's uptake of iodine decreases, and your thyroid gland secretes less thyroid hormone—all factors suggesting hypothyroidism is inevitable at some point if you live long enough. However, other studies have determined that with normal aging there is also a natural decline

**FIGURE 1.4** Hypothyroidism by Age

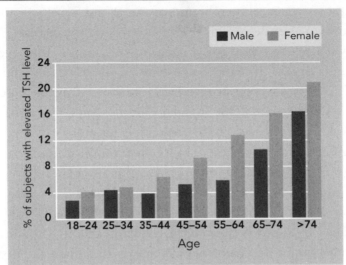

*After age thirty-five, the percentage of people with hypothyroidism increases rapidly, particularly among women. From G. J. Canaris, et al., "The Colorado Thyroid Disease Prevalence Study," Archives of Internal Medicine 160, February 28, 2000: 526–534. Reprinted with permission. Copyright © 2000, American Medical Association. All rights reserved.*

in lean body mass, which means that your body's need for thyroid hormone also declines with age, balancing it with the thyroid's decreased output. Still, physiological changes associated with aging may contribute to the increased risk of hypothyroidism seen with aging.

## Ethnicity

If you are African-American, you are less likely to develop autoimmune thyroid diseases than someone who is white. The third U.S. National Health and Nutrition Examination Survey of people twelve years of age or older (NHANES III), taken between 1988 and 1994, found that concentrations of thyroid antibodies suggest the presence of autoimmune disease in 14.3 percent of whites, 10.9 percent of Hispanic Americans, and only 5.3 percent of African-Americans.

# Risk Factors for Thyroid Disease at a Glance

You are at greater risk for an over- or underactive thyroid if you:

- are a woman
- are over sixty years of age
- are white
- have a family history that includes autoimmune conditions
- are pregnant or have given birth within the last six months
- are iodine deficient or live in a country where iodine deficiency is prevalent
- have been exposed to large amounts of radiation
- smoke
- are taking medications that contain high levels of iodine

## Family History

Autoimmune thyroid diseases, such as Graves' disease, Hashimoto's thyroiditis, and postpartum thyroiditis, run in families. Up to 50 percent of first-degree relatives of patients with these diseases are at risk for an autoimmune thyroid disease. That means that if either of your parents has one of these conditions, there is a substantial chance that you have or will develop an autoimmune thyroid disease. If you or your spouse has this kind of thyroid disease, your children are also at increased risk.

Tracing family history is particularly important when it comes to thyroid disease, because its symptoms are often indistinct. It is possible that you may learn that you have a thyroid disease because your mother or your daughter is diagnosed—usually, but not always, a female relative is affected. All of a sudden, your vague symptoms make sense. If your family members keep each other informed about health conditions that run genetically within your family, the result can be early diagnosis and treatment of conditions that become more severe without treatment. You might also avoid a misdiagnosis, a widespread problem among people who suffer from thyroid diseases.

Keep in mind, too, that if you or a close family member have an autoimmune thyroid disease, you are also at risk for developing another autoimmune disease, including pernicious anemia, type 1 diabetes, adrenal insufficiency, and rheumatoid arthritis.

## Pregnancy

If autoimmune diseases or thyroid disease runs in your family, you are at increased risk for developing thyroid problems during and after pregnancy. Graves' disease or Hashimoto's thyroiditis are more likely to appear during the first trimester of pregnancy, and thyroid problems during pregnancy can be harmful to your baby. Postpartum thyroiditis occurs within six months after delivery. If you or a family member have had thyroid disease, be sure to have your obstetrician check your thyroid function levels before, during, and after pregnancy.

## Diet

The only significant dietary contributor to thyroid disease is iodine. Too little or too much iodine can trigger a thyroid problem. One of the first signs of iodine deficiency is a goiter. As your thyroid tries to produce more thyroid hormone, it gradually enlarges and in severe cases leads to hypothyroidism. Iodine deficiency is generally not a problem in the United States, but it still plagues numerous developing countries and affects more than a billion people, which makes it one of the largest public health problems worldwide. Severe iodine deficiency in children leads to mental retardation and varying degrees of growth and developmental abnormalities. The most severe form of thyroid disease causes cretinism, an extreme form of neurological damage from fetal hypothyroidism that is characterized by gross mental retardation along with short stature, deaf mutism, and spasticity.

If you develop a goiter and live in the United States, chances are that it is unrelated to iodine deficiency. Since the 1920s,

Americans have been steadily consuming iodized salt, the solution to iodine deficiency. During World War I, Army physicians noticed that many recruits had swollen necks, particularly those who came from the Great Lakes region, which became known as the "Goiter Belt." Since then, iodine has also been added to supermarket breads and milk. In recent years, there has been some concern about a decline in iodine consumption among a small portion of Americans. NHANES III found that twenty years after an initial survey taken during the late 1970s, the average per capita consumption of iodine in the United States decreased by 50 percent but to levels that are still considered safe. Initial results of a more recent government survey indicate that these levels have not continued to drop but are stabilizing. The government is continuing to monitor iodine levels.

The reason for the steep decline experienced after the 1970s may have to do with changing eating habits. U.S. salt producers are not required by law to iodize salt, and many specialty salts, such as kosher salt and sea salt that contain no iodine, are now available. Most mass-produced breads are iodized, but nowadays, it is popular to buy fresh breads from bakeries, and these breads do not contain iodine. Processed foods, a staple for many Americans, are indeed high in salt, but most makers of processed foods do not use iodized salt.

Some foods, called goitrogens, interfere with iodine absorption. But you would have to consume these foods in extremely high quantities to pose a risk. One goitrogen is cassava, which is a major source of nutrition from plants in some parts of Africa. (Cassava, yams, taro, and plantains are from the roots and tubers families.) Goitrogens also include bamboo shoots, sweet potatoes, lima beans, cauliflower, cabbage, broccoli, and other foods from the cruciferous family.

Too much iodine can also lead to problems if you are either at high risk for developing thyroid problems or have a preexisting thyroid condition. A healthy thyroid gland can control the amount of iodine taken in, even if it is excessive. However, if you already have an overactive thyroid, even a small excess can cause a change in your thyroid function. You may briefly experience a decrease in thyroid function, followed by an "escape" from the suppressive effect of iodine, leading to increased thyroid function. If you are hypothyroid due to Hashimoto's thyroiditis, you are extremely sensitive to moderate or large amounts of excessive iodine exposure, which can worsen your disease.

You need to consume about 2 grams of iodized salt per day to meet the Recommended Dietary Allowance (RDA) of 150 micrograms (mcg) of iodine per day for adults, and that's only if you're not consuming other sources of iodine, such as packaged breads and milk products. Most people get plenty of iodine. (See Table 1.2 for the recommended daily intake of iodine.) The Institute of Medicine's Food and Nutrition Board finds that the median intake of iodine from food in the United States is approximately 240–300 mcg a day for men and 190–210 mcg a day for women. If you are pregnant, you need 220 mcg of iodine per day. Check to make sure that your prenatal vitamin contains anywhere from 150–220 mcg of iodine, as not all formulas do.

## Radiation Exposure

Exposure to large amounts of radiation during childhood can be harmful to your thyroid. If you received X-ray treatments to your head and neck for enlarged tonsils and adenoids, an enlarged thymus gland, acne, or ringworm as a child during the 1940s and

**TABLE 1.2** Recommended Daily Allowance for Iodine

| Age | Amount |
| --- | --- |
| Adults, ages 14 and older | 150 mcg |
| Pregnant women | 220 mcg |
| Breast-feeding women | 290 mcg |
| Children, ages 9–13 | 120 mcg |
| Children, ages 1–8 | 90 mcg |

Source: Dietary Reference Intakes for Vitamin A, Vitamin K, Arsenic, Boron, Chromium, Copper, Iodine, Iron, Manganese, Molybdenum, Nickel, Silicon, Vanadium and Zinc, Institute of Medicine's Food and Nutrition Board, The National Academy of Sciences, 2002.

# Kelp Supplements: Myth Versus Fact

**Myth:** Eating kelp or taking kelp supplements is a good way to prevent thyroid disease.

**Fact:** Kelp is a kind of seaweed that contains levels of iodine well above the recommended daily allowances. With regular consumption, kelp can lead to changes in thyroid function if you are susceptible to thyroid disease because of your family history or if you have preexisting thyroid disease. If you have underlying chronic thyroiditis, you can become hypothyroid after excessive iodine exposure, while if you have a nodular goiter and sometimes Graves' disease, you may become hyperthyroid after such exposure. The amount of iodine in kelp supplements can range well above the RDA of 150 mcg. The content and purity of dietary supplements are not government regulated. If you live in the United States, you generally do not need to supplement your diet with iodine because this mineral is so readily available in common foods. However, if you are pregnant, you need 220 mcg daily and are advised to take prenatal vitamins that contain iodine.

1950s, you may be at an increased risk for thyroid problems. The level of risk depends on how often and/or how much radiation you were exposed to. The worry here is the development of nodules that can be cancerous.

Exposure to radiation from nuclear fallout also increases the risk of thyroid cancer later in life if you were exposed during childhood. Studies conducted by the National Cancer Institute have found increased thyroid cancer rates in populations affected by the accident at the Chernobyl nuclear reactor in Ukraine in 1986 and by atomic bomb testing in the United States during the 1940s, 1950s, and 1960s. If you believe you were exposed to either harmful X-rays or fallout, talk to your doctor about a thyroid evaluation. The level of radiation used in routine X-rays for dental exams or other diagnostic purposes is not high enough to have an effect on your thyroid gland.

## Smoking

Smoking is a well-known risk factor for heart disease and cancer. Here is another reason not to smoke: numerous studies have confirmed an association between smoking and Graves' disease in people who are genetically predisposed to developing thyroid diseases. One study found that not only was Graves' disease more likely among those who smoked, but that among people with Graves' disease, those who smoked are four to fourteen times more likely to develop eye complications. Smoking has also been linked to triggering or worsening postpartum thyroiditis.

## Medications

Certain medications can induce thyroid disease. For example, *lithium*, a drug widely used to treat bipolar disease (also known as manic depression), interferes with the production of thyroid hormone and decreases the amount of thyroid hormone secreted into the bloodstream. Long-term treatment with lithium results in goiter in up to 50 percent of patients; mild hypothyroidism (often referred to as "subclinical" hypothyroidism) in up to 20 percent; and overt, or obvious, hypothyroidism in up to 20 percent. Less commonly, it can result in a condition that is indistinguishable from thyroiditis.

*Amiodarone*, an iodine-containing drug used to treat heart rhythm disturbances, can affect the thyroid in different ways depending on who is taking it. It leads to thyrotoxicosis (too much thyroid hormone) in up to 23 percent of patients, both those with and without underlying thyroid conditions. In some cases, amiodarone results in thyroid hormone leakage, causing a resolving thyroiditis. In other cases, it may cause excessive thyroid hormone production that does not resolve spontaneously. However, in up to 32 percent of heart patients, amiodarone induces the opposite problem—hypothyroidism. In some of these cases, excessive iodine inhibits production of thyroid hormone.

Two drugs used to treat hepatitis, multiple sclerosis, and some forms of cancer can cause hypothyroidism. *Interferon* and *inter-*

*leukin* are protein hormones called *cytokines* that are produced naturally in the body and play an important role in your immune system. An unfortunate side effect, however, is that in addition to damaging cancer cells, these drugs can damage the thyroid. If you must use these drugs, your doctor should monitor your thyroid function.

Many other drugs can interfere with thyroid function. Routine use of medications with high levels of iodine can trigger either hyperthyroidism or hypothyroidism if you have a preexisting condition such as an underlying autoimmune condition. Your doctor will probably warn you if you are taking a medicine that may harm your thyroid, but you should always read labels carefully. (See Table 1.3 for the iodine content of some medications.) Remember to pay particular attention to micrograms versus milligrams. The RDA

**TABLE 1.3** Iodine Content of Some Medications

| Substance | Amount of Iodine |
|---|---|
| **Cough Expectorants** | |
| Iophen | 25 mg/ml |
| Organidin (iodinated glycerol) | 15 mg/tablet |
| R-Gen | 6 mg/ml |
| **Antiasthmatic Drugs** | |
| Mudrane | 195 mg/tablet |
| Elixophyllin-KI (theophylline) elixir | 6.6 mg/ml |
| **Antiarrhythmic Drugs** | |
| Amiodarone | 75 mg/tablet |
| **Antiamebic Drugs** | |
| Iodoquinol | 134 mg/tablet |
| **Topical Antiseptic Agents** | |
| Povidone-iodine | 10 mg/ml |
| Clioquinol cream | 12 mg/gram |
| **Douches** | |
| Povidone-iodine | 10 mg/ml |

From M. I. Surks and R. Sievert, "Drug Therapy: Drugs and Thyroid Function," *New England Journal of Medicine*, 333: 1688–1694. Copyright © 1995 Massachusetts Medical Society. All rights reserved. Adapted with permission 2005.

for iodine is 150 mcg per day, yet many medications list milligrams. Remember that each mg contains 1,000 mcg.

If you are taking either lithium or amiodarone or are being treated for cancer with interferon or interleukin, be sure that your doctor is monitoring your thyroid function. If you are taking any of the iodine-containing products listed in Table 1.3 on a regular basis, talk to your doctor.

# CHAPTER 2

# Life in the Slow Lane: Down and Under with Hypothyroidism

Thyroid hormone keeps your body working at the right speed. If your thyroid hormone levels decrease to below-normal levels, it is known as hypothyroidism. Hypothyroidism makes the cells throughout your body slow their activity (see Figure 2.1). As a result, many systems in your body slow down, creating a wide range of symptoms that include fatigue, depression, weight gain, constipation, and dry skin, all of which can be misinterpreted as other problems.

Most people do not connect these symptoms to thyroid disease. Nearly ten million people have hypothyroidism, and it is believed that a substantial portion of people with the condition don't know they have it. In 2000, blood tests were performed on twenty-six thousand visitors to a statewide fair in Colorado. Researchers found that almost 10 percent of those tested had elevated TSH levels, many of whom had previously undetected hypothyroidism.

Hypothyroidism occurs in more than one in eight women between the ages of fifty-five and seventy-four. Yet the disease is

**FIGURE 2.1** Hypothyroidism

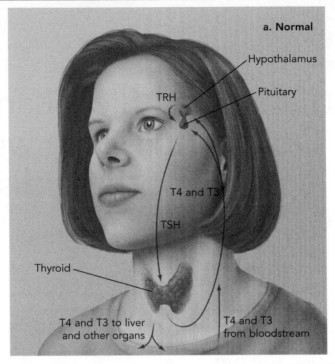

In contrast to a normal thyroid (a), hypothyroidism occurs when too little thyroid hormone (T4 and T3) is generated by the thyroid gland (b). In response, changes in the hypothalamus and the pituitary gland lead to increased TSH production in an effort to increase the thyroid's output. But the diseased thyroid gland continues to lag in production of thyroid hormone, causing the body's metabolism to slow down. Some portions of the damaged thyroid gland might become enlarged, leading to a goiter.

probably recognized the least in older people. That is because the symptoms are known to be far more elusive in that age group.

People over age sixty are much less likely to experience classic multiple symptoms than younger people with thyroid disease have. They sometimes have only one symptom, such as memory loss or depression, both of which are easily attributed to normal aging or other problems. In older women who do experience more classic symptoms of weight gain and fatigue, these symptoms of hypothyroidism can be easily mistaken as typical signs of middle age. On the flip side, physicians must have a high index of

**FIGURE 2.1** *continued*

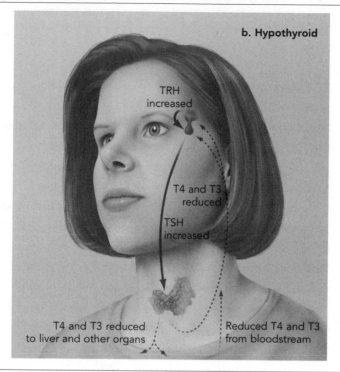

suspicion to make a diagnosis of hypothyroidism in older patients since thyroid disorders can often suggest a disorder of another system.

Only blood tests can confirm whether you are hypothyroid, so it is important that you are aware of the symptoms and ask your doctor for a thyroid evaluation if you are over sixty, exhibit symptoms, or are at risk due to any risk factors mentioned in this book (see Chapter 1). Thyroid tests are not routinely done unless your doctor believes you are at risk or you are symptomatic. If left untreated, hypothyroidism can have serious consequences over time. It increases your risk for high cholesterol, high blood pressure, atherosclerosis, and a heart attack. Eventually, a condition of severe hypothyroidism called *myxedema* can also develop, which occurs when the body slows down to the point that it starts to shut down and potentially falls into a coma.

## Hypothyroidism and Your Heart

Hypothyroidism can result in the following heart and circulation problems.

- **Slow heart rate.** Low levels of thyroid hormone can slow your heart rate.
- **High blood pressure.** Low levels of thyroid hormone make your arteries narrower and less elastic, which can increase the pressure needed to circulate blood around your body.
- **Atherosclerosis.** An underactive thyroid can cause your cholesterol levels to jump. This change may lead to narrowed, hardened arteries, which are a precursor to heart disease and stroke.
- **Diminished pumping ability.** The combination of reduced blood volume, weaker muscular contractions, and a slower heart rate means that the heart can't pump as well as it should. This can reduce blood flow to your skin, kidneys, brain, and other vital tissues.

Getting the proper diagnosis is the hard part with hypothyroidism. The condition is very easily treated with *levothyroxine sodium*, a synthetic version of thyroxine (T4). With proper treatment and routine checkups you can resume a normal life, usually free of symptoms.

## Recognizing Signs and Symptoms

The signs and symptoms of hypothyroidism are quite variable. Two people with the same condition may have entirely different symptoms. One person may become hypothyroid quickly over a few months, while another develops symptoms slowly over many years, making it even more difficult to detect. Generally speaking, the lower thyroid hormone levels become, the more pronounced symptoms will be. Some cases of mild hypothyroidism will progress to more severe disease, and some won't. Still, a person with severe disease may not experience severe symptoms. This is particularly true among older people.

The following sections describe both the classic symptoms experienced by people with hypothyroidism and the symptoms typically experienced by older people. If you are experiencing any of these symptoms, have your doctor check your thyroid.

## Classic Signs and Symptoms of Hypothyroidism

The following symptoms are the classic signs of hypothyroidism.

- **Fatigue.** If you are low on thyroid hormone, you are low on energy. If there is one classic symptom for hypothyroidism, it is utter exhaustion. Some people report that they want to sleep all day even though they slept all night.
- **Feeling chilly.** As your cells slow down, they need less energy and therefore your body produces less heat. You may find that you are always the one who wants to turn up the heat when those around you are comfortable. Cold weather may be intolerable and you may always need one more layer of clothing than those around you.
- **Loss of appetite.** Since your energy needs have decreased, your body requires less calories, so you naturally experience a loss of appetite. Still, many people who are hypothyroid gain weight or find it more difficult to lose weight even though they are eating less.
- **Slow pulse.** You probably will not notice changes in your heart rate unless you take your pulse. Low levels of thyroid hormone can slow your heart rate and may even cause bradycardia, an unusually slow heart rate of fewer than 60 beats per minute.
- **Weight gain.** It is normal for someone who is hypothyroid to gain weight. Even though you may experience a dip in

your appetite, you consume more calories than you metabolize because your body has slowed down and your cells convert less and less of those calories into energy. Therefore, more energy is stored as fat, and you gain weight. In addition, some weight gain may be the result of fluid retention. However, even though a few extra pounds can be blamed on hypothyroidism, the condition does not lead to obesity.

- **Enlarged thyroid gland.** If your hypothyroidism is caused by Hashimoto's thyroiditis or iodine deficiency, you may develop an enlargement called a goiter.

- **Depression.** Hypothyroidism and depression share many of the same characteristics. Fatigue, loss of appetite, and weight gain are often symptoms of depression. Some people who are hypothyroid also experience a perpetual state of unhappiness, or dysphoria, that is often misconstrued as clinical depression. It is not uncommon for a physician to prescribe antidepressants to a person whose underlying problem is really an underactive thyroid. You may also have trouble concentrating, experience memory loss, and seem to care less about what is normally important to you. One study estimates that autoimmune thyroiditis, with or without coexisting symptoms of hypothyroidism, occurs in 20 percent of patients with depression, compared with 5 to 10 percent of the healthy population.

- **Dry skin and brittle fingernails.** Your sweat glands provide your skin with natural moisture. But when your body produces less heat, you sweat less and develop dry skin. If you are hypothyroid, your skin may become chronically dry and flaky. Cracked skin may appear on your elbows and knees. Your nails may also become brittle with rough grooves.

- **Hair loss.** You may notice patchy hair loss, mild or severe, on your scalp. You may also lose body hair.

- **Constipation.** As your digestive processes lag with a slowed metabolic rate, you are likely to experience signs of constipation: hard, dry stools and abdominal cramps that are relieved by bowel movement.

- **Vague aches and pains.** You may experience muscular aches and pains in and around your joints that resemble the pain of rheumatoid arthritis.
- **Menstrual changes.** If you are a younger woman, your periods will tend to become heavier and more frequent. This can even lead to changes in ovulation that may make it difficult to conceive.
- **High cholesterol level.** An underactive thyroid can cause your cholesterol level to jump. This happens when low levels of thyroid hormone cause the liver to make fewer LDL receptors. These are the molecules that pull LDL or "bad" cholesterol out of the blood. If you are older, high cholesterol may be the only sign you experience; as a result, the problem may be diagnosed as a cholesterol disorder rather than hypothyroidism.
- **Carpal tunnel syndrome.** Many people associate carpal tunnel syndrome with long hours spent typing on the keyboard of a computer or doing other repetitive hand movements. Yet this condition often accompanies certain diseases, including hypothyroidism. If you have this symptom, you might feel tingling in your wrist and fingers that is due to swelling in the soft tissues and ligaments supporting the bones surrounding the median nerve that passes through the wrist.

## Signs and Symptoms of Hypothyroidism in People over Sixty

Some people over age sixty with an underactive thyroid are more likely to have few if any classic symptoms of hypothyroidism, while others experience the classic symptoms as a younger person would. Still others may experience a symptom that is not considered typical at all, which makes diagnosis even more difficult. Any of the following, alone or in combination, are typical symptoms of hypothyroidism in older people.

- **Unexplained high cholesterol.** This symptom may stand alone and is an indication for a thyroid evaluation.
- **Congestive heart failure.** Reduced blood volume, weaker muscular contractions of your heart, and a slower heart rate, all caused by low thyroid hormone levels, may contribute to congestive heart failure, a serious condition that results from decreased blood flow to muscle tissues and organs throughout your body. The ineffective pumping also causes blood to back up into the veins that return blood to your heart. Blood backs up all the way into your lungs, which causes them to become congested with fluid. Symptoms of congestive heart failure include breathlessness, swelling in your ankles, weakness, and fatigue.
- **Bowel movement changes.** You may have constipation because of decreased movement of stool through the bowels. Less commonly, you may have frequent bouts of diarrhea, which is more typically a symptom of hyperthyroidism. This is rare, however, and should prompt the investigation of other causes of diarrhea or malabsorption, such as sprue, which is more common in patients with autoimmune thyroid disease.
- **Arthritis.** Vague joint pain is a classic symptom of hypothyroidism and is sometimes the only symptom of hypothyroidism if you are an older patient. However, you may experience an overall muscular aching, particularly in large muscle groups, that does not occur near the joints.
- **Psychiatric problems.** As with younger people, clinical depression is common among older people with an underactive thyroid. The difference is that if you are older, it can be the only symptom. You could also develop psychosis and exhibit either delusional behavior or suffer from hallucinations.
- **Dementia.** Debilitating memory loss can occur alone or, more often—but not always—accompanied by depression or some kind of psychosis. If you or a loved one is being

evaluated for dementia, be sure your doctor has assessed your thyroid function.

* **Problems with balance.** Abnormalities in the cerebellum at the back of the brain that occur in hypothyroidism may lead to walking disturbances.

## Communication Between Family Members Leads to Early Diagnosis and Treatment

Debra, a forty-eight-year-old editor who lives in Massachusetts, has her mother to thank for sharing medical information that helped her catch her own hypothyroidism early. Debra's mother has Hashimoto's thyroiditis along with related autoimmune conditions, including lupus, rheumatoid arthritis, and scleroderma. As Debra can attest, knowing your family medical history can make all the difference when it comes to thyroid diseases, the symptoms of which are often missed. This is her story.

My mother was diagnosed with hypothyroidism when she was forty. I was in my teens when she said to me, "The doctor told me this is hereditary. So just be on the lookout. You probably won't get it, but I just want you to be aware."

For years, every time I went for a checkup, I would always say to my doctor, "Do you think it's time to check my thyroid?" and my doctor always did and my tests always came back negative, so I just never thought about it. When I was about thirty-five, I began developing gynecological problems and I just started feeling awful. I had fibroid tumors surgically removed, but even after that, there was just this kind of pervasive feeling that something was up. I had very heavy periods. I had these months where I felt like PMS was eight times worse than it had been. I started gaining weight. My hair was starting to get thinner, but it didn't thin out to the point where I had a bald spot.

It was then that I became aggressive about checking my thyroid. Still, my thyroid tests always came back normal until two years ago when I had to have my ovaries surgically removed for other reasons. It may have been a coincidence, but after that, my TSH levels were in abnormal ranges. Ever since I was diagnosed, I've been on a low dosage of levothyroxine and I don't feel horrible anymore.

## What Is Causing My Hypothyroidism?

Hypothyroidism is usually caused by an underlying disease or by some previous medical treatment that left the thyroid incapable of functioning properly. Sometimes hypothyroidism is permanent and sometimes it is reversible, depending on the cause.

### Hypothyroid for Life

The most common causes for chronic hypothyroidism are as follows.

- **Autoimmune disease.** The most common cause of permanent hypothyroidism is Hashimoto's thyroiditis, a chronic autoimmune condition in which white blood cells, known as lymphocytes, make antibodies that slowly and gradually disable your thyroid gland. Another autoimmune condition, atrophic thyroiditis, can also cause low thyroid hormone production. In this case, antibodies cause the thyroid gland to shrink.
- **Surgery.** Surgery to partially or entirely remove the thyroid is sometimes required in people who have thyroid nodules, goiter, thyroid cancer, or Graves' disease. If your entire thyroid is removed, you will become hypothyroid and require total thyroid hormone replacement. You may also become hypothyroid if you have your thyroid partially removed. Sometimes, however, if the remaining part of the gland is functioning properly, it may be able to make enough thyroid hormone to keep your blood levels normal.

- **Radiation treatment or exposure.** If you have hyperthyroidism, you may be treated with radioactive iodine that destroys part or all of your thyroid gland. This leads to hypothyroidism. If you have Hodgkin's disease, lymphoma, or cancers of the head and neck and are treated with radiation, you can lose part or all of your thyroid function.
- **Disorders of the pituitary gland.** The pituitary gland, the messenger that tells your thyroid how much thyroid hormone to produce by sending TSH into the bloodstream, can also have problems that cause it to erroneously cease or slow down production of TSH, prompting your thyroid to underproduce. The most common causes of pituitary gland damage are a tumor, radiation, or surgery.
- **Congenital hypothyroidism.** Sometimes, a baby is born without a thyroid, with a partially formed thyroid, or with a thyroid that isn't in the right place. In some cases, a baby is born with a complete thyroid that doesn't function properly.

## Just Passing Through
Temporary hypothyroidism can arise for a variety of reasons.

- **Thyroiditis.** Thyroiditis, an inflammation of the thyroid gland caused by an autoimmune attack or sometimes by a virus, floods your system with too much thyroid hormone, which leads to symptoms of hyperthyroidism, followed by a period of hypothyroidism. Compared to Hashimoto's thyroiditis, which is a chronic form of thyroid inflammation, thyroiditis may be a relatively short-lived condition.
- **Medications.** Medicines such as amiodarone, lithium, interferon, and interleukin can trigger hypothyroidism, particularly if you have a genetic tendency toward autoimmune thyroid disease.
- **Too much iodine.** Taking in too much iodine can cause hypothyroidism if you are at risk for autoimmune disease, or

it can make your existing hypothyroidism worse. (For the iodine content of some medications, see Table 1.3.)

- **Too little iodine.** Iodine deficiency (see pages 14–16) causes hypothyroidism that can be corrected by increasing your iodine intake. Iodine deficiency is uncommon in the developed world, but severe deficiency can lead to permanent damage. In children, it can lead to growth problems and mental retardation.

## Diagnosing Hypothyroidism

When should you have a thyroid test? The American Thyroid Association (ATA) recommends that all adults be screened for thyroid problems with a TSH blood test beginning at age thirty-five and every five years thereafter. Still, there is deep disagreement within the medical community about the cost-effectiveness of screening, so you may or may not be screened routinely by your primary care doctor. You may not even be tested for a thyroid problem if you complain of gaining weight, feeling tired, or feeling depressed, since these are common symptoms most people encounter from time to time and could be indicative of a host of different problems. This is why many people with thyroid disease easily slip through the cracks.

### Ask to Be Tested

To help catch undiagnosed thyroid disease, the ATA and the American Association of Clinical Endocrinologists (AACE) are appealing to patients directly. In a joint public awareness campaign, the groups ask you to ask your doctor to test your thyroid if you are thirty-five or older and either exhibit any symptoms of thyroid disease or are at risk due to any of the risk factors listed in Chapter 1.

Most primary care physicians can diagnose and treat hypothyroidism. In certain situations, however, the AACE recommends consultation with or referral to a clinical endocrinologist, a doctor who specializes in treating the glands and hormones in your body, known collectively as the endocrine system. You may even be referred to a thyroidologist, an endocrinologist who specializes in thyroid diseases. You will probably be referred to a specialist if you:

- are pregnant
- are a cardiac patient
- have a goiter, nodule, or other thyroid structural abnormality
- have a coexisting disease
- have not been successfully treated
- are under eighteen years of age

A test that measures TSH levels in your blood is the best indicator of a thyroid problem. In addition to blood tests, your doctor will want to assess the size of your thyroid by feeling around your neck area and check for any physical signs of hypothyroidism, such as coarse hair or hair loss, dry or yellowish skin, or a pale and puffy appearance. The doctor may also check your reflexes to see if they are delayed. Your weight, cholesterol levels, and blood pressure should also be checked. If your TSH is abnormally high, a blood test to check your thyroxine level (T4) will also be done. If that is low, you are hypothyroid. Many people learn that they have an elevated TSH, but a normal T4. This indicates the presence of mild disease, which may or may not progress to overt hypothyrodism. If your doctor wants to confirm the cause of your hypothyroidism, you might have a blood test to check for the presence of antibodies, which would confirm thyroiditis.

## Mild Thyroid Disease

Suppose you go in for a routine checkup and your doctor decides to test your thyroid function. You've experienced no thyroid disease symptoms, yet the TSH level in your blood is above the normal range. But your T4 level is normal. The results mean that you have mild, or "subclinical," hypothyroidism, a condition that does not meet the diagnostic criteria for overt hypothyroidism but has sparked disagreement among physicians about whether to treat such patients with medication.

The importance of this question cannot be overestimated because of the large number of people who are diagnosed with subclinical thyroid disease. Studies estimate that as many as 20 percent of all women over sixty and between 4 percent to 8.5 percent of the general population have subclinical hypothyroidism.

The treatment guidelines for subclinical disease that have been developed for primary care doctors have been inconsistent over the years, and confusion within the medical community has led to debates over routine screening. One of the arguments against routine screening versus testing only people with symptoms or risk factors is that screening uncovers many mild cases that may not require or necessarily benefit from treatment. Some cases of subclinical hypothyroidism may never progress to overt disease. Only 2.6 percent of all people with mild disease who do not test positive for anti-TPO antibodies, which suggests an underlying autoimmune disease, progress to overt disease each year. The risk of progression is higher for those with mild disease who do have anti-TPO antibodies. Among that group, 4.6 percent of people with mild disease progress to overt disease each year.

Overtreatment—for example, treating someone with subclinical disease who may not need treatment at all or giving excessive amounts to someone who would benefit from less—comes with its own risks. In some cases, a person could develop *thyrotoxicosis*, which means "toxic thyroid," or too much thyroid hormone. (See "Fast Fact: Thyrotoxicosis Versus Hyperthyroidism" in Chapter 3.)

Long-term complications that result from overtreatment can include cardiac problems and bone loss. Most doctors agree that people with subclinical hypothyroidism who exhibit symptoms may benefit from thyroid hormone replacement, but even this hasn't been proven. However, patients with no symptoms present a quandary. Some research over the years has shown that treatment of mild disease is needed to protect patients from the possible consequences of untreated mild disease, including high cholesterol, heart disease, and psychiatric problems along with the risk of progression to overt hypothyroidism.

In 2000, researchers in Rotterdam, The Netherlands, published a large groundbreaking population study of 1,149 women aged fifty-five and older. The researchers recommended treatment for this population after finding that women who had aortic atherosclerosis and a history of heart attacks were more likely to have subclinical hypothyroidism than those who did not. The prevalence of heart disease was highest among women who tested positive for both subclinical disease and the presence of anti-TPO antibodies. The same study reported that subclinical hypothyroidism is as great a risk factor for heart disease as other well-established risk factors, including high cholesterol, smoking, hypertension, and diabetes.

However, in an effort to come to a consensus over what to do with subclinical disease, a large panel of endocrinologists sponsored by the ATA, the AACE, and the Endocrine Society put together its own recommendations for primary care physicians based on a review of all published research on the subject. In that report, published in the *Journal of the American Medical Association* (*JAMA*) in January 2004, the investigating panel found that research linking subclinical hypothyroidism to heart attacks and other cardiac problems was either flawed or inconclusive. For instance, the panel found that the Rotterdam study, a population study based on surveys, did not establish a cause–and–effect relationship between subclinical and aortic atherosclerosis. In other words, other factors, such as lifestyle, socioeconomic status, and access to medical care, may explain the result. The panel also found that there is no clear-cut evidence that treatment of patients with mildly underactive thyroids improves symptoms, reduces cholesterol levels, or prevents progression to overt disease.

So who, if anyone, should be treated for mild disease? It really depends on your individual circumstances. One factor is just how mild your mild disease is. If your serum TSH level is elevated to anywhere between 4.5 and 10 mU/L and your T4 is normal, the panel "recommends against routine treatment" but suggests routine monitoring for progression to overt disease every six to twelve months. (See Table 4.1 for ranges of normal blood test results.) If your serum TSH level is higher than 10 mU/L and your T4 is normal, your disease is still mild, but your chances for progressing to overt disease are greater than those with lower serum TSH levels. The panel considers treatment for this group "reasonable."

Pregnant women deserve special consideration, the panel found, because an underactive thyroid, even mildly so, in a mother has been linked to impaired brain development in her fetus. The consensus panel recommends treating all pregnant women with mild hypothyroidism but did not recommend routine screening of all pregnant women for thyroid disease. Instead, the panel urged the testing of all pregnant women with a family history of thyroid disease, a personal history of an autoimmune disorder, prior thyroid disease, or any signs and symptoms of thyroid disease.

The consensus panel advises against routine screening for the entire population, citing lack of evidence to support any preventative benefit. But it did recommend checking anyone who fell into a high-risk category, which would include all women over age sixty. The panel's review was backed up by the U.S. Preventive Services Task Force, which issued its own report in January 2004. That body found the evidence "insufficient" to recommend for or against routine screening for thyroid disease in adults.

Reports from these panels are hardly the final word on the subject. Already the AACE, a cosponsor of the consensus panel, has issued a response that is at odds with the consensus panel findings. The group is sticking to its own recommendations, issued in 2002, which advise physicians to treat patients with TSH levels greater than 5 mU/L if the patient has a goiter or if thyroid antibodies are present. (The consensus panel did not recommend testing for antibodies in patients with mild disease, even though positive results indicate a higher chance that disease will progress, because the presence of antibodies changes neither the diagnosis of subclinical hypothyroidism nor the treatment recommended.) The AACE also cautions against relying solely on medical studies and ignoring clinical experience and suggests that physicians decide on whether treatment is warranted based on a comprehensive history and physical examination of the patient.

If you haven't been evaluated for thyroid disease, keep in mind that because routine screening in the general population has not been recommended, it may be up to you to ask for a thyroid function test if you are experiencing symptoms and/or are at risk for thyroid disease.

## Treating Hypothyroidism

If you've been diagnosed with clinical hypothyroidism, a sigh of relief may be warranted. The treatment of your disease is as uncomplicated as the symptoms are difficult to recognize. You may be happy to put a name to what has been making you feel miserable and to know that it can be effectively treated.

Your doctor will prescribe a medication that replaces the thyroid hormone that your body is missing. The goal of thyroid hormone replacement is to closely replicate normal thyroid functioning. Pure synthetic thyroxine, called levothyroxine sodium, works in the same way your own thyroid hormone would work. If your condition is permanent, you must take medication for the rest of your life. Some say that this is a small sacrifice, considering the dramatic improvement they experience once their hormone levels are restored to normal. With just one dose per day, you can basically go on with your life with your disease in check. There is no special diet to follow. There is no need to modify your lifestyle in any way.

Since synthetic thyroid hormone is replacing a hormone that naturally occurs in your body, side effects or allergic reactions are rare. If you have a goiter as a result of Hashimoto's thyroiditis, thyroid hormone may help to shrink the goiter or to prevent it from growing.

## Determining Your Dose

Your initial dose of levothyroxine sodium is carefully selected based on your weight, your age, and any coexisting medical conditions. A general guideline for full thyroid hormone replacement is 0.8 mcg for every pound of weight (or 1.6–1.8 mcg for every kg of weight). Your doctor may decide on a lower or higher dose depending on your individual circumstances.

If you are older, your treatment will begin gradually because of an increased risk of underlying heart disease. Full hormone replacement achieved too quickly may put stress on your heart or central nervous system. If medication begins gradually, your heart and central nervous system gradually adjust to a faster pace. For instance, your doctor may start you with 12.5–25 mcg of levothyroxine sodium per day and increase the dose every four to six weeks until laboratory tests show that your TSH and T4 levels are within the normal range. Doctors will prescribe an even more gradual dosing schedule for patients who experience symptoms of congestive heart failure, angina, or anxiety.

The dose is also based on the severity of your hypothyroidism. For instance, if you have autoimmune-induced hypothyroidism, you may only require partial replacement because your thyroid is still producing some hormone. But if your thyroid has been removed, it requires total hormone replacement, which on average means a higher dose. If you have cancer, a higher dose also serves as therapy to prevent recurrence.

Another important factor in determining dose is whether you are on any medication that may interfere with the absorption or metabolism of your thyroid medication. For instance, if you are on estrogen therapy, certain antidepressants, or birth control pills, you may need a higher dose. (See Table 2.1 later in this chapter to compare dosages of different pills.) Therefore, it's important to tell your doctor if you are taking any other medication or if you begin to take other medication after you start taking your thyroid pills.

Think of your initial dose as an estimate of your need. There is likely to be a bit of trial and error, because your thyroid hormone needs are very precise, and you will likely need adjustments until your TSH level is within the normal range. The doctor will probably begin with a low dose because too much thyroid hormone may cause symptoms of hyperthyroidism, such as nervousness, anxiety, or a racing heart. If you experience any of these symptoms, contact your doctor immediately.

Once the initial dose has been decided, remember that it may take several weeks before you experience any changes in your system. Thyroxine is a slow-acting hormone, and you are not likely to feel its effects immediately. Generally, anywhere between six to eight weeks after you begin taking your medication, your doctor will want to check your TSH level and adjust the dose accordingly. If, at that point, your TSH level still is not within the normal range, the dose will be adjusted until your range is normal and your symptoms have improved. Once the appropriate dose has been established, you will have a TSH test, and sometimes a test for free thyroxine (the T4 that is not bound to proteins, but available for use by your cells), every six months to a year. (See "TSH [Thyroid-Stimulating Hormone] Test" and "T4 [Thyroxine] Tests" in Chapter 4.)

## Precise Dosing: Why It's Important to Stick with the Same Name Brand

Synthetic versions of the natural hormone thyroxine, which are widely used today, were developed in the 1920s and have been on the market since the late 1960s. But it wasn't until fairly recently that manufacturers of these drugs were required to seek approval from the Food and Drug Administration (FDA). That's because the development of the drug predated the Food, Drug and Cosmetic Act of 1938, which for the first time required that new drugs be tested for safety. And when these synthetic versions of thyroxine entered the market in 1961, they were not perceived as new and therefore did not require FDA approval. Instead, they were grandfathered in—permitted to stay on the market without going through the approval process.

## Side Effects

Potential side effects of thyroxine medication result if you take more than your body needs, which could lead to thyrotoxicosis and put additional demands on your heart. Side effects may be particularly serious if you have underlying heart problems. Doctors would typically opt to start you on a low dose and gradually increase it to give your cardiovascular and central nervous systems time to adjust to an increased metabolism. If you experience any of the following symptoms, contact your doctor immediately:

- chest pain
- trouble breathing
- irregular heartbeat
- signs of hyperthyroidism (see pages 54–57)

If you are allergic to the dyes used in the color-coding of thyroid medication, your doctor can prescribe 50 mcg tablets, which are almost always white and free of dyes.

Over the next several decades, complaints about levothyroxine sodium pills were filed with the FDA, citing problems with the consistency of strength from pill to pill. By 1997, the agency concluded that no marketed levothyroxine preparation was shown to have consistent potency and stability and therefore could not be recognized as "safe and effective." In light of this, the FDA issued a notice requiring manufacturers to get approval for thyroid drugs; therefore, all brand name and generic versions of levothyroxine sodium have had to undergo potency testing since 1997 to become FDA approved.

Of all the brand names of thyroid drugs on the market, one is as good as the next. However, problems can occur when you switch brands. Each brand is manufactured slightly differently from the next. For instance, they all have the same active ingredient—levothyroxine sodium—but the inactive ingredients that determine a drug's consistency may vary. These small differences can have a significant effect on the drug's bioavailability, meaning how much thyroxine your body absorbs. Your body's needs are so precise that even slight changes in the levels of thyroxine absorbed may affect your overall health. For instance, if you are taking 100 mcg of one brand, your thyroid hormone levels may be normal. But if you switch to 100 mcg of a different brand, your levels could go into a high thyrotoxic range or a low range, making you hypothyroid—depending on how much of the drug your body absorbs. Switching brands is therefore not recommended. Even if you have the best intentions, however, you may have to switch for one reason or another. If you must switch brands, tell your doctor so that you can have your TSH level measured after an appropriate interval and make any necessary adjustments to your dosage.

Changes in the thyroid drug market occur now and then, so be aware of any that affect you. For instance, people who took Levothroid were advised by the drug's new manufacturer, Forest Pharmaceuticals, to have thyroid blood tests performed eight to twelve weeks after they began taking a new reformulated version of the drug that came on the market in 2004. The old formula is no longer available. If you are taking the new formula, you will know because the shape of the pills changed from round to oval and some of the pill colors changed.

## What About Generic Thyroid Drugs?

In general, generic versions of many types of drugs offer a less-expensive quality alternative. However, this is not the case with thyroid drugs. The issue is not one of quality, as generics must undergo the same potency tests that brand names do. Instead, it has to do with the amount of thyroid hormone that is available for use by the body with any given formulation, which is dependent on the dose in addition to how well you absorb it. If you take a generic version of levothyroxine sodium, you may not necessarily get the same generic product with each refill, because generic products may be interchanged. This may throw off your TSH and T4 levels. The drug dispensed by the pharmacist may be based on what the pharmacist has in stock and the cost to the pharmacy. You must be able to ask for the product by name so that you receive the same formula consistently. To do this, the ATA and the AACE recommend choosing a brand name and staying with that same brand indefinitely.

## Color Codes

Levothyroxine sodium is available in a wide range of strengths, from 25 mcg to 300 mcg. Four brand names reviewed at the time of publication, as well as some generics, use color codes to differentiate among the strengths. (See Table 2.1.) It may be easier to remember that you are taking the yellow pill than it is to remember that you are taking 100 micrograms. But you really cannot rely on color alone when ordering a prescription. Mistakes can be made, for instance, if you or your pharmacist confuses light blue with blue or green with mint green.

**TABLE 2.1** What Color Is Your Thyroid Pill?

Use this chart of the doses and colors of common brands of levothyroxine sodium to see what strengths are available or, if you are switching brands, to compare color codes.

| Strength (mcg*) | Levothroid | Levoxyl | Synthroid | Unithroid |
|---|---|---|---|---|
| 25 | Orange | Orange | Orange | Peach |
| 50 | White | White | White | White |
| 75 | Violet | Purple | Violet | Purple |
| 88 | Mint green | Olive | Olive | Olive |
| 100 | Yellow | Yellow | Yellow | Yellow |
| 112 | Rose | Rose | Rose | Rose |
| 125 | Brown | Brown | Brown | Tan |
| 137 | NA** | Dark blue | Turquoise | NA** |
| 150 | Blue | Blue | Blue | Blue |
| 175 | Lilac | Turquoise | Lilac | Lilac |
| 200 | Pink | Pink | Pink | Pink |
| 300 | Green | Green | Green | Green |

*Dosage may be listed in milligrams rather than micrograms. There are 1,000 micrograms in 1 milligram. (Thus, 0.137 mg is the same as 137 mcg.)

**Not available in this strength

## Taking Your Medication

Taken once a day, thyroxine tablets result in very stable levels of thyroid hormone in your bloodstream. The best time to take your medicine is first thing in the morning on an empty stomach. But if that doesn't work for you, remember that it is most important to be consistent and take your pill the same time every day. If you forget one day, it is usually best to take the missed dose as soon as you remember. One good way to avoid skipping a dose is to get a daily pill organizer.

Certain drugs, such as iron or calcium supplements, antacids, and cholesterol-lowering medications, can interfere with the absorption of thyroxine tablets (see Table 2.2). Be sure to tell your doctor about anything that you are taking that may interfere with your thyroid medication. You may be advised to take your thyroid tablet several hours before or after these medications.

Too much soy, which has become a very popular alternative source of protein in recent years, can also interfere with absorption.

## Thyroid Hormone from Animals

Long before the development of synthetic thyroxine tablets, people with thyroid conditions were treated with extracts of animal thyroid glands. This treatment was developed in 1891 and was considered one of the first real cures for disease before the penicillin era. Back then, patients were injected with sheep thyroid extract. Later, instead of getting injected with animal thyroid, patients ate ground or fried sheep thyroid. Eventually, animal thyroid was dried and powdered so that it could be taken in pill form, a preparation known as desiccated thyroid. This was the most common form of thyroid treatment before the structure of the hormone thyroxine was identified, clearing the way for the development of synthetic versions of thyroid hormone (levothyroxine sodium). Still, desiccated thyroid remained the mainstay of therapy for underactive thyroid; it wasn't until 1962 that levothyroxine entered the market after doctors realized that it offered important advantages to patients.

## TABLE 2.2 Drug Interactions

The following medicines and therapies can affect the effectiveness of thyroid medicines in one or more of the following ways: by interfering with the absorption of thyroid hormone, by binding thyroid hormone to binding proteins, and by interfering with thyroid hormone metabolism.

| Cancer Therapies | Cardiovascular Therapies | Cholesterol Therapies |
|---|---|---|
| Fluorouracil | Amiodarone* (Cordarone) | Bile acid sequestrants, including cholestyramine (Questran),* colestipol (Colestid),* and clofibrate (Atromid-S) |
| Asparaginase | Furosemide (Lasix) | |
| Tamoxifen | Heparin | |
| Bexarotene* | Oral anticoagulants | |
| Interferon* | | Slow-release nicotinic acid |
| Interleukin* | | |

| Gastrointestinal Therapies | Hormonal Therapies | Neurologic/Psychiatric Therapies |
|---|---|---|
| Antacids, such as aluminum hydroxide | Androgens/anabolic steroids | Sertraline* (Zoloft) |
| Sucralfate | Estrogens (Prempo, Premarin, and others) | Lithium* |
| Cation exchange resins | Growth hormone | Other antidepressants and antipsychotic agents, including quetiapine (Seroquel), clomipramine (Anafranil), and methadone (Dolophine) |
| Charcoal | Glucocorticoids, such as prednisone (Deltasone, Meticorten, and others) | |
| | Dopaminergic drugs, including bromocriptine (Parlodel) and cabergoline (Dostinex) | Anticonvulsants, including phenytoin (Dilantin),* phenobarbital (Bellatal, Luminal, and Solfoton),* and carbamazepine (Atretol, Carbatrol, Tegretol)* |

| Nutritional Supplements | Other Medicines |
|---|---|
| Calcium carbonate | Sulfonylureas |
| Ferrous sulfate (iron) | Nonsteroidal anti-inflammatory drugs (NSAIDS), such as meclofenamate, mefenamic acid, and phenylbutazone |
| Multivitamins (presumably because of their iron and calcium content) | Radiographic agents, such as contrast agents containing iodine, in addition to ipodate* and iopanoic acid* |
| Iodine,* including kelp supplements | Salicylates (high doses of aspirin and salsalate) |
| Soy* | Sulfonamides, such as acetazolamide and sulfisoxazole |
| | Antituberculous, such as rifampicin and ethionamide |
| | Propanolol (Inderal, Inderal LA) |
| | Orphenadrine (Norflex) |

*The impact on effectiveness is potentially significant.

Today, synthetic thyroxine is the preferred choice among doctors because it provides stable levels of the hormone and it is well absorbed. Desiccated thyroid, now made mostly from pig thyroid gland, is still prescribed by some doctors. Its proponents value it as a "natural" alternative to levothyroxine sodium. Some people have reported that they feel better using this product than synthetic T4. But there are a number of problems with desiccated thyroid tablets.

For one thing, potency of desiccated thyroid can vary from one batch to another depending on several factors, including such environmental influences as the animal's diet. Pills made from animal thyroid are not purified. They contain hormones and proteins that don't normally exist outside the thyroid gland. Some patients develop allergic reactions to the animal protein. And animal thyroid pills are not entirely natural. They contain unnatural chemicals, called binders, used to make the tablets. Allergic reactions are far less common among those who use synthetic T4.

Another difference is that desiccated thyroid contains both T4 and T3 (triiodothyronine). T3 is the more active of the two hormones, and normally it is principally made naturally in the body from T4, a conversion that takes place mainly in the liver but in other tissues as well. The body also makes T3 from synthetic T4. So the T3 in the desiccated thyroid pills can lead to toxicity or can cause some people to develop temporary symptoms of hyperthyroidism. They are temporary because T3 has a short, but powerful, life span in the body. On the other hand, this boost of T3 may be the reason some people prefer desiccated thyroid and report that they have more energy and generally feel better than they do on pure synthetic T4.

## Synthetic T4/T3 Combinations

There are synthetic versions of pills that contain pure T3 (the active ingredient is liothyronine sodium), but these are not recommended as a therapy alone because they can potentially lead to thyrotoxicosis. However, a regimen that combines synthetic versions of T4 and T3 has gained attention recently. Either a combination of T4 and T3 or a single pill that contains both T4 and T3, called *liotrix*, are sometimes prescribed to an occasional patient who simply does not feel well despite being treated with pure T4. But again, there are problems with the potency and short life of T3. Liotrix, sold under the name Thyrolar, contains a preparation of T4 and T3 in a ratio of four to one, which is more T3 than is produced naturally within the body. Just after taking liotrix, there are very high levels of T3 for a short time and then the levels fall off very rapidly; this surge of excess thyroid hormone may lead to some temporary hyperthyroid symptoms.

Questions remain over whether people truly experience improved symptoms by adding T3 to their regimen. Some studies have confirmed that certain patients do feel better when they use the combination of T4 and T3. One study in particular, published in the *New England Journal of Medicine* (*NEJM*) in February 1999, found that the T4/T3 combination improved mood, depression, low energy, anger, and cognitive function in half of thirty-three patients who were randomly assigned a combination of T4 and T3. Such symptoms did not improve in the other half of the group, which was given pure T4.

More recent studies have not confirmed the *NEJM* study. A study published in *JAMA* in December 2003 divided forty-six people into two groups. One group received a combination of T4 and T3, the other took T4 alone. In the end, the group taking the T4/T3 combination did not show any improvement in symptoms as measured by scores on a thyroid-specific health questionnaire nor any improvement in neuropsychological tests. At least two other studies have yielded similar results.

The biggest problem with combination T4/T3 regimens is that it is difficult to replicate the ratio of T4 and T3 naturally produced in the body. The recent studies have been criticized for not having administered truly physiologic ratios of T4 and T3. Replicating such levels of thyroid hormone in animal studies have required continuous infusions of both T4 and T3, according to the *JAMA* study, which suggested that a sustained-release form of T3 might come closer to replicating natural ratios. This sustained-release T3 drug doesn't exist yet, but scientists are working on developing one. For now, the most efficient way to approximate your body's natural ratios is to take pure T4, from which your body naturally produces T3 at a steady pace that cannot be copied by a dose of T3.

While the combination therapy may prove beneficial in certain people, it also may be risky, and it certainly isn't a magic pill for all those who still suffer from fatigue or depression despite treatment that puts their hormone levels within normal ranges. If you still experience symptoms and your thyroid hormone levels are normal, discuss it with your doctor, who may prescribe a combination of synthetic T4 and T3. The doctor may recommend taking the T3 portion of your combination in split doses to smooth out the surge in T3 levels that could result from taking a substantial amount of T3 at once.

Keep in mind, too, that the symptoms you are experiencing may not be related to the thyroid. You may, for example, need to make some lifestyle changes that could improve your mood and energy levels, such as a change in your diet or starting an exercise regimen.

## Thyroid Medications: Myths and Facts

There are a number of common perceptions about thyroid medications. Let's separate the myths from the facts.

### Thyroid Hormone Medication and Osteoporosis: Is There a Link?

**Myth:** Taking any amount of thyroid hormone medication puts you at risk for osteoporosis. Postmenopausal women taking levothyroxine should also take estrogen.

**Fact:** If you have too much thyroid hormone in your system, you are at an increased risk for osteoporosis, a disease that usually occurs in women after menopause or in elderly men. Osteoporosis results in weakened bones and makes you more susceptible to fractures. Excess thyroid hormone abnormally speeds up the activity of certain bone cells, called osteoclasts, that are responsible for removing old bone. Normal levels of thyroid hormone keep the balance between the cells that form new bone, osteoblasts, and the osteoclasts. So if you are taking thyroid hormone replacement pills and your thyroid function levels are normal, you are at no more risk for osteoporosis than you would be if you weren't on the medication.

At one time, some doctors recommended estrogen replacement therapy to women to offset any potential damage to bones caused by excess thyroid hormone. Estrogen therapy is no longer recommended for this purpose because of recent studies linking it to an increased risk of breast cancer. Studies also show that estrogen therapy does not protect against heart disease as was previously thought. As long as your thyroid hormone levels remain normal, thyroid medication will not lead to bone loss. So be sure to have your blood levels routinely monitored. Taking other measures to prevent osteoporosis, such as consuming adequate amounts of calcium and vitamin D and exercising, is always a good idea at any age. Talk to your doctor about ways to protect yourself from bone loss.

## Hypothyroidism and Obesity: Is There a Link?

**Myth:** Hypothyroidism leads to obesity, and people with thyroid troubles have a harder time losing weight than others, even when they are on appropriate levels of thyroid hormone.

**Fact:** There is a widespread belief that an underactive thyroid causes obesity, folklore that no doubt emerged because hypothyroidism can lead to some weight gain. While experts acknowledge the weight gain connection, obesity is a whole different question. Your metabolism is indeed slower if you have an underactive thyroid. Your body uses less energy, and unused excess calories are stored as fat. But just as your metabolism slows down, so does your appetite. If you are hypothyroid, you may gain three to ten pounds—or you may not gain any weight at all. But hypothyroidism is not to blame for obesity, a condition that likely involves a number of contributing factors, including genetics, psychology, diet, and exercise habits.

Obesity is a major health problem in this country that affects both those with and without thyroid problems, and obesity rates increase every year. It's no news that many Americans live on fast food and have a sedentary lifestyle. Some 64 percent of Americans are overweight and 30 percent are obese, according to a report issued recently by the Centers for Disease Control and Prevention. The FDA reports that obesity is poised to surpass smoking to become the leading cause of preventable deaths in the United States.

While it is true that some people seem to clearly have a harder time losing weight than others, there is no scientific proof that thyroid patients who are being treated appropriately have a unique problem keeping weight off.

## Thyroid Drugs for Weight Loss: Not a Good Idea

**Myth:** One way to lose weight is by increasing your thyroid medication.

**Fact:** Difficulty losing weight is a very common complaint from those whose medication has put them within normal thyroid hormone ranges. You might assume that it is your thyroid that is preventing you from shedding the unwanted pounds. It is logical to take this one step further and surmise that if your thyroid medication were increased, you would have an easier time losing weight. The higher dose would make your metabolism burn more calories and you would lose more weight. After all, one of the symptoms of too much thyroid hormone is weight loss in most people. This may be true in the short term. One study of nine people taking thyroid medication found that small changes in their T4 dose can have significant impact on what is known as resting energy expenditure, meaning how much energy is used when you are resting. But experts believe that this effect would not continue to play out long-term because of your body's ability to adapt. In other words, small increases in T4 will likely increase

49

your appetite, and while you may lose weight initially, increased calorie consumption and other adaptations such as decreased exercise, will eventually cancel out any increase in metabolic rate. However, the long-term effect of modest excess T4 or T3 has not been studied.

In addition, it isn't just fat that comes off when T4 is increased. A hyperthyroid state can lead to a breakdown in muscle mass. Excess thyroid hormone is dangerous and it is more likely to cause thyrotoxicosis than weight loss.

A wealth of both credible information and misconceptions about hypothyroidism, its treatment, and its relationship to weight gain abounds on the Internet and in the popular press. (Reputable Internet sources are listed in the Additional Resources section.) As you wade through what seems like an endless sea of information on the subject, remember to consult your doctor, who is your best source of reliable information. You should discuss your concerns over something you've read, or what seem to be new developments in treatment, with your physician.

# 3

# Hyperthyroidism: Help, I Want to Slow Down!

The word *hyper* can mean "above, over, and excessive" or "high-strung and keyed up." Both definitions describe the effect hyperthyroidism has on your body. In the words of Jerry, a hyperthyroid patient whose story is told later in this chapter, "You have this constant feeling of being tense, frantic, and irritable, like you will explode at any given minute. You feel as though you've had eight cups of coffee and you're just jazzed up all the time."

This feeling comes from having too much thyroid hormone in your system. Just as an underactive thyroid produces too little thyroid hormone and slows your metabolism, an overactive thyroid produces too much thyroid hormone and speeds your metabolism. It doesn't respond to decreased TSH levels, but continues to overproduce. If you are a typical hypothyroid patient, you suffer from sleepiness, cold intolerance, dry skin, weight gain, loss of appetite, constipation, and a low pulse, while if you are a typical hyperthyroid person, you endure sleepless nights, heat intolerance, excess sweating, weight loss, a voracious appetite, loose bowels, and a high pulse (see Figure 3.1).

Despite such polar-opposite effects, however, the diseases are similar in many ways. The most common cause for each disease involves the presence of antibodies that target and attack the thy-

**FIGURE 3.1** Hyperthyroidism

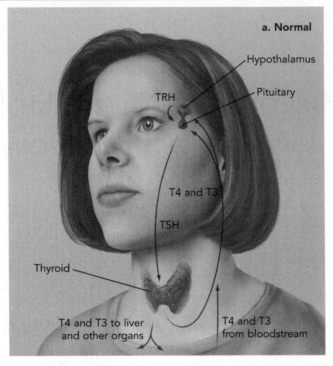

*In contrast to a normal thyroid (a), in hyperthyroidism the thyroid enlarges and produces too much thyroid hormone (b). A wide variety of symptoms appear, including sweating, a fast pulse, and weight loss. Excessive thyroid hormone creates changes in the hypothalamus and pituitary gland, which lead to decreased thyroid-stimulating hormone (TSH), but the diseased, overactive thyroid gland does not respond to this signal and continues to overproduce thyroid hormone.*

roid gland. These conditions, in which a malfunctioning immune system attacks healthy body tissues, are known as autoimmune diseases.

Hyperthyroidism is considerably less common than hypothyroidism, but they are both more prevalent in women than men. The risks for hyperthyroidism increase as you age, with one exception. Graves' disease, the most common cause of hyperthyroidism, tends to strike women in their reproductive years on, from between the ages of twenty and fifty. Both hypothyroidism and hyperthy-

**FIGURE 3.1** *continued*

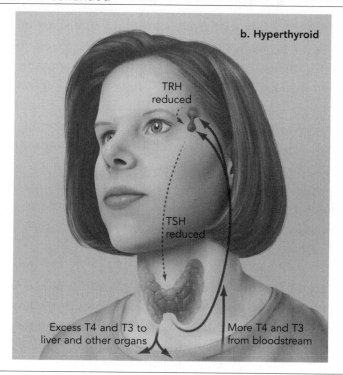

roidism cause fewer detectable symptoms in older people. As these diseases present themselves in subtle ways in this age group, they may seem like another disease altogether, masquerading as heart disease, psychiatric problems, or bowel problems.

Hyperthyroidism can have serious consequences if left untreated. It puts you at risk for osteoporosis, and, as too much thyroid hormone makes your heart work faster and harder, it can lead to heart difficulties.

Most people who experience a variety of classic symptoms are treated with drugs that suppress the production of thyroid hormone, with radioactive iodine that destroys part of the thyroid gland, or with surgery before life-threatening complications or permanent heart damage occurs. In older patients, however, a heart problem is often the first sign of hyperthyroidism.

## Recognizing Signs and Symptoms

The symptoms of hyperthyroidism tend to come on slowly, and they vary from person to person. It's not always obvious that symptoms, such as excess thirst or an increased appetite, are an indication that something is wrong. Often, people don't see a doctor until they experience palpitations or shortness of breath. The following sections describe both the classic symptoms most typically experienced in hyperthyroidism and the symptoms more commonly encountered by older people.

### Classic Signs and Symptoms of Hyperthyroidism

The following are the most common signs and symptoms experienced by people with hyperthyroidism.

- **Enlarged thyroid gland.** As your thyroid produces more and more hormone, your thyroid enlarges and can protrude from your neck to form a goiter. If the goiter is noticeable enough, it may feel lumpy.
- **Heat intolerance.** A speeded-up metabolism leads to an increase in your body temperature. You may be the only one in the room who wants to open a window, or you may find yourself in short sleeves while others are wearing sweaters.
- **Exhaustion.** Your body is perpetually in overdrive, which essentially tires out every one of its systems. You may find yourself out of breath after crossing the street or climbing the stairs.
- **Emotional changes.** Your body's exhausted state coupled with an overstimulated central nervous system can lead to a variety of emotional changes, such as anxiety intermixed with depression, insomnia, and irritability.
- **Perspiration and thirst.** As your body temperature rises, your sweat glands tend to overproduce and you feel the need to continually replenish fluids.
- **Constant hunger.** As your body uses up energy, it tends to cry out for more, which can lead to an insatiable appetite.

- **Unexplained weight loss.** Even though you may find yourself constantly eating, you could lose weight, usually between five and ten pounds. If you have severe thyrotoxicosis, you can experience extreme weight loss.

- **Racing heart.** Hyperthyroidism causes abnormal heart rhythms. Out of nowhere, you may suddenly feel your heart race. This can occur when you are exerting yourself or when you are relaxing.

- **Fast pulse.** If you habitually take your own pulse as part of your exercise regimen, you will notice a more rapid pulse than normal. If, for example, your normal pulse is between the 60 to 70 beats per minute range, you may find your heart is beating 80 to 100 times a minute.

- **Hand tremors.** You may notice your hands shaking. It might be subtle or it could be to the point where you can't carry a drink across the room without spilling it. This is the result of overstimulated nerves.

- **Muscle weakness.** Excess thyroid hormone tends to break down muscle. You are likely to experience a feeling of weakness, particularly in your arms and legs. If you are a physically active person, you may notice marked changes in your athletic performance.

- **Diarrhea.** An overactive thyroid causes your digestive system to speed up, and this leads to frequent, loose bowel movements.

- **Eye problems.** Particularly if you have Graves' disease, you may experience eye problems, and they can be quite severe. The most common eye symptom is a retraction of the eyelids that makes your eyes appear to bulge or stare dramatically. Your eyes may also be puffy and watery, and you may experience double vision.

- **Menstrual changes and infertility in women.** If you are a woman of childbearing age, your periods may be lighter or you may skip periods. This can lead to changes in your ovulation cycle and infertility.

- **Infertility, decreased libido, and enlarged breasts in men.** If you are a man, hyperthyroidism also interferes with your sperm cycle, causing temporary infertility. Decreased libido may stem from the weakening effect of hyperthyroidism, along with a relative decline in testosterone. Enlarged breasts (known as gynecomastia) result from a relatively high level of estrogen.
- **Hives.** You might notice an itchy rash that can be relieved with antihistamines.

## Signs and Symptoms of Hyperthyroidism in People over Sixty

If you are over sixty years old, a diagnosis of hyperthyroidism may be delayed because you tend not to experience the number of symptoms that younger people do. One study, conducted in France and published in 1996, compared signs and symptoms in older hyperthyroid patients to those in patients under age fifty. The study identified seven features—hyperactive reflexes, increased sweating, heat intolerance, hand tremors, nervousness, excessive thirst, and increased appetite—that occur less frequently in older patients.

While you may experience classic symptoms of hyperthyroidism, it is more typical that you would show a few or only one of the following symptoms.

- **Depression.** As an older person with hyperthyroidism, you are more likely than a younger person with the disease to develop depression that may appear as apathy. Though depression is sometimes cited as a feature of hyperthyroidism in younger people, it is usually intermixed with anxiety in younger people. On the other hand, as an older person with hyperthyroidism, you would tend to experience depression alone. If you exhibit this symptom, you will often feel sad and lethargic and have little interest in either yourself or your surroundings.

- **Congestive heart failure.** Your most prominent sign of hyperthyroidism could be congestive heart failure, the symptoms of which include breathlessness, swelling in your ankles, weakness, and fatigue. In the case of an overactive thyroid, backup in blood flow and ineffective pumping result from the heavy burden hyperthyroidism places on your heart.
- **Fast pulse.** The French study found that an abnormally fast pulse, known as *tachycardia*, of over 100 beats per minute occurred in 50 percent of older patients. It occurs in 90 percent of younger patients. This sign may go unnoticed unless you have seen a doctor.
- **Atrial fibrillation (racing and irregular heartbeat).** The French study found that 35 percent of older patients experienced the disorganized heart rhythms characterized by *atrial fibrillation* while only 2 percent of younger patients did.
- **Nervousness and exhaustion.** You may be one of the approximately 20 percent of older people who feel the nervousness and anxiety typically experienced by younger patients with an overactive thyroid. On the other hand, you may also feel lethargic.
- **Excessive weight loss.** A younger person with hyperthyroidism may experience some weight loss, but you may tend to lose even more weight, to the point where you could appear malnourished.
- **Muscle weakness.** If you have lost a lot of weight, you are likely to have profound muscle weakness due to an accelerated breakdown of your muscles.

## What's Causing My Hyperthyroidism?

Hyperthyroidism is usually caused by an underlying thyroid condition. Other times, it is triggered by certain medications or excessive doses of iodine. The following are the causes of hyperthyroidism.

## Graves' Disease

This disease, named after Dr. Robert Graves of Dublin, who first discovered it more than 160 years ago, is by far the most common cause of hyperthyroidism in both younger and older people. The cause of Graves' disease is believed to be a combination of factors, including genetic predisposition, your immune system, your age, sex hormones, and stress. The immune system abnormalities that occur with Graves' disease promote thyroid growth as well as hyperfunction to variable degrees. For instance, you could develop a barely enlarged thyroid gland that produces an enormous amount of thyroid hormone or a fairly big goiter that only over-produces a modest amount of thyroid hormone. Graves' disease is discussed in detail in Chapter 5.

## Toxic Multinodular Goiter

Toxic multinodular goiter, also known as Plummer's disease, is a common cause of hyperthyroidism in people over sixty, but it remains second to Graves' disease in all populations. It is charac-terized by an enlarged thyroid gland, or goiter, that has nodules that generally overproduce thyroid hormone in varying degrees. In most cases, this kind of lumpy goiter develops from an enlarged thyroid that has been present for many years, although it may have been inconspicuous. The thyroid gradually becomes more and more overactive until you become hyperthyroid. What causes these kinds of goiters to become overactive is not fully understood.

## Hot Nodule

Hot nodules are certain nodules that can develop in the thyroid gland that independently produce thyroid hormone and lead to hyperthyroidism.

## Thyroiditis

Thyroiditis leads to a temporary phase of thyrotoxicosis, during which time you may experience symptoms of hyperthyroidism because your thyroid essentially leaks thyroid hormone into the bloodstream. Then your thyroid runs low and produces insuffi-

## Fast Fact: Thyrotoxicosis Versus Hyperthyroidism

If the thyroid hormone levels in your system are abnormally high, you may hear your doctor refer to your condition as thyrotoxicosis rather than hyperthyroidism. Medically speaking, thyrotoxicosis refers to too much thyroid hormone, whether it be due to too much thyroid hormone medication, a thyroid that is leaking thyroid hormone, or an overactive thyroid. The term *hyperthyroidism* is reserved for excess thyroid hormone caused specifically by an overactive thyroid. But often these terms are used interchangeably.

cient amounts of hormone, leading to hypothyroidism, which is usually temporary.

### Too Much Thyroid Medication

If you are being treated for hypothyroidism and your dose is too high, you likely will develop thyrotoxicosis and the symptoms of hyperthyroidism. If you develop this condition because you are taking too much hormone, the problem is easily reversed when you begin taking the appropriate dose.

### Too Much Iodine

Taking too much iodine, either through your diet or through medications and supplements that are high in iodine, can lead to hyperthyroidism if you are predisposed to the condition. (See Table 1.3 for a list of medicines that contain high amounts of iodine.)

## Diagnosing Hyperthyroidism

As with hypothyroidism, a TSH blood test can confirm the presence of hyperthyroidism. This sensitive test and the other tests used when diagnosing your condition are discussed in Chapter 4. Symptoms of hyperthyroidism are often vague. However, if you experience certain "classic" symptoms of hyperthyroidism—a rac-

## Hyperthyroidism and Your Heart

Hyperthyroidism makes your heart work harder and can result in several heart conditions.

- **Abnormal heart rhythms.** Several rhythm disturbances can result from thyroid overstimulation. The most common are sinus tachycardia, an abnormally fast heart rate that can top 100 beats per minute, and atrial fibrillation, a disorganized rhythm in the heart's upper chambers. Atrial fibrillation in turn causes irregular beating of your heart's lower chambers or ventricles, which pump blood from your heart to the rest of your body. A related symptom is *palpitations*, a sudden awareness of your heart's contractions.
- **High blood pressure.** High systolic pressure (the top number of a blood pressure reading) is common if you have hyperthyroidism, especially if you are older.
- **Chest pain.** An excess of thyroid hormone makes your heart beat more forcefully and pump more blood. That increases the heart muscle's need for oxygen. If clogged, coronary arteries can't carry the extra blood your heart demands, and the result is chest pain, known as *angina*.
- **Heart failure.** By forcing your heart to work at a faster pace, an overactive thyroid can overtax it and cause heart failure, a condition in which your heart can't pump enough blood to meet your body's needs.

ing heart, anxiety, breathlessness—a trip to the doctor's office is warranted. Your doctor may or may not check your thyroid function during a routine visit, so it's up to you to notice any symptoms and be aware of any risk factors you may have, then ask your doctor to test your thyroid function.

Your primary care physician may diagnose your condition, or you may be referred to an endocrinologist or thyroidologist, an endocrinologist who specializes in thyroid disorders. Your doctor will ask about your symptoms, feel around your neck area to check for a goiter, and examine your eyes for signs of eye problems suggestive of Graves' disease. Your doctor will look for other physical signs of the disease and will ask you about your family history of thyroid or other autoimmune diseases.

If your TSH test comes back abnormally low, indicating that your pituitary gland is signaling your thyroid gland to cut back production of thyroid hormone, you will have a free T4 test or a series of tests that estimate free T4 (see page 74). If your free T4 levels are elevated, you have too much thyroid hormone in your system, which indicates you may be hyperthyroid. A blood test to check whether your T3 level is elevated may also be warranted, along with a blood test to check for the presence of antibodies that cause Graves' disease.

To diagnose hyperthyroidism, you may have to undergo tests that use small amounts of radioactive iodine. The radioactive iodine uptake (RAIU) test measures how efficiently your thyroid gland absorbs iodine. The radioactive iodine scan is used if there is a structural problem, such as a nodule. This scan shows whether the nodule is "hot" or whether it is producing thyroid hormone.

## Treating Hyperthyroidism

The goal of treatment is to stop the thyroid from overfunctioning, and there are three different ways of doing this. Radioactive iodine may be used to destroy part of your thyroid. Medication could be used to block your thyroid's ability to produce hormone. And surgery to remove all or part of your thyroid is sometimes an option.

If you were diagnosed with hyperthyroidism by your primary care doctor, you will likely be referred to an endocrinologist or thyroidologist. Unlike hypothyroidism, which can usually be treated by your primary care doctor, hyperthyroidism is less common and treating it is more complex. The specialist will outline the different therapy options for you.

The final decision on your treatment plan will rest on a number of factors, including your age, the cause of your condition, how severe it is, and whether you have any coexisting medical problems. It is important to understand the benefits and drawbacks of your therapy and to seek a second opinion if you are not comfortable with your doctor's recommendation. The following therapies are used to treat hyperthyroidism.

## Beta-Blockers

Regardless of what treatment turns out to be right for you, your doctor may initially prescribe a beta adrenergic blocking agent, commonly known as a *beta-blocker*, which will not cure your hyperthyroidism but will relieve some of its symptoms.

Beta-blockers are typically prescribed to treat hypertension, angina, and coronary artery disease, but they are also useful as part of a treatment plan for hyperthyroidism. Beta-blockers do not reduce the levels of thyroid hormone in your bloodstream, but they do block the action of thyroid hormone on your tissues and can bring you relief within hours. While you are waiting for more permanent measures of therapy to take effect, beta-blockers will help your heart to relax. They slow your heart rate, reduce palpitations and tremors, and may diminish nervousness.

Propranolol was the first beta-blocker developed, but your doctor can choose from more than ten different varieties of this class of drug that have since been developed. Some beta-blockers that have entered the market more recently stay in your system longer and require only one or two doses a day. Some forms of propranolol must be taken up to four times a day.

Although beta-blockers are generally safe, they can have side effects (see Table 3.1). They may reduce the strength of your heart muscle contractions, which can lead to fatigue or exercise intolerance. If you are diabetic, beta-blockers can mask some of the warning signs of low blood sugar. They could also make the symptoms of asthma worse. If you are taking a beta-blocker, call your doctor right away if any of the following symptoms persist or are severe: increased shortness of breath, wheezing, difficulty

TABLE 3.1 Medications Commonly Used to Treat Hyperthyroidism

| Generic Name | Brand Name | Side Effects |
| --- | --- | --- |
| **Beta Blockers** | | |
| Atenolol | Tenormin | Dizziness, fatigue, headaches, nightmares, difficulty sleeping, nausea, heartburn, diarrhea or constipation, skin rash, sudden weight gain, or vomiting. In some patients with heart problems, diabetes, or asthma, these drugs can cause increased shortness of breath, wheezing, difficulty breathing, irregular heartbeat, swelling of the feet and lower legs, and chest pain. |
| Metoprolol | Lopressor, Toprol-XL | |
| Nadolol | Corgard | |
| Propranolol | Inderal, Inderal LA | |
| Timolol | Blocadren | |
| **Antithyroid Drugs** | | |
| Methimazole | Tapazole | Rashes, itching, joint pain; can lower white blood cell count, making you more susceptible to infection; liver damage (rare) indicated by yellowing eyes, dark urine, and abdominal pain. |
| Propylthiouracil (PTU) | Propyl-Thyracil | |

breathing, a skin rash, an irregular heartbeat, swelling of your feet and lower legs, chest pain, vomiting, or severe diarrhea. Note that these drugs are not recommended for long-term use during pregnancy or to women who are breast-feeding.

## Radioactive Iodine Therapy

The administration of radioactive iodine, a procedure sometimes called *radioiodine ablation*, is a safe and effective way to resolve your hyperthyroidism. This therapy is the most widely used treatment for hyperthyroidism in the United States. Radioactive iodine destroys a significant portion of your thyroid, thereby reducing the production of thyroid hormone. Ideally, the goal is to make you *euthyroid*, a medical term used to describe a thyroid that is producing just the amount of thyroid hormone your body needs to function normally. Most likely, however, you will become hypothyroid and be dependent on thyroid hormone for life, which, in the long run, will keep your thyroid hormone levels normal and, ultimately, leave you feeling well. Your doctor will attempt to estimate how much radioactive iodine will cure your hyperthyroidism. But it is next to impossible to be exact. Even if the exact dose were achieved, your normally active thyroid would likely become over-active again in time. So most physicians err on the aggressive side. If the dose falls even slightly short of curing you, you will still be hyperthyroid and require another round of treatment.

The treatment is simple. You take a drink or capsule contain-ing radioactive iodine, just as you might for a radioactive iodine uptake test, except that this radioactive iodine typically comes from a different kind of radioactive isotope of iodine than that used in testing. I-123, which is generally used in testing, emits radiation that can be traced by a camera and is harmless to your thyroid. In treatment, a larger amount of the more potent I-131 is used to destroy overactive thyroid cells. The dosages are usually measured in units of radioactivity called *curies*, named after the French physicist Pierre Curie, who, with his wife Marie, won a Nobel prize for discoveries in radioactivity. One curie equals a thousand millicuries. Doses are sometimes measured in *becquerels*, a unit named after Henri Becquerel, who discovered radioactivity.

Typically, a dose of I-131 to treat hyperthyroidism ranges from 5–30 millicuries (mCi) or 185–1,100 megabecquerels (MBq). (One MBq is equal to one million becquerels. To convert mCi to MBq, multiply by thirty-seven.) A larger dose of 30–75 mCi (or 1,100–2,775 MBq) may be used to shrink larger thyroid glands that are causing problems with breathing. However, surgery is usually preferred if you have a compressive goiter, which causes symptoms by compressing structures close to the thyroid, such as the esophagus, trachea, and the large veins in the neck and upper chest. Larger doses of radioactive iodine are reserved for cases where surgery isn't an option, either because the patient refuses or surgery is considered risky, as is sometimes the case in elderly or frail patients.

Your thyroid is naturally programmed to take in iodine, and, because it is overactive, it is likely to take up a substantial dose. Beginning about a week prior to treatment until two days after-ward, you may need to stay on a low-iodine diet or to at least avoid major sources of iodine so that your thyroid is "hungry" for iodine. (For low-iodine diet guidelines, see Chapter 8.) This means avoiding all iodized salt. Keep in mind that sodium is okay as long as it is not iodized, so this is the time to pull out the kosher salt.

Once you ingest the treatment, the radioactive molecules will begin to destroy your thyroid cells. Within days of your treatment, the radioactive iodine that has not been picked up by your thyroid passes from your body in urine or is mostly reduced to a harmless nonradioactive state. It generally takes at least six to twelve weeks for your thyroid levels to drop to normal. You may then become hypothyroid anytime from that point on to more than ten years later. When this occurs, you will need to begin thyroid hormone replacement.

The radioactive iodine procedure is painless, although you may feel some tenderness in your neck, particularly when the dose of radioactive iodine is on the higher end. Your mouth may feel dry afterward, because saliva glands are sometimes disrupted during the treatment; however, this is unusual for the typical doses of radioactive iodine used in the treatment of hyperthyroidism.

When this form of treatment was first used more than sixty years ago, doctors and patients were concerned about the risks that radioactive iodine could pose in causing cancer, infertility, or birth defects in children. As it turns out, authorities who have studied this in all these years say that such risks are negligible. Still, women are cautioned to wait for six months and men for at least two months following treatment before starting a pregnancy. The procedure was once considered too risky for children, but nowadays more and more children are being treated with radioactive iodine. However, it should not be used to treat pregnant or breast-feeding women.

As perfect as this treatment sounds, it is not without risks. Radioactive iodine treatment may lead to a radiation-induced inflammation, or thyroiditis. In this case, your hyperthyroidism may worsen temporarily, sometimes accompanied by neck pain. This kind of thyroiditis is likely to last a few days, and your doctor can prescribe medicine to relieve the symptoms. If you have Graves' disease, you may experience an exacerbation of your eye problems after radioactive iodine. You are at highest risk for this if you are a smoker with severe, unstable eye disease and if your thyroid levels are not well regulated after receiving radioactive iodine.

After radioactive iodine treatment, you'll need to follow a few precautions over the next few days (outlined in Chapter 8) to prevent exposing others to the radiation present in your bodily fluids. In particular, you should stay away from pregnant women and small children, who are more sensitive to radiation exposure.

## Antithyroid Drugs

Drugs known as antithyroid agents block the thyroid gland's ability to make thyroid hormone and thus reduce the level of thyroid hormone in your body.

Antithyroid drugs may be the only therapy recommended if you have Graves' disease. With Graves' disease, removing your thyroid is typically not required if your thyroid gland isn't enlarged to the point that it is compressing any structures in your neck. Usually, there are no potentially worrisome nodules that have to be excised. Additionally, in the absence of nodules that are overproducing thyroid hormone, antithyroid drugs create a chance for spontaneous remission. However, most people with Graves' disease opt for radioactive iodine therapy, which has a better long-term track record.

The upside of antithyroid drugs is that you may go into a long-term remission from your disease without damaging your thyroid gland. The downsides are that there is uncertainty as to how long you'll need to take them before remission takes effect and that they can have serious side effects.

Using antithyroid drugs for about one to two years leads to remission in 20 to 30 percent of patients with Graves' disease who opt for this treatment. Those who do go into remission can relapse. If you aren't having success, your doctor will likely recommend radioactive iodine therapy, which has minimal risks and a much better success rate.

Antithyroid drugs can also be used before treatment with radioactive iodine or surgical removal of the thyroid. This combination of therapies is usually recommended if you are a heart patient or if you are an older patient, with greater cardiovascular risks. Due to the effect that changes in thyroid hormone levels can have on your heart, your doctor will want to observe your cardiac function closely as the antithyroid drugs are used to gradually bring your hormone levels down to normal before radioactive iodine therapy or surgery. Doing so minimizes the risk of severe thyrotoxicosis, which would result from inflammation caused by radioactive iodine or from surgical manipulation of the thyroid gland.

There are two types of antithyroid drugs commonly used in the United States, methimazole (Tapazole) and propylthiouracil (PTU). Once you begin taking either type, it may take between one and three months for you to begin feeling better and your thyroid function to return to normal.

Methimazole and PTU each work a little bit differently, so your doctor may prescribe one over the other, depending on your situation. If you are pregnant, for instance, PTU is generally prescribed in the United States because it appears less likely to enter the bloodstream of the fetus and has not been linked with the birth defects *aplasia cutis*, a rare scalp malformation, and *choanal atresia*, an abnormality of the nasopharynx (upper part of the pharynx, or cavity, that connects the nose to the mouth), which have been associated with the use of methimazole.

Some physicians consider PTU the drug of choice for those who have severe hyperthyroidism because it inhibits the conversion of T4 to T3, the more active of the thyroid hormones. It is usually prescribed at a daily dose of 300–400 mg, taken in several doses because it is only potent for about eight hours. Methimazole, usually prescribed in daily doses of 30–40 mg, can usually be taken once a day because it has a much longer duration of action than PTU. It may also be less likely to cause some unusual but serious adverse effects.

In some people, antithyroid drugs cause allergic reactions, such as rashes, itching, and joint pain. In one in five hundred or so patients, antithyroid drugs substantially diminish the number of white blood cells in the bloodstream, lowering that person's resistance to serious infection. In the most extreme form of this condition, known as *agranulocytosis*, the white blood cells completely disappear.

To be sure that your white blood cell count remains normal, your doctor will want you to hold off on taking your medication and have a blood test if you develop any type of infection or signs of infection, such as a fever or a sore throat. If your white blood cell count appears to be down due to PTU or methimazole, you may not resume taking the drug.

Another rare side effect is liver damage. If you notice any signs of liver damage, such as yellowing eyes, dark urine, severe fatigue, or abdominal pain, stop taking the drug and call your doctor.

## Surgery

Another way to cure hyperthyroidism is to have all or part of the thyroid gland removed in a procedure known as a *thyroidectomy*. However, with the success of radioactive iodine therapy, surgery is typically reserved for those who have very large goiters or nodules that are causing breathing or swallowing difficulties. It is also useful for people who are relatively resistant to radioactive iodine treatment. Surgery may also be a good choice for pregnant women whose conditions cannot be controlled with conservative doses of antithyroid drugs and for patients who are allergic to antithyroid medications. Due to concerns over the safety of radiation therapy, thyroidectomy is more popular outside the United States, in places such as Japan and parts of Europe.

Antithyroid drugs or iodine drops, which work like antithyroid drugs, are sometimes administered prior to surgery to help control hyperthyroidism. Iodine drops, however, are typically reserved for use in severe hyperthyroidism or hyperthyroidism that needs to be quickly controlled, such as in critical heart conditions or in preparation for emergency surgery. During thyroidectomy, the thyroid gland is removed through an open incision. Minimally invasive surgical techniques that involve small incisions and the insertion of tubes for the passage of surgical instruments are sometimes employed but this is not typical.

Thyroid surgery is safe and highly effective. Major complications occur in less than 2 percent of patients operated on by an experienced thyroid surgeon. Complications that can occur include damage to the parathyroid glands surrounding the thyroid, which control your body's calcium levels. There could also be damage to your laryngeal nerves on each side of your neck that control your vocal cords, and you could either become hoarse or lose most or all of your voice. If there is damage to one of the nerves, your loss of voice is typically temporary or partial. Bilateral damage is more severe, and you would be less likely to spontaneously recover.

After your thyroid surgery, you will most likely become hypothyroid and require thyroid hormone replacement for life. If your entire thyroid is removed, you would have nothing left to make thyroid hormone. If you have only part of the thyroid left, you may be lucky enough to be euthyroid. Still, you'll need to have blood tests periodically to be sure.

## Remembering What It's Like to Feel Good

Jerry's story is a classic case of hyperthyroidism, in which a combination of symptoms came on so gradually that he didn't put them together until they interfered with his favorite hobby, mountain climbing. A spinal surgeon with a demanding schedule and highly active life, fifty-one-year-old Jerry makes time to climb Mount Washington, the highest peak in the Northeast, at least once every winter, when snow covers its massive rocks. But on one routine climb, it came as a surprise to him that he was out of breath and gasping for air. This is Jerry's story.

> The conditions were perfect that day. I expected my climbing time to be three and a half to four hours and it was more like five and a half. This just didn't make any sense. I couldn't figure out why I had no endurance.
>
> So I decided to look at my own life and see what else was going on. There were two other things that were odd.

One is that I was constantly thirsty. I would come home every night and I would drink three to four glasses of water. The other thing is that my pulse had been running high. Now most people aren't tuned in to their own pulse, but ever since I ran marathons fifteen years ago, I became compulsive about taking my pulse. Back then, it was always low—in the upper 40s or low 50s. As I got older, my normal resting pulse was about 60. And now, when I checked it, my pulse was in the 80s and that was kind of weird. And I remembered that occasionally, in recent months, I could feel my heart race. So it was the combination of drinking a lot, high pulse, and zero endurance that made me wonder what was going on.

Now I wasn't smart enough to realize that the lack of endurance would be a sign of hyperthyroidism. But it was the high pulse that led me to check my thyroid function, because that's a classic sign of thyroid disease. Drinking a lot—that's a classic symptom of diabetes. Lack of endurance can be a lot of things. Since I'm a physician, I was able to run my own blood work. So I checked my blood count. I checked my blood sugar and I checked my thyroid function, and when I looked at the results, my thyroid function tests looked kind of strange. That's when I contacted my physician, who said, "Come in and we'll repeat the tests," and the same results came back. I had other tests, and it turned out I had Graves' disease.

It wasn't until after I was diagnosed that I realized there were other symptoms, but I hadn't put them in the picture. I've always been a little warmer than the next person, but over the last year and a half, it got worse, and I was always hot. It got to the point where I was sweating so much in the operating room that I had to wear a sweatband. And nobody else in the room complained of the heat. Of course, that's a classic sign of hyperthyroidism, but I didn't put it in the picture. I also had been experiencing hand tremors. In the operating room, I manipulate very small instruments. When your hand is out in space you always have a little tremor. But this seemed to be worse to the point where a nurse was saying, "Are you sick or something?"

Another symptom that I didn't initially recognize is that when I got up and walked into the next room, I'd be out of breath. This is the same symptom I experienced on Mount Washington, except it was with a trivial exertion. My appetite also seemed insatiable. I'm an active person, and I normally like to eat a lot and eat well, but I noticed I was constantly hungry. I would have breakfast, and then by nine o'clock I would want lunch, and still I would keep snacking all day and sometimes eat three bowls of cereal before I went to bed.

I was first treated with beta-blockers, just to relieve some of the symptoms until I was treated with radioactive iodine, which was a very simple procedure. I just had to swallow a capsule and then go home. My doctor warned me about "the crash." Typically, at some point, perhaps days or weeks after treatment, you crash into a hypothyroid state. But he also told me that before crashing, my hyperthyroid symptoms could become worse. That's what happened. I was continually monitored, and after a couple of weeks, I became clinically more toxic [hyperthyroid] to the point that it was quite unpleasant. I continued to take the beta-blockers but they didn't help much. My heart rate was up to 80 beats per minute. I continued to lose muscle mass. When I tried to exercise, I was gasping for air. I just felt awful.

Then, suddenly, about six to seven weeks after my treatment, I felt better. It happened instantaneously, like someone turned on a switch. Suddenly, I didn't feel as hot. I felt cold. What a good feeling! My thirst decreased and my appetite decreased. It was confirmed in the lab that I had become hypothyroid, and it was then that I was put on thyroid hormone replacement. Ever since, I have felt great. I no longer feel as though I am going to explode at any given moment. I always had this constant feeling of being tense and frantic and irritable. I had to work to hold in my feelings. It's as though someone has put me on a tranquilizer. No longer do I constantly seek food and water. I used to spend my day figuring out how to find food. I always made sure I had something to eat and drink in the car. After I was cured I had to stop and say, wait a minute, it's been a few hours and I haven't had to eat something. My pulse was much more normal, in the low 50s to low 60s.

The best way to describe what I'm feeling now is to say that I had no idea how badly I felt for so long until I was finally able to feel good. I've put on six or seven pounds. And I'm back on track, exercising for about an hour a day. I'm running, biking, or kayaking, lifting weights and climbing mountains. I'm trying to build my endurance back, particularly because I've arranged a trip to Mount Rainier in a couple of months. It's the highest peak in the continental United States—a 14,000-footer, so I have a lot of work to do.

Whether you are treated with surgery, radioactive iodine, antithyroid drugs, or a combination of these therapies, hyperthyroidism requires long-term follow-up. You'll need to watch for signs and symptoms of hypothyroidism (as discussed in Chapter 2) and your doctor will monitor your TSH, T4, and T3 levels, first at frequent intervals and then every six months to a year. (See the next chapter for information on these blood tests.)

If you develop hypothyroidism, as most people in this situation eventually do, you must continue to see your doctor for blood tests even after your medication is prescribed because your body's needs may change over the years.

# 4

# A Guide to Thyroid Tests

New thyroid patients are introduced to a parade of acronyms that sound more like a top secret code than medical tests. Yet, because thyroid problems involve continual follow-up and monitoring over the years, you'll soon find yourself quite familiar with tests that measure TSH, T4, FT4, T3, and FT3, to name a few.

Thyroid testing typically involves blood work, tests that use radioactive iodine, and imaging tests. Most tests are used to determine how well your thyroid is functioning. Imaging tests are also sometimes needed to investigate any structural problems, such as a nodule or goiter.

## Blood Tests

Functional thyroid diseases, including hypothyroidism and hyperthyroidism, are diseases characterized by hormones that are out of balance with each other. Consequently, for each part of the hypothalamic-pituitary-thyroid axis discussed in Chapter 1, there are hormonal tests to determine whether the axis is working normally. By observing these hormone levels together, doctors can usually tell what your problem is and what is causing it. However, nodules and goiters may throw off your hormone balance, so imaging tests may be required to evaluate any structural thyroid disease. Here are some of the blood tests your doctor may ask for if thyroid disease is suspected.

## TSH (Thyroid-Stimulating Hormone) Test

Doctors will first look at thyroid-stimulating hormone (TSH), the hormone secreted by the pituitary gland that determines how much hormone your thyroid makes. A newer, more sensitive TSH test that was developed in recent years has become the single best screening test to determine if you have thyroid disease, assuming that you do not have an unusual disorder of the pituitary gland that interferes with the normal production of TSH.

If this test comes back normal, it means that the levels of TSH circulating in your bloodstream are within normal ranges (see Table 4.1 for normal ranges). If it comes back high, your pituitary gland is sending a loud message to a failing thyroid that is not producing enough hormone, and you are hypothyroid. If your TSH levels are below the normal range, you have too much thyroid hormone circulating, and you are hyperthyroid.

These results apply to new patients who have never been on thyroid medication. But if you are being treated for an overactive or underactive thyroid, you will encounter this test periodically, with potentially different implications. For instance, if you've been taking too high of a dose of thyroid hormone and recently adjusted the dose, the test results may indicate a low TSH level for weeks or even months until your body adjusts to the change. If you recently began treatment for hyperthyroidism, your TSH levels may also be low for a while.

## T4 (Thyroxine) Tests

Thyroxine (T4), the hormone produced solely by the thyroid gland, circulates in two forms. Once secreted by the thyroid, most T4 is "bound" to protective binding proteins and not readily available for use by your cells. A very small percentage—well under 1 percent—of all of the circulating thyroxine is not bound to proteins and is therefore "free" and available for immediate use

**TABLE 4.1** Thyroid Blood Test Results for Most Commonly Used Tests (for People Not Yet Taking Thyroid Medication)

| Condition | TSH Level | FT4 Level or FT4 Index | FT3 Level or FT3 Index |
|---|---|---|---|
| Normal (euthyroid) | Within normal range of 0.45 and 4.5 mU/L* | Within normal range of 0.8–2.0 ng/dL* | Within normal range |
| Hypothyroidism | High | Low | Not useful |
| Hyperthyroidism | Low | High | High |
| Secondary hypothyroidism (indicating a pituitary disorder) | Low | Low | Not useful |
| Secondary hyperthyroidism (indicating rare pituitary tumor that is producing TSH) | High | High | High |
| Subclinical (mild) hypothyroidism | High | Within normal range | Not useful |
| Subclinical (mild) hyperthyroidism | Low | Within normal range | Within normal range |

*The normal range of TSH, T4, and T3 in the bloodstream slightly varies from lab to lab. A 2004 consensus report gives the normal range of TSH in the bloodstream as between 0.45 and 4.5 mU/L, and lists the normal range of free T4 as between 0.8 and 2.0 ng/dL. No range was cited for T3. Unit abbreviations are mU/L (milliunits per liter) and ng/dL (nanograms per deciliter).

by your cells. Enough free T4 must be present to keep up with the demands of your cells. Bound T4 acts as a circulating reservoir that is continually replenished by hormone that is secreted by the thyroid in equilibrium with the amount of free T4 needed by your cells. Since bound T4 constitutes the vast majority (more than 99 percent) of T4 in the body, a total T4 test essentially establishes how much T4 is circulating in your body.

A free T4 (FT4) test, considered most important for determining how the thyroid is functioning, measures only the amount of T4 available for use. In combination with a TSH test, a free T4 test gives a precise account of how your thyroid gland is functioning and helps determine the cause of the problem. For instance, if you have an elevated TSH and low FT4, you have primary hypothyroidism—the term used when the problem lies within the thyroid—due to disease that involves your thyroid gland.

If you have a low TSH and low FT4, your problem lies with a faulty pituitary gland and is considered secondary hypothyroidism. This term is used when the problem lies outside of the thyroid in the area of the hypothalamus or pituitary gland, the regions of the brain that influence and produce TSH.

A low TSH combined with an elevated FT4 means that you have too much thyroid hormone in your system. In that case, another test, called a radioactive iodine uptake (RAIU) test, may be performed (see "Radioactive Iodine Uptake [RAIU] Test" in this chapter). This test will confirm whether your thyroid is over-producing thyroid hormone, referred to as hyperthyroidism, or whether another problem has led to excess hormone, otherwise known as thyrotoxicosis, the medical term used to denote thyroid hormone excess of any kind. For instance, your thyroid may be leaking the hormone it produces, or perhaps you are taking too much thyroid hormone.

High levels of TSH and normal FT4 levels indicate that you have mild, or subclinical, hypothyroidism, which may or may not be causing symptoms. There is considerable debate over whether mild hypothyroidism should be treated.

Older thyroid function tests may sometimes be used in combination to calculate the amount of free T4, but these tests are not used as often as the free T4 tests, simply because the older method involves two tests instead of one. This combination of tests, which includes a T3 resin uptake (T3U) and total T4 test, provides an estimate of the percentage of thyroid hormone that is free and available to act on tissues. This figure is known as a free T4 index.

## T3 (Triiodothyronine) Tests

As with thyroxine tests, there are several tests that measure the amount of triiodothyronine (T3) in your bloodstream. Just as T4 is principally bound to protective proteins, the majority of T3 is also bound to them. One test, called a total T3 test, measures the total amount of T3 circulating in your body, and another test, called a free T3 test (FT3), measures the T3 that is freely circulating and available for use by your body. Another reliable way to determine the amount of free T3 is to calculate the free T3 index, which combines the results of a total T3 test with the T3U test. The combination of tests is preferred because the free T3 index is easily calculated and has a more widely recognized and better-established normal range than free T3 tests do.

T3 tests are not typically used in the diagnosis of hypothyroidism because if you have an underactive thyroid, your T3 levels are the last to fall. You can be severely hypothyroid and have a normal T3. T3 can, however, sometimes help doctors diagnose hyperthyroidism or determine how severe hyperthyroidism is. If you are hyperthyroid, your free T3 level is likely to be elevated. In some people who are hyperthyroid, the TSH test comes back low and the FT4 test comes back normal, and it is only the free T3 index that is elevated. This too indicates hyperthyroidism, which may be confirmed with a RAIU test.

## Thyroid Antibody Tests

Antibody tests are used to determine whether an autoimmune disorder is causing your thyroid disease. If your TSH and free T4 tests reveal that you are hypothyroid, your doctor may want to test for the presence of anti-Tg and anti-TPO antibodies. Anti-Tg antibodies work against a protein called thyroglobulin that is made by the thyroid and is vital to the production of thyroid hormone. Anti-TPO antibodies are directed against thyroid peroxidase, the main enzyme involved in thyroid hormone synthesis. The presence of these antibodies indicate that Hashimoto's thyroiditis, an autoimmune disease, is behind your hypothyroidism.

If you are diagnosed with hyperthyroidism, your doctor may test for the presence of antibodies that work against the TSH receptor on the thyroid gland. The presence of these antibodies confirms Graves' disease. TSH, or thyrotropin, receptor antibodies (TRAb) may be classified as those that stimulate the thyroid, known as TSH receptor-stimulating antibodies, and those that block its action, known as TSH receptor-blocking antibodies. An example of a stimulating antibody is thyroid-stimulating immu-noglobulin, or TSI. An example of a blocking antibody is TSH-binding inhibitory immunoglobulin, or TBII.

## TRH (Thyrotropin-Releasing Hormone) Test

Thyrotropin-releasing hormone (TRH) is the hormone that is secreted by the hypothalamus to stimulate TSH production in the pituitary gland. In most cases, a blood test that involves the administration of TRH is not needed. But if your doctor suspects that the source of your thyroid woes involve either problems with your pituitary gland or with your hypothalamus, this test may be used. This test was once more routinely used in cases where TSH test results were questionable. These days, however, TSH tests are ultrasensitive, giving such reliable results that a backup TRH test is usually not used.

The TRH test is a bit different than other blood tests. A blood sample for TSH is drawn and then TRH is injected intravenously. Blood samples for TSH are then drawn at certain time intervals.

## Radioactive Iodine Tests

Radioactive iodine tests capitalize on the thyroid's ability to pull iodine from your bloodstream and to use it to make thyroid hormone. These tests are typically used to determine when levels of thyroid hormone in your system are high or to investigate a nodule. You are given a small amount of radioactive iodine orally. Once in your system, your thyroid cells concentrate this kind of iodine just as they would dietary iodine. However, in this case, the radioactivity emitted from the substance enables doctors to use special machinery to trace it, which allows them to see how well your thyroid concentrates iodine.

If you're like most people, you may worry about the effects radioactive iodine might have on your health and on your thyroid in particular. You can rest assured that the minimal amount and type of radioactive material (I-123) typically used in these tests are harmless to the thyroid. The type usually used to destroy thyroid tissue in the treatment of hyperthyroidism and thyroid cancer is called I-131, which, when used to treat thyroid conditions, is given in a much higher dose than the dose of radioactive iodine used in tests.

Elements such as iodine exist in both radioactive and nonradioactive forms. The radioactive forms, which give off radiation, are known as radioactive isotopes. These two types of radiation, I-123 and I-131, are two different radioactive isotopes.

I-123 is a radioactive isotope that emits gamma rays that do not damage thyroid cells. This is the kind most commonly used in testing, and it is used in very small amounts. The I-131 isotope, which is used in medicine to destroy harmful thyroid tissue, emits high-energy beta rays known to produce cell damage or death. Some doctors still use I-131 in testing at a dose too small to be considered harmful.

I-123 also has a substantially shorter half-life than I-131. The medical term *half-life* is used to describe the time required for half the amount of a substance to be out of your system. I-123 has a half-life of thirteen hours as opposed to I-131, which has a half-life of eight days. Still, if you are pregnant or nursing, you should not have these tests.

There is no need for radioactive iodine tests in the diagnosis of hypothyroidism, because blood tests alone confirm the disease and its underlying cause. But if you're suffering from thyrotoxicosis, a doctor can use the RAIU test to measure how much iodine is taken up and concentrated in your thyroid. This measurement helps doctors distinguish whether your thyroid is truly hyperthyroid, or overproducing thyroid hormone; whether it is leaking hormone, indicating a transient or resolving form of thyroiditis, such as postpartum thyroiditis (if you are not nursing); or whether you are taking too much thyroid hormone.

If there is a structural concern, such as a nodule, you may have both the uptake test and a thyroid scan. For either test, you must not eat for several hours beforehand. You may even be instructed not to eat the night before the test. Check with your doctor. If you are taking antithyroid medication, you must stop taking it three to five days before the test.

## Radioactive Iodine Uptake (RAIU) Test

If you have the radioactive iodine uptake test, you will be given a tiny amount of radioactive iodine, usually contained in a small capsule that is easy to swallow. Doctors are able to measure how much radioactive iodine is taken into your thyroid by using a special machine that is placed directly over your thyroid gland (see Figure 4.1). The test isn't painful. It is done in the sitting position and requires you to remain still with your neck extended for about two minutes at a time. The entire test takes about ten minutes and is usually performed twenty-four hours after you swallow the tracer. In some cases, earlier measurements are performed instead of or in addition to the twenty-four-hour measurement.

The test result is expressed as a percentage of iodine concentrated from the total amount of iodine you are given. If the test shows that your thyroid gland has taken in an abnormally small

**FIGURE 4.1** Radioactive Iodine Uptake Test

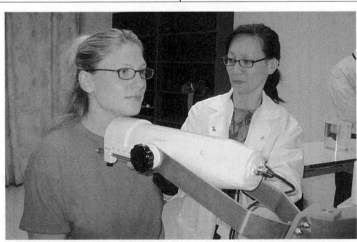

*To help diagnose thyroid disease, you may be asked to undergo this test to determine whether your thyroid gland is absorbing too much or too little iodine.*

percentage of the iodine, even though you have elevated levels of thyroid hormone in your system, it may indicate that your thyroid gland is leaking excessive amounts of thyroid hormone rather than overproducing it. On the other hand, the test may simply show that there is an excessive amount of iodine in your body. This is because the thyroid needs a certain amount of iodine in order to function. When excessive amounts of iodine are present, the thyroid only requires a small percentage of the total iodine pool, as reflected by a low radioactive iodine uptake, for it to perform its functions.

Abnormally high levels of radioactive iodine absorbed by the thyroid also have several implications. If your thyroid hormone levels are high, it may indicate that your thyroid gland is overproducing thyroid hormone instead of leaking it and you have hyperthyroidism. On the other hand, a high uptake may simply reflect a deficiency of iodine in your body regardless of what your blood tests show.

If you are taking thyroid hormone medication, the RAIU test is sometimes done if your TSH levels are abnormally low to indicate whether you are taking too much hormone or whether you have a hot nodule—a nodule that is overproducing thyroid hormone. A RAIU that was normal or high in combination with a scan that shows an area that concentrates radioactive iodine quite well in the region of a thyroid nodule would determine whether you did have a hot nodule.

## Radioactive Thyroid Scan

This test is sometimes done to assess any structural abnormalities. It is similar to the RAIU test in several ways. You are given a tiny amount of radioactive iodine, usually in the form of a capsule but sometimes in the form of an injection of technetium, which is also a radioactive substance. For this test, however, a special camera takes pictures of your thyroid gland from three different angles. An abnormal thyroid scan may show either a small or large thyroid gland. It can also show areas in the thyroid gland where there are high and low areas of activity. A thyroid scan is also done to assess whether or how actively nodules are functioning, to determine whether you have a hot nodule or a "cold" one, which produces little or no thyroid hormone. The procedure takes about half an hour. You must remain still for this test with your neck extended, which can cause some discomfort.

## Thyroid Ultrasound

If you have a nodule or goiter or your thyroid is irregularly shaped, making it difficult to examine physically, you may have a thyroid ultrasound. During ultrasound, high-frequency sound waves are used to create an image of your thyroid. During the procedure, you will lie on an examining table. A technician or a doctor will put a warm gel on the front of your neck where your thyroid is located and will then place an instrument called a trans- ducer, which conducts the sound waves, on your neck so that an image of your thyroid can be obtained painlessly.

Doctors use tests but also rely on clinical experience when diag- nosing thyroid conditions, particularly when there is mild disease and the decision to treat it may depend on other factors, such as whether there are symptoms. During each visit, your doctor will perform a physical exam, ask about symptoms, and check for any signs of thyroid disease, such as abnormal blood pressure, changes in your heart rate, changes in the size of your thyroid, and changes in the speed of your reflexes.

# CHAPTER 5

# An Immune System Run Amok: Thyroiditis, Graves' Disease, and Related Problems

As you go about your day and even as you sleep, your immune system is quietly and constantly patrolling your body to detect and destroy invaders. It is your most powerful protector, working tirelessly around the clock to keep you safe. But occasionally, for reasons only partially understood, the immune system mistakenly turns on the very body it is designed to protect, resulting in conditions known as autoimmune diseases.

Hashimoto's thyroiditis and Graves' disease, the most common types of hypothyroidism and hyperthyroidism respectively, are examples of autoimmune conditions of the thyroid. If you've been diagnosed with hypothyroidism or hyperthyroidism and you live in the United States or another region where iodine intake is adequate, there is a good chance that you have one of these conditions that are the result of a faulty immune system. And since genes handed down through generations are believed to be at least partly responsible for the development of autoimmune diseases, it is likely that someone else in your family—perhaps one of your parents, your child, or even an aunt or an uncle—has either a thyroid problem or an autoimmune condition of another organ or system.

But not everyone with a family history of thyroid problems or related conditions develops an autoimmune disease. You needn't assume that you'll inherit the condition if someone in your family has it. While there is certainly a genetic component involved, it's only one ingredient in the mix. There also has to be a trigger. Specific triggers have not yet been identified, but there are theories, which are outlined in this chapter. For instance, because women, particularly premenopausal women, are affected at about three times the rate men are, scientists suspect that hormones are somehow involved, but it is not clear how. Infection with bacteria and viruses, exposure to toxins or certain drugs, long-term stress, aging, and pregnancy may also influence an individual's susceptibility to develop an autoimmune disease.

## Your Immune System

To understand what happens when you develop an autoimmune condition of the thyroid, it helps to understand some basics about how your immune system works.

Normally, your immune system protects you from the ceaseless assaults of bacteria, viruses, fungi, and parasites, which are all considered disease-causing pathogens or germs. Your immune system does so through a coordinated response, often referred to as the *immune response*, which is essentially a complex set of biochemical interactions.

To cause disease, a germ that is entering your body must reproduce in sufficient numbers before it is overwhelmed by the body's immune response. Once the battle between the germs and the immune response has begun, the result of this race determines whether the outcome is sickness or health. Most of the time you have no idea of the battle raging inside of you.

Your body's first line of defense is your skin. As the largest organ your body has, it is a formidable barrier to infection, teeming with good bacteria with their own important functions, one of which is to provide an unfriendly environment for germs that can harm you. However, the skin doesn't provide perfect protection. If a germ passes through the initial barriers of your skin and mucous membranes, it triggers a sophisticated, well-orchestrated backup plan, known as the *innate immune system*, which has several strategies of its own for protecting you. One of these involves a group of white blood cells known as *phagocytes*. Cells in the phagocyte family, including *neutrophils*, *macrophages*, and long-armed *dendritic cells*, engulf and destroy pathogens by chemically chewing them up. But the phagocytes have another important role: they must send for help from other cells in the immune system. They do this in two ways, by sending out danger signals and by chopping up the disease-causing germ and displaying pieces of it— known as *antigens*—on their cell surface with a *major histocompatibility complex* (MHC) molecule. These molecules serve as a kind of photo ID tag for the phagocyte.

This is where a sophisticated group of *lymphocytes* (another kind of white blood cell), known as *B cells* and *T cells*, come into play. These are part of what's known as the *adaptive immune system*, which gets its name because it adapts itself during the first exposure to a germ so that it can destroy the same pathogen the next time it appears. B cells and T cells each have a different way of fighting infection. And there are different categories of T cells, each of which tackles problem pathogens in its own way (see Figure 5.1).

## Lifestyles of B Cells and T Cells

B cells and T cells start life in the bone marrow. B cells are home-bodies and stay in the bone marrow to mature. T cells, on the other hand, leave the bone marrow and move to the thymus, an important organ of the lymph system that is located in the upper chest. The young T cells mature in the thymus (hence the *T* in T cells). After they reach maturity, B cells and T cells travel via the bloodstream to the peripheral lymphoid tissues: lymph nodes, spleen, tonsils, adenoids, Peyer's patches (located in the small

FIGURE 5.1 Adaptive Immune Response: T Cells

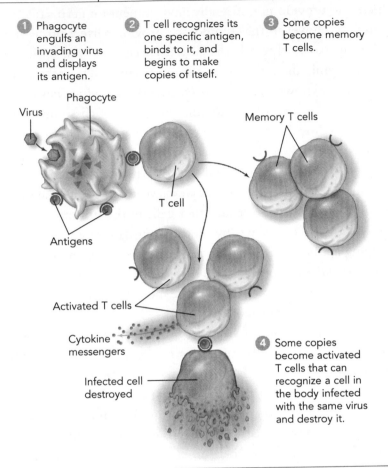

1. Phagocyte engulfs an invading virus and displays its antigen.

2. T cell recognizes its one specific antigen, binds to it, and begins to make copies of itself.

3. Some copies become memory T cells.

Phagocyte

Virus

Memory T cells

T cell

Antigens

Activated T cells

Cytokine messengers

Infected cell destroyed

4. Some copies become activated T cells that can recognize a cell in the body infected with the same virus and destroy it.

*T cells attack and destroy invaders, then multiply to prepare for a future invasion of the same germ.*

intestine), appendix, and so on, where some remain. The others circulate in the blood, migrating from lymphoid organ to lymphoid organ.

## Recognizing the Enemy

There are thousands of different kinds of T cells, each of them born to recognize one particular antigen. The recognition of one special antigen by a single T cell is arguably one of the most astounding aspects of the adaptive immune response. The human immune system can recognize countless antigens on the surface of phagocytes. Based on that recognition, the adaptive immune system is able to customize its terminator strategy to a particular antigen.

Since each T cell is born to recognize one antigen, this provides the body with a huge repertoire of cells predestined to recognize any of the germs likely to invade the body. But out of all the microorganisms that might enter the body, and all the T cells designed to respond to those microorganisms, how does that one special T cell get activated and copied when its pathogen enters? It looks for two kinds of signals from the phagocytes of the innate immune system. The first signal is called the recognition signal. As mentioned above, the phagocytes—such as the long-armed dendritic cells as well as the macrophages and neutrophils—engulf the germ; chop it into pieces, called *peptides*; and display these small pieces as a signal or antigen on the cell surface. These phagocytes, which are known as *professional antigen-presenting cells*, next travel to a nearby lymphoid organ, where the appropriate T cell recognizes the antigen signal.

The second signal is the danger signal. It takes the form of changes on the surface of the antigen-presenting cells as well as the release of chemical messengers. This second signal tells the T cells to multiply and to ramp up their fighting forces. With this signal, a phagocyte, such as a dendritic cell, essentially says, "Look out, I'm showing you a foreigner that shouldn't be here." Without this danger signal, there would be no serious immune counterattack.

Once the antigen is presented to its matching T cell in a lymphoid organ, the antigen selects and activates the T cell by locking onto an antigen receptor on the T cell's surface. This is like a key fitting a customized lock. Binding with the antigen causes the T cell to start making clones—identical copies of itself that are able to recognize that specific antigen only. Over the course of three to five days, a small army of T-cell clones comes into being. This army organizes itself into subunits with assigned tasks. Some are designated to kill infected cells; some to activate other lymphocytes to multiply; still others to remember the antigen and wait quietly for its return visit at a later date. Because these T cells are so specific, once a T cell recognizes its antigen, it can launch an attack that is specifically tailored to the way that pathogen operates. It anticipates, for example, whether the pathogen will operate inside or outside a cell and can launch an attack based on that information.

B cells, on the other hand, recognize their specific antigen in the surface of the invading pathogen. Then a similar process happens as with the T cells. Some B cells clone into B cells that remember that particular antigen, while others multiply as *plasma cells*, which generate molecules called *antibodies* that bind with the pathogens and block them from entering your healthy cells.

This explosive increase in the number of lymphocytes, both B cells and T cells, from just a few to millions is called *clonal expansion*. It's what gives your immune system its extraordinary might and specificity.

## Memory: Long-Term Protection

The clonal expansion of lymphocytes not only fights off the invading germs but also makes sure your immune system remembers and recognizes a villain the next time it comes back to town. When lymphocytes multiply during clonal expansion, some of them are destined to live on as "memory" B cells and T cells. These clones are a subset of the expanded number of B cells and T cells that develop from your first exposure to a germ, and they protect you against subsequent attacks by the same germ. Because of this increase in memory cells, your immune system's responses to subsequent attacks are faster and greater than to the first. This explains why once you've had an infectious illness, you don't get sick when you're exposed to it the next time around. You may get "the flu" again, but it would have to be caused by a different form of the influenza virus than the last time. You can't get sick from the same one you had before.

## Recognizing Self

An immune response is activated when the immune system alerts the body to the presence of foreign or "nonself" microorganisms. Conversely, a normal immune system does not attack "self" cells.

Normally, when the cells of your body display protein fragments on their surface as part of the routine recycling that goes on all the time, your immune system ignores your body's own self cells. When the immune system malfunctions and attacks self cells, the consequences can be disastrous, leading to thyroid diseases or other autoimmune conditions such as lupus and rheumatoid arthritis.

Unresponsiveness, or immunologic tolerance to self, is therefore very important. The major safeguard that prevents a normal immune system from attacking its own cells is the rigorous screening of T cells during their development in the thymus. It's been estimated that less than 5 percent of T cells pass muster and go on to join the ranks of the functioning immune system. A policy of programmed cell death rids your immune system of those T cells that would mistakenly treat your normal cells as foreign. After this culling, the immune system should have only those T cells that can recognize the foreign or nonself antigens presented to them by antigen-presenting cells.

## Autoimmune Disease

When components of the adaptive immune response, namely B cells and T cells, fail to distinguish between "self" and "nonself," they attack the body's own tissues in the same way they would attack invading germs. Normally, immature T cells that fail to learn the difference between "self" and "nonself" are eliminated. Theoretically, your body should have no lymphocytes that can't make the distinction. But the process isn't perfect. Some failing-grade cells slip past this weeding-out process and remain in circulation, which means they have the potential to produce autoantibodies and autoreactive T cells that can go on to wreak havoc on your tissues.

If these cells are directed against nerve tissue, the result can be multiple sclerosis, while if they are directed against the pancreas,

# Examples of Autoimmune Diseases and Their Target Organs

**Blood**

Autoimmune hemolytic anemia

Autoimmune thrombocytopenia

Pernicious anemia

**Blood Vessels**

Antiphospholipid syndrome

Behçet's disease

Temporal arteritis

Uveitis

Wegener's granulomatosis

**Endocrine Glands**

Addison's disease

Autoimmune oophoritis and
    orchitis

Graves' disease

Hashimoto's thyroiditis

Hypoparathyroidism

Type 1 diabetes

**Gastrointestinal System**

Autoimmune hepatitis

Celiac disease

Crohn's disease

Chronic active hepatitis

Primary biliary cirrhosis

Ulcerative colitis

**Multiple Organs/
    Connective Tissues**

Ankylosing spondylitis

Dermatomyositis

Polymyositis

Rheumatoid arthritis

Systemic lupus
    erythematosus

Scleroderma

Sjögren's syndrome

**Nervous System**

Autoimmune neuropathies
    (e.g., Guillain-Barré
    syndrome)

Multiple sclerosis

Myasthenia gravis

**Skin**

Dermatitis herpetiformis

Pemphigus vulgaris

Psoriasis

Vitiligo

you could develop type 1 diabetes. In systemic lupus erythematosus and rheumatoid arthritis, cells are directed against multiple organs and connective tissues. If these cells are directed against the thyroid, you can develop one of several forms of thyroiditis or Graves' disease. Experts believe that as many as fifty million Americans, or one in five people, may be afflicted with an autoimmune disease.

## Autoimmune Thyroid Disease

In thyroid conditions, the antithyroid immune response begins with the activation of T cells that are specifically programmed against certain thyroid antigens. Researchers are unsure of how these antigens develop, but they have theories. One theory is that T-cell activation results from an infection with a virus that has a protein similar to a thyroid protein. The thyroid protein resembles the viral protein so much that it is mistaken for the viral protein, and the T cells mount their attack against the thyroid protein. This theory is referred to as *molecular mimicry*, but it has yet to be proven.

Another theory holds that some thyroid antigens are generated from thyroid cells themselves, specifically, from the cells that line the thyroid's hormone-producing units, called follicles. The theory is that these cells, like phagocytes, may present their own intracellular proteins to T cells in the form of antigens. This view is supported by the finding that thyroid cells in patients with autoimmune thyroiditis express MHC molecules. These are the molecules that normally attach to phagocytes that display an antigen to T cells. In patients who don't have the disease, thyroid cells do not express these molecules.

Whatever the mysterious mechanism that presents antigens may be, once a passing T cell recognizes an antigen as a match, an immune response is activated and clonal expansion occurs. During this process, the T-cell action induces B cells to secrete thyroid antibodies.

In patients who develop various forms of autoimmune thyroid disease, three main target antigens for thyroid antibodies have been identified. They are peroxidase, a thyroid enzyme instrumental in synthesizing thyroid hormone; thyroglobulin, a thyroid protein where thyroid hormone is stored; and the TSH receptor, a protein complex located on the surface of thyroid cells. The

TSH receptor has TSH-binding sites that enable the thyroid to receive TSH signals from the pituitary gland.

In blood tests, the antibodies that are most frequently measured in people with various forms of thyroiditis are those that work against peroxidase. Accordingly, these are called antithyroid peroxidase (anti-TPO) antibodies. The presence of high levels of these antibodies is frequently associated with overt hypothyroidism or is a predictor that it will develop over time. Other antibodies that attack thyroglobulin are called antithyroglobulin (anti-Tg) antibodies. These antibodies contribute to thyroiditis but are not the direct cause of it.

Antibodies that attach themselves to the TSH receptor and stimulate overproduction of thyroid hormone are most frequently seen in patients with Graves' disease. These antibodies, known as thyrotropin receptor antibodies (TRAb), are a mix of TSH stimulators and blockers. In the vast majority of cases where these antibodies are present, the stimulators are dominant and the patient becomes hyperthyroid, because the thyroid is essentially tricked into producing thyroid hormone. However, in 10 percent of people with Hashimoto's thyroiditis, blocking antibodies dominate the TSH receptor, thereby tricking the thyroid into slowing down production of thyroid hormone. In addition, these antibodies may contribute to shrinkage of the thyroid rather than enlargement, which explains why a number of patients with autoimmune hypothyroidism have atrophic thyroiditis, a condition that involves no goiter but a smaller than usual thyroid gland.

The following conditions are types of thyroiditis that can occur when these antibodies are present, with one exception. Only subacute thyroiditis, a condition that typically follows an upper respiratory infection, does not seem to involve autoantibodies.

## Hashimoto's Thyroiditis

Hashimoto's thyroiditis is a fancy name for the most widespread cause of hypothyroidism in the United States. It's not unusual for people to be diagnosed with this type of hypothyroidism but never hear the name of the Japanese physician who first described it in 1912. Yet, it's important to distinguish Hashimoto's thyroiditis from other types of hypothyroidism because of its importance to you and your family's medical history.

Dr. Hakaru Hashimoto originally reported the condition in four women who had a goiter that appeared as if it had transformed into lymphoid tissue. Scientists now know that the thyroid's unusual appearance was due to an assault by lymphocytes, but it wasn't until the 1950s that antithyroid antibodies were discovered in patients with this condition. With a better understanding came more scientific names that are now used interchangeably in medical journals with Hashimoto's thyroiditis, including chronic lymphocytic thyroiditis (lymphocytic refers to the accumulation of lymphocytes) and chronic autoimmune thyroiditis, both the atrophic and goitrous forms.

If you or a family member have a history of thyroiditis or the other autoimmune diseases listed in the sidebar "Examples of Autoimmune Diseases and Their Target Organs," you are predisposed to developing Hashimoto's thyroiditis. However, there are other factors that determine who develops the disease and who doesn't. How much dietary iodine you take in is one such factor. If thyroid autoantibodies are present in your system and you routinely take kelp supplements or medicines with high amounts of iodine (see Table 1.3), you may trigger hypothyroidism. If you consume a lot of salt or iodine-containing foods, such as fish or milk, you typically don't have to worry.

Iodine as a trigger for hypothyroidism may seem counterintuitive, given that iodine is an important ingredient in thyroid hormone production and lack of iodine is the number one cause of hypothyroidism worldwide. Yet population studies have shown that if you are predisposed to hypothyrodism due to autoantibodies, too much iodine enhances your antibody activity. Similar studies show that Hashimoto's and other forms of thyroiditis are more prevalent in iodine-sufficient regions, such as the United States, than in iodine-deficient areas.

Gender is also a determinant. Women are five to seven times more likely than men to develop Hashimoto's thyroiditis, most typically after age forty-five when the concentration of antibodies appears to increase. While scientists don't fully understand the impact of estrogen, this hormone is known to enhance the immune system response.

To confirm the presence of Hashimoto's thyroiditis, you will probably have a blood test for antibodies in addition to other thyroid function blood tests (discussed in Chapter 4). Some studies have shown that anti-TPO antibodies are present in up to 95 percent of people with Hashimoto's thyroiditis and that up to 60 percent of patients test positive for anti-Tg antibodies. When diagnosing Hashimoto's thyroiditis, doctors prefer testing for anti-TPO over anti-Tg antibodies because the former are more frequently positive than the latter in those with this condition.

Most people with hypothyroidism in this country have a mild form that may never progress to overt disease. Out of the 4.6 percent of people in the United States who have hypothyroidism, 4.3 percent have mild disease while 0.3 percent have overt disease. If you have mild disease and test positive for antithyroid antibodies, however, there is a better chance that you will develop overt disease, so you should be monitored periodically by your physician.

Once overt hypothyroidism is present, thyroid hormone replacement is the treatment of choice. Sometimes hormone replacement is used to treat patients with mild disease and a high thyroid antibody concentration, because these patients are most at risk for developing overt hypothyroidism. In this case, the goal of treatment would be to normalize the TSH level.

For patients with a large goiter, larger doses of thyroid hormone replacement are prescribed to shrink the goiter. It usually takes months for any noticeable decrease in size. How much a goiter shrinks with therapy and how long it takes for reasonable results varies widely from person to person.

## Postpartum Thyroiditis

Every mother knows that during the first month or so after giving birth, as you answer to the cries of a fussy newborn around the clock, your world can become a roller coaster of emotions.

The combined effect of hormone level changes, sleep deprivation, love for your new baby, and trepidation over your new responsibilities may leave you feeling exhausted, sad, and anxious. Thus, if you are of the 10 percent of women who develop postpartum thyroiditis during this period, you may not notice as the symptoms of this disease, which lead to their own kind of highs and lows, creep in.

Postpartum thyroiditis, which can occur one to six months after pregnancy, is characterized by a phase in which your thyroid leaks thyroid hormone to the point where your system is dominated by too much of it, followed by a hypothyroid phase when the thyroid has drained itself.

During the initial thyrotoxic phase, which lasts from one to three months, you may experience some of the signs and symptoms of hyperthyroidism (discussed in Chapter 3), although they may not be as intense. These symptoms can include heart rhythm disturbances, heat intolerance, or anxiety. Since this phase is short-lived, you shouldn't display some of the symptoms that occur with prolonged hyperthyroidism, including substantial weight loss or severe muscle weakness.

As your body's thyroid hormone levels shift from too much to too little, the fatigue, malaise, and impaired concentration brought on by hypothyroidism may prevail. Carelessness and depression are also common. Although depression is usually not the result of hypothyroidism caused by postpartum thyroiditis, it often coincides with it. These symptoms can last for four to six months.

Most women, about 80 percent, recover their normal thyroid function within a year, but if you have had this condition, you are statistically more at risk for developing permanent hypothyroidism in the future, so you should be periodically monitored by your doctor. If you have had postpartum thyroiditis, you have a 70 percent chance of developing it again after any subsequent pregnancies.

Postpartum thyroiditis occurs more frequently in women who have another autoimmune disease, particularly those with type 1 diabetes mellitus. But, as with other thyroid diseases, other factors are also at play. Changes that occur during pregnancy can trigger this disease. During pregnancy, the immune system must adapt to the growing fetus. Both B-cell and T-cell function are believed to be suppressed by the high levels of circulating estrogen during pregnancy. The rebound of B cells and T cells from this immune system suppression after delivery is thought to trigger the disease. Several environmental factors may also be at play. Smoking is a known trigger, and excess iodine intake may influence the severity of your disease.

Postpartum thyroiditis may not require any treatment if it is mild. But if your symptoms are bothersome, you may be treated with a class of drugs called beta-blockers to relieve some of your symptoms during the thyrotoxic phase and with thyroid hormone replacement during the hypothyroid phase, until your endocrinologist determines that the condition has resolved.

If you have a family history of thyroid disease, your obstetrician can test your blood for antithyroid antibodies during the first trimester of your pregnancy. If your test is positive, there is a very good chance you will develop this condition, so you should continue to be monitored during and after your pregnancy.

## Silent Sporadic Thyroiditis

As its name implies, silent sporadic thyroiditis, which is also known as painless sporadic thyroiditis, comes without warning and slips out quietly, all the while being so mild that you never know you have it. As with postpartum thyroiditis, it is deemed "painless" to distinguish it from subacute thyroiditis, which leads to a tender, aching neck and fever. Its painless, mild, sporadic, and transient nature makes it difficult for physicians to study, but here is some of what is known.

Painless sporadic thyroiditis follows the exact clinical course as postpartum thyroiditis, with a thyrotoxic phase followed by a hypothyroid phase. The only difference between the conditions is that the latter occurs after pregnancy while the former can occur in men but is more common in women. Some people with painless sporadic thyroiditis develop a small, painless goiter.

Although it typically resolves on its own, 20 percent of patients with this condition develop chronic hypothyroidism. It can recur, but the rate of recurrence has not been well established in scientific studies.

## Subacute Thyroiditis

When you have the flu, you typically aren't concerned with your thyroid. But with subacute thyroiditis, also known as de Quervain's thyroiditis, you may have a fever, sore throat, exhaustion, and a potentially severe aching neck that worsens when you turn your head or swallow. Subacute thyroiditis usually follows an upper respiratory infection, and researchers believe it is caused by an unidentified combination of viruses that attack your thyroid, causing it to leak thyroid hormone. This thyrotoxic phase, including the neck pain, lasts for several weeks, and you may then become mildly hypothyroid. You might be treated with beta-blockers to relieve the symptoms of hyperthyroidism, along with a nonsteroidal anti-inflammatory drug (NSAID), usually aspirin, to reduce inflammation, pain, and fever. If aspirin isn't effective or you don't tolerate it well, ibuprofen or another NSAID may help. As a third resort, your doctor might prescribe a glucocorticoid, such as prednisone. The hypothyroid stage is usually mild and resolves itself. Rarely, permanent hypothyroidism develops and requires lifetime hormone replacement.

# Graves' Disease

The odds of husband and wife both developing Graves' disease are believed to be somewhere between one in ten thousand to one in three million. So when it was determined in 1991 that President George H.W. Bush suffered from the condition, just two years after Barbara Bush was diagnosed with it, it came as somewhat of a surprise to the medical world. Confounding doctors more was the discovery that even the first family's dog, Millie, suffered from lupus erythematosus, an autoimmune disease. This apparent coincidence suggested that something other than genetics was at work.

According to news reports at the time, medical experts searched for an environmental hazard that would link the couple's conditions together. President Bush's doctor ordered testing of the water in the White House, the vice president's mansion (where Bush had lived for eight years prior to residing at the White House), and the Bushes' vacation homes to search for any chemicals or germs that might have brought on the disease. High lead levels were found at the vice president's mansion, but lead does not cause Graves' disease. To this day, doctors don't know why the first couple developed Graves' disease around the same time.

What triggers Graves' disease is largely a mystery. There is no known environmental cause. Even so, it is believed that Graves' disease is determined by a mixture of genetic, environmental, and internal factors, which are together responsible for the emergence of autoreactivity of B cells and T cells to the TSH receptor. In those genetically predisposed to develop an autoimmune condition, particularly women, smoking has been weakly linked with developing Graves' disease in some studies, although smoking more directly affects the worsening of eye complications. Some drugs, such as lithium, can be a culprit. Interferon alpha, a medication used to treat hepatitis C and cancer, can induce Graves' disease, but the medication is more often associated with the development of thyroiditis. Some people develop Graves' disease after treatment for AIDS with highly active antiretroviral therapy (HAART). In this case, however, Graves' disease is not a side effect of the drug but is believed to be the result of a recovered immune system that begins operating as it did before its functions were suppressed by the AIDS virus. So someone with AIDS who develops Graves' disease may have already had it or was already predisposed to it before developing AIDS. Another theory is that in some people who are being treated for AIDS, the recovery process in itself triggers an autoimmune response that results in Graves' disease.

Stress may also play a role. Several studies have found that Graves' disease often follows a stressful event, such as bereavement, a divorce, or a job loss. Yet most people with Graves' disease, like the Bushes, cannot put their finger on a cause.

By the time most people with Graves' disease see a doctor, they are experiencing multiple symptoms of hyperthyroidism that, taken together, leave them feeling awful. However, President Bush's story is a good example of an older person's typical experience. Older people are likely to experience fewer serious symptoms than a younger person does. Graves' disease was diagnosed days after the president, then sixty-six years old, was taken to the hospital for shortness of breath and an irregular heartbeat he encountered while jogging. He underwent numerous heart examinations that ruled out heart function problems and was treated with drugs to regulate his heartbeat. The problem was traced to hyperthyroidism. Eventually, he was treated with radioactive iodine therapy and continued with heart medication until his heart rhythms were normal.

## Graves' Eye Disease

A revved-up thyroid gland is more than enough to handle. Yet some people who develop Graves' disease suffer the additional misfortune of having problems with their eyes.

Graves' eye disease is known by several names, including *thyroid eye disease* and *Graves' ophthalmopathy*. If there is an upside to the misery that comes with it, it is that its symptoms are a tip-off that something is amiss with your thyroid, unlike other vague signs and symptoms that can go undetected for years. So a person with hyperthyroidism may be diagnosed more quickly when the hallmark signs of Graves' eye disease—tearful, sometimes painful eyes that may appear to be bulging or staring—emerge (see Figure 5.2). The condition is usually, but not always, related to Graves' disease and typically emerges within eighteen months of the onset of hyperthyroidism.

Although it seems to enjoy keeping Graves' disease company, Graves' eye disease is considered a separate condition that can occur in the absence of hyperthyroidism, in which case it is referred to as *euthyroid Graves' (eye) disease*, or even months after hyperthyroidism has been treated. It can also occur with Hashimoto's thyroiditis. But when the symptoms are more severe, the

**FIGURE 5.2** The Eyes of Graves' Disease

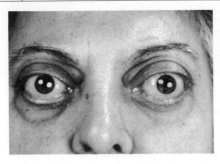

*People with Graves' disease sometimes develop red, irritated eyes that may appear to be staring and protruding.*

condition almost always coincides with Graves' disease. Researchers believe that what bonds these two conditions, and sometimes a third condition of the skin called *Graves' dermopathy*, are common or similar autoimmune antigens found in thyroid tissue, skin cells, and tissues of the eye orbit. Thus, eye symptoms are often related to a separate autoimmune assault on the eyes, although they are sometimes the result of a hyper-functioning thyroid.

One antigen common to all three conditions is believed to be a TSH receptor antigen. That is the antigen believed to trigger the production of an antibody that binds to the TSH receptor, which in turn stimulates the thyroid to overproduce thyroid hormone. In people who have eye symptoms related to an autoimmune assault on the eyes, antibodies are produced that attack the tissue that surrounds the eyeball.

To understand your symptoms, it helps to understand the anatomy of the eye. The globe of your eye sits in your eye socket, which is made of bone that resists expansion (see Figure 5.3). So when antibodies attack the tissues behind the eyes, those tissues swell and expand; in turn, this may force your eyes to shift forward and your eyelids to retract. If the swelling is bad enough, it can put pressure on the optic nerve that conducts visual stimuli to the brain. This can mean impaired vision. The muscles that control your eye movement are also targeted, potentially causing you to see double and your eyes to appear out of line with one another.

## FIGURE 5.3 Anatomy of an Eye Affected by Graves' Eye Disease

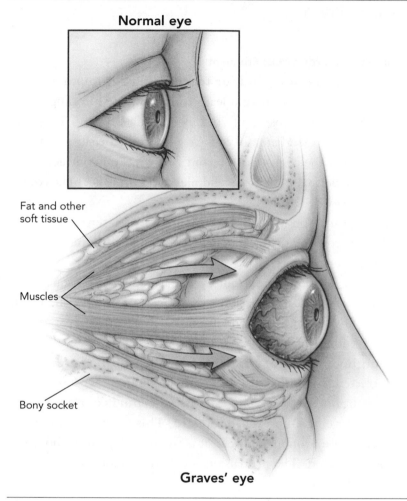

**Normal eye**

Fat and other soft tissue

Muscles

Bony socket

**Graves' eye**

*In Graves' eye disease, the muscles that control eye movement stiffen, potentially causing improper alignment of the eyes and double vision. The soft tissues behind the eyeball swell, pushing the eyeball forward in its socket. This is called proptosis or exophthalmos.*

The following features are characteristic of Graves' eye disease. At the root of these annoying and sometimes debilitating symptoms is inflammation of the muscle and fat that sit behind the eyeball in the eye orbit. In some cases, inflammation can be severe enough to force the eyeballs to protrude and to restrict eye mus-

101

cle movement. Symptoms may occur in only one eye or be worse in one eye than the other.

### Symptoms Occurring Most Frequently

- **Dryness, redness, and/or tearing.** These symptoms can occur when inflammation leads to incomplete blinking or incomplete eye closure of your eyes while sleeping. This can be further exacerbated if you are thyrotoxic because of the effect that the overactive thyroid's state has on contracting the muscle that controls eyelid elevation, thus keeping your eyelid elevated.
- **Irritation.** You may also experience a gritty sensation, as though you have sand in your eyes. This is also due to incomplete closure.
- **Staring appearance.** Your eyes may appear to be staring. This is due to lid retraction, which is usually solely the result of excess thyroid hormone in your system, not a separate autoimmune attack on your eyes.
- **Bulging.** Your eyes may appear to bulge when your lids are retracted. But your eyes may truly be bulging because autoantibodies are causing the tissues behind your eye to swell, forcing your eyeball forward. This protrusion may seem more pronounced than it actually is if your eyelid is also retracted. The protrusion is called *proptosis* or *exophthalmos.*
- **Light sensitivity.** Incomplete blinking may also lead you to become sensitive to light.

### More Severe Symptoms Occurring Less Frequently

- **Double vision and eye malalignment.** For you to see normally, the eye muscles that control movement in one eye must function in exact concordance with muscles of your other eye. If these muscles are swollen enough, movement of one eye may be out of sync with the other eye, causing you to see double. If you are experiencing double vision, your eyes may also appear to be looking in different directions.

- **Blurring or loss of color vision.** If inflammation is causing enough pressure on the optic nerve, your vision may be impaired.
- **Cornea erosion.** If your eyelids don't close all the way, your cornea can become damaged from overexposure to the air. This overexposure leads to dryness, which in turn makes your eye more susceptible to inflammation.
- **Total loss of vision.** This symptom, which rarely occurs, can result from severe pressure on the optic nerve.

*The Eye Exam.* If you have Graves' disease, your doctor will want to examine your eyes. If you have visible signs of Graves' eye disease, you will probably be referred to an ophthalmologist, a doctor who specializes in the diagnosis and treatment of eye problems. An ophthalmologist can measure how far your eyes have protruded with a special instrument called an exophthalmeter. Another instrument called a slit lamp, which looks like a microscope, can be used to examine your corneas. Pictures of tissues behind your eyes that may be inflamed can be obtained through a combination of imaging tests, including ultrasounds of your eyes, a computerized tomography scan (CT scan), or magnetic resonance imaging (MRI).

*Treatment.* Treatment will depend on how severe your eye problems are. Most people have mild to moderate symptoms that improve spontaneously, but even so, it may be anywhere from eighteen months to two years before the condition resolves. In the meantime, the amount of swelling in your eyes can fluctuate.

Your doctor may advise you to take simple measures to alleviate your discomfort. These can include wearing dark sunglasses, avoiding bright sunlight, sleeping with your head raised to alleviate swelling, using lubricating eyedrops and ointments to keep your eyes from drying, and covering your eyes while sleeping. If you smoke, giving up cigarettes, which are known to worsen the eye problems seen in Graves' disease, can improve your condition.

More severe disease, particularly impaired vision, is treated with high doses of steroids either alone or in combination with an X-ray treatment to the eye orbit known as *orbital irradiation*. How effective these X-ray treatments are is unclear. For instance, in one well-known study, researchers found that eye disease in a group of patients only improved slightly after a year of receiving treatments. The study's authors noted that the marginal improvement may have been the result of either natural remission or the X-ray treatments.

The most common surgery, performed by an ophthalmologist who specializes in treating Graves' eye disease, is lid repair to correct lid retraction. Another kind of surgery is aimed at creating space for the protruding eyeball. This can be achieved through a procedure known as *orbital decompression*, during which swollen tissue behind the eyeball or some bone of the socket is removed.

Other surgical procedures may accompany orbital decompression. One, known as *orbital augmentation*, involves pulling the facial bones forward. Two others are operations on the nose: *septoplasy*, an operation on the portion of the nose that separates the right and left nostrils, and *turbinate reduction*, a removal of part of the sidewalls of the nasal cavity.

In addition, surgery on eye muscles may be done to correct problems with eye alignment. Sometimes, plastic surgery is used to correct droopiness around the eyes that doesn't resolve with the disease.

## Graves' Dermopathy

Another condition that can occur along with Graves' disease involves an autoimmune attack against the skin, usually the skin of the lower legs. This condition, known as Graves' dermopathy, occurs much less frequently than Graves' eye disease and is separate from the skin changes that result directly from hyperthyroidism, such as moist, smooth skin. Graves' dermopathy involves a thickening of the skin, called *pretibial myxedema*, usually on the

# Fast Fact: Radioactive Iodine and Graves' Eye Disease

Radioactive iodine therapy, the number one choice in treatment for Graves' disease, can actually bring on or worsen Graves' eye disease, particularly in smokers. This exacerbation is usually temporary and may be prevented with steroid treatment. If you receive radioactive iodine therapy, your doctor may prescribe a daily dose of prednisone that should be gradually tapered down over the course of three months.

shins where areas of skin appear to be bulging or swollen. A few people will develop a more unusual problem known as *acropachy*, which is characterized by elevation of the nail beds and swelling in the hands and feet. Sometimes there is a bulbous enlargement of the fingertips that is known as clubbing.

If you develop these kinds of skin problems, you may be referred to a dermatologist. Graves' dermopathy may be effectively treated with steroid creams. More severe skin problems may benefit from steroid injections. Although these therapies may help relieve discomfort in acropachy, there is no known therapy that effectively reverses its effects. Unfortunately, little is known about the clinical course of the condition, yet it is believed to resolve on its own. Some evidence of that comes from the Mayo Clinic in Rochester, Minnesota, which reported in 2002 that of forty patients who were diagnosed with acropachy at the institution over a twenty-six-year period, none complained of its symptoms in long-term follow-up visits or questionnaires.

## Autoimmune Disease on Three Fronts: Eyes, Thyroid, and Adrenal Glands

Years after being treated for Graves' eye disease, Kathryn, a sixty-four-year-old clinical psychologist, developed hypothyroidism. With these conditions controlled, she never expected to confront Addison's disease, a rare, serious condition that occurs more often in people with thyroid problems, yet may be even more difficult to diagnose. But when exacerbated by injury or illness, it can be fatal if untreated, and it almost cost Kathryn her life. This is her story.

The first sign that I had a thyroid problem was back in 1967. My eye looked like it was severely protruding because my eyelid was retracted. I had a hard time closing it at night and I felt a lot of pressure. It turned out I had mild Graves' disease, but I had no other symptoms but my eye trouble. I was treated by an ophthalmologist with eye medication and the problem subsided. It wasn't until several years later that I began to feel tired all of the time, very anxious, and depressed. I felt this way for some time. I also developed very dry skin. My mother had hypothyroidism. She was on thyroid medication from the time I was a child, but I didn't realize that I was at risk.

I didn't see an endocrinologist until my husband felt a nodule around the early 1980s. After numerous tests, I learned I had a cold nodule. I had a needle biopsy and the nodule was benign. Later, blood tests confirmed that I had mild hypothyroidism and I began taking thyroid hormone replacement pills. I felt a significant change in my mood. I was no longer tired all the time. It was a wonderful change. I was also shocked to learn that my depressed mood was primarily due to my thyroid and not to psychological reasons. In my own psychotherapy practice now, I'm a lot more in tune to people's medical conditions when they come to me because they are depressed.

I was checked regularly. Everything was going along fine until 1995, when I got a divorce. I kind of panicked and for two years I just felt like I was under a lot of stress. I had to open up an office in another town. I was teaching at college, staying up late preparing for classes. I really wore myself out. Within a couple of years, I got involved with someone else who was emotionally volatile. I developed esophageal reflux, which can be stress related. I was treated and it totally disappeared. But a renewed feeling of fatigue didn't.

I was aware of being tired at the time. I attributed it to getting older and my hectic life. But for at least two years, I noticed my skin was getting brown. People would say, "Gee you look so tan." I just attributed it to good pigmentation. Now I know it's one of the signs of Addison's disease. I never mentioned it to my doctor because these things come on subtly and you wind up just explaining them to yourself.

But everything changed the day before Thanksgiving in the fall of 1999. I was shopping for the holiday dinner and I had a moderately painful attack in my stomach. I felt kind of faint. I didn't know it, but I was having a gallbladder attack. So I went home and started throwing up repeatedly. I attributed this to a severe flu. But in reality, the gallbladder attack prompted a full-blown Addison's crisis (acute adrenal gland failure). I was lying on the sofa, feeling as though I had been drained of life. I should have called 911, but my brain really wasn't working right. I thought, none of my doctors would be around because of the holiday and I should wait. I spent the day getting very dehydrated. A friend came over to bring me some soup and I always regret that she didn't think it was something worse than usual. I had a cab take me to the doctor the next day. I saw my primary care doctor and I could barely stand up in his office. I threw up clear liquid in the examining room. They did some quick readings and sent me right to the hospital, where I stayed for two or three days. Apparently I had a very severe infection and what looked like an abscess in my liver. The doctors analyzed where the bacteria came from and determined it was my gallbladder, and they were very concerned. I got heavy doses of antibiotics and was given intravenous fluids so I was hydrated. A lot of tests were done and I was sent home. I was weak. I had no appetite and felt faint and dizzy all the time. I became so sick I went to the hospital again. Again I underwent many tests, but no one knew what was wrong with me. So they rehydrated me for a couple of days and again I went home. They were calling me the mystery lady at that point because they couldn't figure out why I wasn't recovering.

So I went to my primary care doctor because I could barely walk up my stairs. He said, "You are going back to the hospital and you are not leaving until they get a diagnosis." I was seen in the ER again, for the third time. This time it was an endocrinologist who happened to be there and I think he suspected Addison's disease right away. My doctor had apparently already suspected it and tested my cortisol [a glucocorticoid] level. But the result was misleading because my estrogen hormone replacement therapy had influenced the reading. This time, the endocrinologist did a very definitive test that involved injecting a hormone that stimulates the adrenal glands to see if they would produce cortisol. And that's when they figured out what I had. What a great relief it was that I had a diagnosis and that the condition is very treatable. They gave me my first cortisol pill and in less than an hour I could get out of my bed and walk around the hospital floor.

Now, in addition to thyroid hormone, I must take steroid hormones to replace what my adrenal glands can't produce. I've learned how to manage my disease. Within the last two years, both my thyroid and Addison's diseases have stabilized. Due to the Addison's, which I never take for granted, I've adjusted my lifestyle accordingly. I do not have the same energy level as I once did, but I've learned to rest when I need to. I don't see patients back-to-back. I cancel things when I need to. I eat well. I exercise regularly and get plenty of rest. I'm just thankful that I have conditions that can be successfully controlled with simple lifestyle changes and medication.

## Your Family Medical History

Thyroid diseases represent a small number of about eighty autoimmune diseases that can affect specific tissues or organs of the body. If a family member has any condition that falls under the autoimmune umbrella, you are at an increased risk for developing one of these conditions. However, you have a better chance of developing thyroid disease if a family member has an autoimmune thyroid condition. Still, people with thyroid disease often discover other diseases in their family history. But you won't know if you don't ask. Several thyroid disease patients interviewed for this book pointed out that they never knew that an aunt or a cousin had a thyroid or other autoimmune condition until they themselves were diagnosed. That information could have led to an earlier diagnosis. A great way to be sure you don't miss any such close relatives is to create a family tree and leave spaces under each name to list any health problems that each relative may have. You can then take this chart to your doctor. The following are some examples of other autoimmune diseases that sometimes coincide with thyroid disease. (Others are listed in the sidebar "Examples of Autoimmune Diseases and Their Target Organs.")

### Addison's Disease

Addison's disease is characterized by extreme weakness, weight loss, low blood pressure, gastrointestinal problems, and darker pigmentation of the skin. This condition is sometimes caused by an autoimmune attack on the adrenal glands, which produce glucocorticoid hormones that help your body combat stress, particularly illness or injury. If not managed with steroid medications, Addison's disease can be life threatening. The condition is rare, but when it does occur there is often a family history of thyroid disease.

### Celiac Disease

Caused by an autoimmune attack on the intestines, celiac disease leads to the inability of your small intestine to absorb nutrients, called malabsorption. It is triggered by gluten, a protein found in wheat, rye, oats, and barley. Its symptoms include foul-smelling, grayish diarrhea stools, a bloated abdomen, and weight loss.

Several studies have found that this disease is more prevalent in patients with autoimmune thyroid disease than in the general population. One study compared ninety-two patients who had autoimmune thyroid disease and ninety patients who had thyroid structural problems (nodules, goiters, and thyroid cancer) that weren't autoimmune in origin. In the former group, 4.3 percent tested positive for celiac disease versus 1.1 percent in the latter group.

## Diabetes

Type 1 diabetes, sometimes known as juvenile-onset diabetes, is an autoimmune disease in which your body's immune system attacks the cells in the pancreas that secrete insulin. This results in a lack of insulin, a hormone that is required for proper absorption of sugar by cells. If you have an autoimmune thyroid disease, your children and grandchildren are statistically more at risk for developing this type of diabetes. Conversely, type 1 diabetes patients have thyroid dysfunction at a rate two to three times higher than in the general population and are urged by some doctors to undergo annual screening for thyroid disorders.

## Hypoparathyroidism

Parathyroid glands, which sit in close proximity to your thyroid gland, regulate the amount of calcium in your bloodstream. In this condition, which results in below-normal levels of calcium in your blood, the parathyroid glands do not produce enough of their hormone to keep your calcium levels up to par.

## Systemic Lupus Erythematosus

This is an uncommon condition where autoimmune antibodies go on a systemwide offensive, causing inflammation in many body tissues, including the joints, heart, kidneys, lungs, and skin.

Although lupus is rare among thyroid patients, thyroid disease is highly prevalent among lupus patients. So if you have lupus, you should be periodically checked for thyroid problems.

## Pernicious Anemia

Pernicious anemia is a grave form of anemia that may occur in older patients who have Graves' disease or Hashimoto's thyroiditis. It is caused by a faulty autoimmune response that leads to the failure of your digestive tract to absorb vitamin $B_{12}$—an essential ingredient in the production of red blood cells, which carry oxygen through the bloodstream from your lungs to cells in need of it. The disease originates in the cells that line a part of the stomach that produces a substance called *intrinsic factor*, which is responsible for absorbing $B_{12}$ in the small intestine.

## Rheumatoid Arthritis

Rheumatoid arthritis is an autoimmune condition in which antibodies cause inflammation of your joints and tendons. It occurs in 1.7 percent of the general population and in 6.7 percent of thyroid disease patients. Treatment for thyroid disease may alleviate some of the symptoms that are common to both conditions. Other conditions characterized by inflammation or pain in muscles, joints, or fibrous tissue that can occur with thyroid disease include the following.

- **Sjögren's syndrome.** A chronic autoimmune disease that occurs in mostly older women, characterized by dryness of the mucous membranes, particularly of the eyes and mouth.
- **Polymyalgia rheumatica.** A disorder that occurs mostly in the elderly, involving pain and stiffness in the shoulders, neck, and pelvic areas.
- **Relapsing polychondritis.** A disorder affecting the cartilage that results in progressive inflammation of the ears, nose, larynx, trachea, eyes, joints, kidneys, and heart.

## Type 1 Autoimmune Polyglandular Syndrome

Chronic autoimmune thyroiditis occurs in 10 to 15 percent of patients who have this syndrome, which is characterized by at least two of the following problems: hypoparathyroidism, Addison's disease, or chronic mucocutaneous candidiasis—a fungal infection of the skin and mucus membranes, usually of the mouth, vagina, or intestinal tract.

## Type 2 Autoimmune Polyglandular Syndrome

Major components of autoimmune polyglandular syndrome type 2 are autoimmune thyroid disease, type 1 diabetes mellitus, and Addison's disease. At least two major components are required to diagnose this syndrome. The following conditions may also be present: premature ovarian failure; lymphocytic hypophysitis, or autoimmune destruction of the pituitary gland; vitiligo; alopecia areata, or the sudden loss of hair in patches; sprue, which is a chronic digestive disease, sometimes called celiac disease, involving malabsorption; pernicious anemia; serositis, which is an inflammation of tissues that line the lungs, heart, and abdominal organs; and myasthenia gravis, which is an autoimmune disorder of neurologic origin that results in muscle weakness.

In addition to occurring frequently with this syndrome, chronic autoimmune thyroiditis occurs frequently in any of these disorders when they are isolated.

## Vitiligo

Vitiligo, which also occurs more often in families with a history of thyroid disease, is characterized by painless white patches of skin, typically around the knuckles, wrist, and neck.

## Lessons from One Woman's Family History of Thyroid-Related Conditions

Florence was on the lookout for diabetes for most of her life because her father and uncle both had it. Since no one in her family had thyroid disease, she didn't expect to be diagnosed with hypothyroidism or celiac disease, autoimmune diseases that emerged well before a stressful event made her diabetes evident. In the meantime, she struggled with conditions unrelated to thyroid disease, including cancer and heart disease. Yet at eighty-two years of age, with her conditions under control, she still practices law, finds time to play bridge, and exercises at the gym most days. Here is her story.

My father was a diabetic and my uncle died of diabetes. I was very aware of what it meant to have this disease because, by the age of eleven, I had to care for my father since my mother was crippled due to her arthritis.

I grew up with very sick parents. I wanted to make sure I didn't have diabetes so I always told my doctors about it and was tested. I basically grew up waiting to get it, but it didn't occur until later in life.

But more than fifty years ago, doctors discovered I had hypothyroidism after my first pregnancy resulted in a still-birth. I was put on thyroid hormone replacement medication before becoming pregnant again, and although my pregnancies were difficult, they resulted in healthy babies. After having three children, I was taken off thyroid medication and was fine. But somewhere around twenty-five years ago, I began feeling tired and nauseated all the time. It's difficult to recall other symptoms, but I do remember that I just didn't feel well at all. It turned out that it was my hypothyroidism, so I was immediately put back on treatment.

I've had celiac disease since I was a child, but it wasn't diagnosed until around thirty years ago. I remember bouts with the disease even at the age of ten. For example, I remember asking my teacher if I could go to the bathroom and her telling me "no" and then going right there at my seat because I couldn't help it. As I got older, I noticed that my bouts with this condition seemed to coincide with stress I experienced while helping to care for my father. My doctor thought I should have outgrown the condition—the painful, severe diarrhea usually connected to stress—so he sent me to a hospital in Manhattan to partake in a week-long program for undiagnosable conditions. By the end of the week, they still couldn't diagnose it. I should mention that I was also anemic, which is a common complication of celiac disease. But they didn't know back then that gluten —found in wheat, oats, and barley—can spur an attack. Then an interesting medical breakthrough occurred. During World War II, a time when wheat grains were scarce in Holland, a Dutch physician discovered that children with celiac disease, who normally failed to thrive, improved on a diet without wheat. Still, it wasn't until the 1970s, when I switched medical plans, that this discovery helped me. It was a very busy time. I was working and raising three children and saw a recipe for a quick nutritious breakfast that seemed like a great time-saver. It was a milkshake that had, among other ingredients, wheat germ. Suddenly, I developed a kind of dermatitis that is sometimes seen with celiac disease. I was sent to a dermatologist who did a bunch of tests and referred me to a gastroenterologist who did an intestinal biopsy that confirmed celiac disease.

All the while, I had never developed diabetes, until around twenty years ago. I was involved with the biggest real estate transaction of my career and there was a lot of stress involved, which I believe triggered the diabetes. Fortunately, I am familiar with the symptoms, and I was checked and sure enough I had it. I didn't want to take insulin because my father had so many disastrous reactions to it, because back then it was hard to regulate how much you needed, and he often gave himself too much. So I was given oral medication and everything was fine. My blood sugar readings were normal for fifteen months. Then, I was hurt in an automobile accident. It was a stressful situation and in turn, my blood sugar level became very high. My doctor tried all kinds of oral medications, but nothing would bring it down. So I had to begin taking insulin injections and I am on insulin to this day, but because of home medical devices that are available now for self-monitoring, I don't have as many problems as my father had on insulin. Plus the newer kinds of insulin are better.

My son, who is forty-seven, developed Graves' disease about fifteen years ago. He was treated with radioactive iodine and was told that within five years he would probably develop an underactive thyroid and would have to start taking medication. At this point, he has not developed hypothyroidism. My daughter, who is fifty-two, and my other son, who is fifty, have not developed any autoimmune conditions, and neither have my four grandchildren.

Florence also survived multiple cancers of the breast, lungs, and skin, and she manages her coronary artery disease with medication. Her brother and her mother both died in their early fifties from heart attacks. One of her siblings died in early childhood due to rheumatic heart, and her father died at seventy-two from a liver condition. She concludes, "I have a list of many medications that I have to take every day, but at eighty-two, given my family's medical history and all that I have been through, I feel very fortunate just to be here. I attribute my age to advances in today's medicine."

# CHAPTER 6

# Your Thyroid and Pregnancy

Pregnancy, with all the excitement and joy that it brings, is also a prime time for thyroid conditions to emerge or worsen, potentially affecting both your health and the growth and development of your baby. Even before conception, thyroid conditions that have lingered untreated can hinder your ability to become pregnant or can lead to miscarriage. Fortunately, most thyroid problems that affect pregnancy are easily treated. The difficulty lies in recognizing a thyroid problem during a time when some of your chief complaints—fatigue, constipation, heat intolerance, and anxiety—can be either the normal side effects of pregnancy or signals that something is wrong with your thyroid.

Detecting a thyroid problem is important. But it is equally necessary to have your thyroid checked if you already know you have a thyroid condition and you are planning to become pregnant or are pregnant. Whether you were treated for a thyroid condition before becoming pregnant or are diagnosed with one during pregnancy, following a few simple guidelines, outlined in this chapter, will ensure that your body is getting the appropriate amount of thyroid hormone to safeguard a healthy pregnancy.

## Your Thyroid and Infertility

Both hypothyroidism and hyperthyroidism can have a profound effect on a woman's ability to conceive. Hyperthyroidism can also affect fertility in men, although the effects of hypothyroidism are less clear-cut.

The root of the problem in women lies with the effect that thyroid hormone has on the menstrual cycle. Just as your normal thyroid status relies on the precise balance among hormones secreted by your hypothalamus, pituitary gland, and thyroid gland, a woman's menstrual cycle relies on a delicate balance of various reproductive hormones. When that balance is off, menstrual irregularities can occur leading to anovulation—no release of an egg from your ovary. Too much or too little thyroid hormone in your system can upset the balance of reproductive hormones in complicated ways, which in turn, can cause changes in the length of your cycle and frequency of bleeding. The upside here is that irregularities in your menstrual cycle are often a tip-off that something is wrong. While there could be dozens of reasons why your periods are irregular or why you can't get pregnant, it never hurts to have your doctor check your thyroid. Thyroid blood tests should also be repeated periodically if the problem persists. (See "From Infertility to Four Children: One Woman's Success Story.")

Women with hypothyroidism tend toward heavy menstrual flow, called menorrhagia. Women with hyperthyroidism may experience the absence of bleeding, called amenorrhea, or abnormally infrequent, scanty bleeding, called oligomenorrhea. Sometimes the heavy bleeding more typically associated with hypothyroidism can also occur in women with hyperthyroidism.

Studies show that most women with severe hypothyroidism become infertile and that many with moderate disease also have problems conceiving. In fact, severe hypothyroidism rarely complicates pregnancy, because 70 percent of women with this condition do not ovulate and therefore cannot conceive. Among women who do conceive, moderate to severe hypothyroidism results in an increased number of first trimester miscarriages, stillbirths, and premature infants. The effect that mild hypothyroidism has on fertility is not well understood, but it may have some impact. Severe hyperthyroidism is known to cause infertility, but more moderate forms may or may not complicate conception.

Too much thyroid hormone can also lead to male infertility and decreased libido due to the effect it has on male reproductive hormones and, in turn, a man's sperm cycle.

Once effectively treated, thyroid diseases should not affect conception or your pregnancy, but you should be sure that your thyroid function is routinely monitored while you are trying to conceive and during your pregnancy. If you have been treated and you are still having difficulties conceiving, you should see an infertility specialist who can help determine whether other medical problems are to blame.

## From Infertility to Four Children: One Woman's Success Story

At fifty years of age, Susan has very little time to herself. With four children who range in age from four to twelve and a full-time job as a hospital administrator, she is always busy, but she doesn't mind.

Prior to these days when her biggest worries center around getting her children to and from their activities and making sure their homework gets done, Susan's heart was wracked with grief over not being able to have a baby. After many attempts at in vitro fertilization (IVF)—a procedure in which a woman's eggs are fertilized in a lab and then placed back into her uterus—she was diagnosed with a thyroid problem that caused thyroid hormone levels in her bloodstream to fluctuate between high and low. This fluctuation made her condition even more difficult to diagnose than those with clear hypothyroidism or hyperthyroidism. After she was treated with radioactive iodine and put on thyroid hormone replacement, she went on to have four healthy children with minimal intervention. Here is her story.

When my husband and I first tried to have a child, I miscarried. I was already in my thirties and anxious to have a family, so I decided to see an infertility specialist. I really didn't think I'd have any trouble conceiving, since I had already done so once, but as it turned out, I went through fertility treatments for almost five years with no success. This experience was a real roller coaster, but I was determined. I made six attempts with IVF, but only three cycles were completed. The other three had to be cancelled either because I didn't produce enough eggs or the eggs weren't mature enough.

After the sixth attempt I honestly considered giving up. Nothing seemed to be working. I even began the adoption process. But I kept hearing more and more about different infertility clinics from friends, so, even though I knew I was nearing the end of the road, I considered one more consultation at a new IVF clinic. After my physical and blood work the new doctor said to me, "What's up with your thyroid?" I said, "Well nothing." At that point, I figured I had been to so many different specialists and had every conceivable test, so it was unheard of to me that I could possibly have a condition that was undiagnosed. But he said that my blood work indicated that I had an underactive thyroid. I was then referred to an endocrinologist, who repeated the blood work and found that my problem was the reverse of what the first doctor found. This time, I had an overactive thyroid. It took several months of follow-up before the endocrinologist could get a full understanding of what was going on. It turned out I had an uncommon condition that left my thyroid hormone levels fluctuating between too high and too low. The funny thing about it is that I really didn't have any symptoms, except for a short menstrual cycle that came and went periodically. I could have had the condition for years and not known about it.

What was difficult about my condition at the time is that, unlike other thyroid problems, it couldn't be treated with medication because it was sometimes overactive and sometimes underactive. My endocrinologist recommended a course of radioactive iodine, that would probably leave me hypothyroid and then my condition could be controlled with medication. When I considered this, it seemed the right thing to do. The worst thing that would happen is that I would be required to take thyroid hormone pills for the rest of my life. But if this would enable me to conceive, it would be worth it.

After my radioactive iodine treatment, I went on hormone replacement and waited about a month or two before I tried to get pregnant again. This time I did a GIFT cycle. [Gamete Intrafallopian Transfer, or GIFT, involves placing eggs and sperm into a woman's fallopian tube for fertilization.] This time I conceived, but eight weeks later, I miscarried. It was a major disappointment, but at the same time it was encouraging because in prior cycles I never conceived. The infertility specialist thought maybe something else was going on, so more tests were done and he thought I may have a rare autoimmune condition that was causing me to reject my husband's sperm. So I was scheduled to have a procedure that would test for that condition. Since only a few hospitals in my area do this procedure, I had to wait several months. So I asked my doctor if I could undergo intrauterine insemination [IUI] while I waited, just so I was doing something and not just waiting around. I knew I wasn't getting any younger. [IUI is a procedure in which sperm is passed to a woman's uterus while she is ovulating through a catheter that is placed into her cervix.] So, we did an IUI, and I ended up getting pregnant! During this pregnancy, I was followed very closely by my endocrinologist, who made adjustments to my thyroid medication as necessary. Everything went smoothly, and in October of 1991, I had my first baby girl.

I didn't waste any time trying to get pregnant again. My fertility specialist thought I may not need IVF, GIFT, or even IUI, but just a hormonal boost with some fertility drugs. It turned out I had no trouble getting pregnant without these medical procedures. I went on to have three more healthy babies. I had my fourth child when I was forty-six years old. My endocrinologist followed me through each pregnancy, altering my thyroid hormone medication accordingly. When I look back, I remember how I didn't want to see a thyroid specialist. At that point, I had been through the ringer and I thought it was just going to be a waste of time. Obviously, it wasn't.

## Normal Hormone Changes During Pregnancy

Pregnancy is often described as a time when hormones rage. This is no understatement. In fact, pregnancy tests rely on the measurement of a hormone called *human chorionic gonadotropin* (hCG), which becomes increasingly elevated from the day you conceive. Increases in hCG and estrogen normally result in some degree of interference with thyroid hormone levels. In women with healthy thyroid glands, these changes do not result in thyroid diseases, but they can affect thyroid function tests.

HCG increases mildly stimulate the thyroid, resulting in small decreases in your TSH level during the first trimester of your pregnancy. Typically, a TSH test may turn out to be mildly low during the first trimester, but it should be normal for the duration of the pregnancy. The elevated level of estrogen in your system increases the amount of thyroid hormone–binding proteins circulating in your bloodstream, resulting in increases of your total T4 measurement. Free T4 and free T3 measurements are unaffected by these changes, so during pregnancy, your doctors will rely on the measures of free T4 and free T3 test results when checking your thyroid function.

## Hypothyroidism During Pregnancy

When you are pregnant, your body needs enough thyroid hormone to support a developing fetus and your own expanded metabolic needs. Healthy thyroid glands naturally meet your increased thyroid hormone requirements. If you have Hashimoto's thyroiditis or an already overtaxed thyroid gland, your thyroid hormone levels may decline further. So if you have an undetected mild thyroid problem, you may suddenly find yourself with pronounced symptoms of hypothyroidism after becoming pregnant.

Although estimates vary, hypothyroidism complicates as many as 2.5 percent of all pregnancies. Hypothyroidism develops more frequently after pregnancy in women with type 1 diabetes mellitus and Hashimoto's thyroiditis, who previously did not have hypothyroidism. Most pregnant hypothyroid women have Hashimoto's thyroiditis. Others, who have been treated for hyperthyroidism but are normal prior to pregnancy, are prone to develop hypothyroidism during pregnancy because of their diminished thyroid hormone reserve. Among women who are already being treated for hypothyroidism, the condition can worsen during pregnancy and their hormone replacement needs will likely increase.

Iodine deficiency, a chief cause of hypothyroidism in other parts of the world, rarely causes the condition in pregnant women who live in the United States. However, a small percentage of women may not be getting enough iodine in their diet.

### Your Risks

In the United States, most women who develop hypothyroidism during pregnancy develop mild disease and may experience only mild symptoms or sometimes no symptoms. However, if you had a mild, undiagnosed condition before becoming pregnant, your condition may worsen. You may experience a range of signs and symptoms but be unaware of some that can be easily written off as normal features of pregnancy. If you have untreated hypothyroidism, even a mild version, you may be at risk for pregnancy complications. Treatment with sufficient amounts of thyroid hormone replacement significantly reduces your risk for developing any of the following pregnancy complications associated with hypothyroidism.

- **Abruptio placentae.** This is a premature detachment of the placenta from the wall of the uterus.
- **Anemia.** This condition occurs when your hemoglobin level falls below normal. Hemoglobin is a protein in your red blood cells that transports oxygen throughout your body. If you develop this condition and it becomes severe, you may experience fatigue, breathlessness, fainting, palpitations, and pallor.
- **Preeclampsia.** This is a serious condition that occurs in late pregnancy and that is characterized by excessive weight gain, generalized edema that causes your face and hands to become puffy, high blood pressure, and vision problems.
- **Postpartum hemorrhage.** If you are hypothyroid, you may have a loss of uterine tone. This can result in excessive bleeding either during delivery or during the postpartum period.
- **Premature birth.** A baby born more than three weeks early is premature. A recent study found higher rates of preterm birth in women with mild hypothyroidism.
- **Miscarriage.** If you are hypothyroid, you are most at risk for miscarriage during your first trimester.

## Your Baby's Risks

Thyroid hormone is critical for brain development in a fetus. A fetus depends solely on its mother for its thyroid hormone for most of the first trimester of pregnancy. So when deprived of adequate amounts of thyroid hormone, particularly in cases where maternal hypothyroidism is moderate to severe, a baby is at an

# Unmasking Hypothyroidism Disguised as Normal Pregnancy

Pregnancy provides a good cover for an underactive thyroid because many of its symptoms are in line with the symptoms of hypothyroidism. The following are signs and symptoms common to both hypothyroidism and normal pregnancy:

- carpal tunnel syndrome
- constipation
- emotional changes
- fatigue
- fluid retention
- loss of appetite (usually during the first trimester when morning sickness is common)
- muscle cramps
- weight gain

Some common signs and symptoms that distinguish hypothyroidism from pregnancy are:

- cold intolerance
- delayed reflexes
- dry skin
- hypertension
- low pulse

increased risk for impaired neural development. It has long been known that severe hypothyroidism in a mother can lead to mental retardation in her offspring. This is mainly seen in parts of the world where maternal hypothyroidism is caused by severe iodine deficiency.

The impact that more mild forms of hypothyroidism has on a developing fetus is not fully understood, but some research has shown that even mild hypothyroidism during pregnancy may have a negative effect on a baby's intelligence. One study that drew a lot of attention was published in the *New England Journal of Medicine* in 1999. It found that children born to women who had even a mildly underactive thyroid in pregnancy are four times as likely as others to grow up with significantly lower IQs. The study involved first an analysis of stored blood samples collected from more than 25,200 pregnant women between 1987 and 1990 and then a follow-up of intelligence tests in the children once they reached seven to nine years old. One reassuring aspect of the study is that women who were being treated for overt hypothyroidism but still had mild disease during their pregnancy had children with normal intelligence. But one question the study didn't answer is whether treatment of mild hypothyroidism discovered during pregnancy reverses the condition's effect on the baby's brain, which is believed to occur during the early weeks of pregnancy.

Preliminary results of a newer study suggest that preterm birth, not early brain development, may explain the link between mild hypothyroidism and lower IQs. That study, conducted by researchers at the University of Texas Southwestern Medical Center, found a higher incidence of premature births in women with mild thyroid disease than in women with healthy thyroids. Prematurity is a recognized cause of neuropsychological problems in children.

More research must be done before doctors know for sure whether mild maternal hypothyroidism causes mild developmental problems in their offspring. In the meantime, if you discover that you have hypothyroidism, mild or overt, and you are pregnant, there is no need to panic. Most hypothyroid pregnancies have very good outcomes. Treatment with thyroid hormone therapy increases the likelihood of success, so be sure to start your medication as soon as you are diagnosed.

## Who Should Be Tested?

Despite the impact thyroid diseases can have on a mother and baby, whether to test every pregnant woman for them remains controversial. As it stands, doctors recommend that all women at high risk for thyroid disease or women who are experiencing symptoms should have a TSH and free T4 blood tests and other thyroid blood tests if warranted. You are at high risk if you have a history of thyroid disease or thyroid autoimmunity, a family history of thyroid disease, type 1 diabetes mellitus, or any other autoimmune condition. If you have any of these risk factors, be sure to tell your obstetrician or family physician. Ideally, you should be tested prior to becoming pregnant at prenatal counseling and again shortly after becoming pregnant.

Some physicians will perform thyroid antibody tests in addition to testing thyroid hormone levels. If you have detectable antithyroid antibodies, you are at risk for developing postpartum thyroiditis. Studies also show that women with antithyroid antibodies are at an increased risk for miscarriage. Keep in mind that just because you are more at risk does not mean that you will have either of these complications. It just means that you have more of a chance than someone who doesn't have these antibodies and that your doctor may want to monitor you more closely.

Unfortunately, many women at risk for thyroid diseases are missed because, for example, they may be unaware of their family history. Some groups of physicians, representing thyroid specialists, are pushing for more widespread screening. Other groups representing obstetrician-gynecologists argue that there is no compelling evidence that all pregnant women should be tested when only 2.5 percent have hypothyroidism and most cases are mild. Thyroid specialists are pushing for pilot screening programs to assess the efficacy, costs, and benefits of more widespread screening. As this book was published, a group of medical researchers based in Cardiff, Wales, was embarking on one such program. The Controlled Antenatal Thyroid Screening Study (CATS) involves a randomized prospective evaluation of 22,000 women who are less than sixteen weeks pregnant.

## Treating Hypothyroidism During Pregnancy

There is no difference between treating hypothyroidism when you are pregnant than when you aren't. Levothyroxine sodium pills are completely safe for use during pregnancy. They will be prescribed in dosages that are aimed at replacing the thyroid hormone your thyroid isn't making so that your TSH level is kept within normal ranges. For complete information on thyroid hormone replacement, see "Treating Hypothyroidism" in Chapter 2. Once you begin taking your thyroid hormone pills, you will be monitored closely until your TSH level is within normal ranges. Once it is, your doctor will want to check your TSH level every six weeks or so. Your doctor may also counsel you to take your thyroid hormone pills at least one-half hour to one hour before or at least three hours after you take iron-containing prenatal vitamins or calcium supplements, both of which can interfere with the absorption of thyroid hormone.

## What If I Already Take Thyroid Hormone Medication Before I Become Pregnant?

If you are being treated for hypothyroidism, it is extremely important to have your thyroid checked as soon as your pregnancy is detected so that medication adjustments, typically required before eight to ten weeks of pregnancy, can be made expeditiously. Your TSH level may be checked within one to two weeks after your initial dose adjustment to be sure it is normalizing. Once it drops, you'll need to be checked less frequently during the rest of your pregnancy. Your thyroid hormone needs are likely to increase throughout your pregnancy. As many as 80 percent of all patients may require dose adjustments ranging from 10 percent to greater than 100 percent. Most women have their dosages adjusted anywhere between 30 to 60 percent. The goal of therapy is to keep your TSH level within normal ranges. Once you deliver, your doctor will adjust your dose back to its preconception level.

## Preventing Hypothyroidism During Pregnancy

Although iodine nutrition in the United States is generally adequate, the government's third National Health and Nutrition Examination Survey (NHANES III) found that some women of childbearing age may be at an increased risk for mild iodine deficiency. The U.S. Institute of Medicine's recommended daily allowance (RDA) for pregnant women is 220 mcg daily. This corresponds approximately to a urinary iodine concentration of 15 mcg/dL. The median urinary iodine level among pregnant women reported in NHANES III was 14.1 mcg/dL. Surprisingly, 6.9 percent of women were found to be iodine deficient with urinary iodine levels below 5 mcg/dL.

Your iodine needs increase during pregnancy. During the first trimester, your thyroid must make enough thyroid hormone for you and your baby, but even after that, when your baby begins to make thyroid hormone, he or she relies on the iodine you ingest.

The American Thyroid Association strongly encourages all pregnant women who are not being treated for thyroid disease to take a prenatal vitamin that contains 150 mcg of iodine each day to help meet your RDA of 220 mcg per day. (The RDA for nursing mothers is 290 mcg.) Many brands of prenatal vitamins do not contain iodine, so be sure to read labels when choosing yours.

## Hyperthyroidism During Pregnancy

Graves' disease tends to strike women during their reproductive years, so it should come as no surprise that it occasionally occurs in pregnant women. Reports on pregnancies lasting longer than twenty weeks suggest that Graves' disease occurs in 2 per 1,000 pregnancies, or 0.2 percent of all pregnancies. Pregnancy may worsen a preexisting case of Graves' disease. Graves' disease can also emerge for the first time, typically during the first trimester of pregnancy. The disease is usually at its worst during the first trimester. It tends to then improve in the second and third trimesters and flare up again after delivery.

Another form of hyperthyroidism, called *gestational transient thyrotoxicosis* (GTT), occurs only during pregnancy and results from direct stimulation of the thyroid gland by high levels of hCG. GTT is actually more common than Graves' disease but is typically milder, and women usually do not need any treatment for it as the condition resolves on its own. Some women with GTT develop *hyperemesis gravidarum*, a syndrome characterized by nausea, vomiting, and weight loss during early pregnancy. While many patients with hyperemesis gravidarum have elevated thyroid hormone levels, a significant percentage do not. Although there appears to be a connection between hyperemesis gravidarum and the thyroid, additional factors such as high hCG levels and high estrogen levels appear to have a major role in its development.

Two other less-frequent forms of hyperthyroidism that occur only rarely in pregnancy are *solitary toxic adenoma* (see "Autonomous Nodules" in Chapter 7) and *toxic multinodular goiter* (see "Multinodular Goiter" in Chapter 7).

## Your Risks

If you have hyperthyroidism during pregnancy, you are at an increased risk for experiencing any of the signs and symptoms of hyperthyroidism. And unless your condition is mild, if it is not treated promptly, you could miscarry during the first trimester; develop congestive heart failure, preeclampsia, or anemia; and, rarely, develop a severe form of hyperthyroidism called *thyroid storm*, which can be life threatening. Mild hyperthyroidism or hyperthyroidism caused by GTT do not usually lead to these problems.

## Your Baby's Risks

Mild hyperthyroidism does not typically result in any harm to the fetus. Overt hyperthyroidism, if untreated, can lead to stillbirth, premature birth, or low birth weight. Sometimes it leads to *fetal tachycardia*, which is an abnormally fast pulse in the fetus. If you have Graves' disease, an autoimmune condition, TRAb antibodies can cross the placenta and interact with your baby's thyroid gland. If your antibody levels are high enough, your baby could develop fetal hyperthyroidism, or neonatal hyperthyroidism, although this is not common.

Your baby may also be at risk for developing hyperthyroidism if you have been treated for Graves' disease in the past, even if you are presently hypothyroid. This is because antibodies that are capable of crossing the placenta and stimulating your baby's thyroid may still be present. Be sure to tell your doctor if you have ever had Graves' disease, so that your and your baby's condition can be monitored appropriately.

## Diagnosing Hyperthyroidism During Pregnancy

As with hypothyroidism, diagnosing hyperthyroidism based on symptoms can be tricky because pregnancy and hyperthyroidism share a host of features. Still, you should be aware of the symptoms and bring them to the attention of your doctor if you are experiencing them. For instance, feeling your heart flutter or suddenly becoming short of breath, both symptoms of hyperthyroidism, can be normal in pregnancy, but your doctor still may want to investigate these symptoms. If you have any risk factors for thyroid disease, be sure that you are tested (see "Who Should Be Tested?").

While hyperthyroidism can easily be diagnosed through blood tests, finding out what's causing it may require scanning tests that use minimal amounts of radioactive iodine. During pregnancy, however, scanning tests are not done because small amounts of radioactivity may cross the placenta and become concentrated in your baby's thyroid gland. Antibody tests can be used to distinguish Graves' disease from other causes. A physical exam can help diagnose or distinguish a toxic adenoma or toxic multinodular goiter.

## Treating Hyperthyroidism During Pregnancy

Mild hyperthyroidism usually does not require treatment, only routine monitoring with blood tests to make sure the disease does not progress. More serious conditions require treatment. However, treatment options are limited for pregnant women. Radioactive iodine, which is typically used to treat Graves' disease, cannot be used during pregnancy because it easily crosses the placenta, potentially damaging the baby's thyroid gland and causing hypothyroidism in the baby.

## Unmasking Hyperthyroidism Disguised as Normal Pregnancy

As with hypothyroidism, symptoms of hyperthyroidism may lurk unnoticed because they can be mistaken for normal pregnancy. The following are signs and symptoms common to both hyperthyroidism and normal pregnancy:

- emotional changes
- excessive sweating
- heat intolerance
- fatigue
- increased appetite
- palpitations
- nervousness
- shortness of breath
- tachycardia
- urinary frequency

Features that distinguish hyperthyroidism from normal features of pregnancy are:

- eye problems
- hand tremors
- hypertension
- goiter
- frequent bowel movements
- loosening of nails from the nail bed (onycholysis)
- muscle weakness
- weight loss or inadequate weight gain

Antithyroid drugs are typically the choice of treatment, but this regimen must be monitored carefully because of some risks. While antithyroid drugs cross the placenta and have the potential to harm your baby's thyroid gland, propylthiouracil (PTU) is pre-

## Fast Fact: Taking Antithyroid Drugs While Breast-Feeding

The antithyroid drugs PTU and methimazole have proven to be safe to take while breast-feeding, although PTU is preferred because smaller amounts of PTU cross into breast milk than of methimazole. If you decide to breast-feed your baby while taking antithyroid drugs, be sure to tell your pediatrician or family physician. Although the chances of problems are small, that way the doctor will know that your baby's thyroid function or immune system may be affected by these medications and will be prepared to do the proper testing when indicated. Despite evidence about the drugs' safety, some physicians remain reluctant to encourage patients who are taking antithyroid drugs to nurse because of the concern over adverse affects and the requirement for additional monitoring.

ferred to methimazole (Tapazole) because it is highly protein bound and crosses the placenta less efficiently. Methimazole has in the past been associated with a birth defect of the skin called *aplasia cutis*. More recently, it's been linked with *choanal atresia*, another birth defect that results in a failure of the back of the nostril to open into the nasopharynx.

Due to its potential risks, the goal of treatment is to use the minimal amount of antithyroid drugs possible to maintain your T4 and T3 levels at or just above the upper level of normal, while keeping your TSH levels suppressed. When hormones reach the desired levels, the drug doses can be reduced. This approach controls hyperthyroidism while minimizing the chances of your baby developing hypothyroidism.

Beta-blockers can be used to control severe palpitations and tremors, but they must be used sparingly. In studies of pregnant women with hypertension, beta-blockers have been linked with intrauterine growth problems, fetal cardiac distress, neonatal hypoglycemia, and fetal bradycardia—an unusually slow heart rate.

If you are allergic to antithyroid drugs, surgery is an option, but it is not the preferred choice because of the risks associated with anesthesia.

## Goiters and Nodules During Pregnancy

In areas of the world where iodine deficiency is a problem, developing a goiter is commonplace during pregnancy. Initial observations of this phenomenon come from ancient Egypt, where it was customary to tie a snug reed around a newly married woman's neck. If the reed broke, it was a sign that she was pregnant. In the United States and in places where iodine intakes are generally sufficient, it is unusual for women to develop goiters; it is possible, however, as some women may be at risk for iodine deficiency. If you think that you may have a goiter, be sure to let your doctor know so that the appropriate thyroid function tests can be done.

Thyroid nodules also tend to creep up during pregnancy. However, the incidence of thyroid cancer in pregnant women is 1 per 1,000. If you develop a nodule, your doctor may recommend a fine needle aspiration (FNA) to evaluate it. Scanning techniques are contraindicated because they involve ingesting radioactive iodine, which can be harmful to your baby. If your nodule is benign, your doctor will continue to monitor it and perhaps perform a subsequent FNA biopsy if it enlarges. Thyroid cancer may require surgery, but because thyroid cancer is often slow growing, surgery can usually be delayed until after your baby is delivered. The safest time for surgery during pregnancy is during the second trimester.

# 7

# A Guide to Thyroid Lumps: The Harmless and the Worrisome

The discovery of a lump on your neck can shake up the most cool and collected among us. If you're like most people, you immediately fear the threat of cancer. Thankfully, not all lumps are created equal, and in the case of your thyroid, the vast majority—more than 90 percent by most estimates—do not contain cancerous cells and typically require no treatment.

A lump that appears on the thyroid is called a nodule, which by definition means an abnormal growth of thyroid cells. Nodules are extremely common, although most of them are benign. If you start talking about thyroid nodules with your friends, chances are that it won't be long until you find that someone you know has had a nodule that probably turned out to be benign. Of course, thyroid cancer, discussed in the next chapter, does become a reality for some. More than twenty thousand cases of thyroid cancer are diagnosed annually in the United States. So if you see or feel a lump or your doctor discovers it during a routine exam, you must have it evaluated to be sure that it is not cancerous. No matter how minimal the odds for cancer are, lumps should never be ignored.

## Thyroid Lumps from A to Z

Nodules come in varying sizes and consistencies, and they can be as mysterious as they are varied. Doctors do not know what causes most benign nodules to grow. In some cases, lack of iodine prompts their growth, but this rarely occurs in the United States where iodine intake levels are adequate. More often, nodules seem to just appear sporadically and then sit there like bumps on a log with no purpose. Some do interfere with thyroid function and lead to hyperthyroidism, while others can occur as part of hypothyroidism, particularly with Hashimoto's thyroiditis (see Chapter 5). When diagnosing and treating nodules, doctors must look at your case individually in the context of your and your family's medical histories, the type of nodule, its size, and whether it is causing any harm. A thyroid lump may also turn out to be a goiter or part of a goiter. The following are descriptions of various types of thyroid lumps you may encounter.

### Autonomous Nodules

Autonomous nodules have a mind of their own and contain active thyroid cells. As they form, they independently produce thyroid hormone, and in some cases, they do so with complete disregard to the pituitary gland that tells the thyroid how much hormone to produce. So thyroid hormone levels in your bloodstream could increase to beyond what is required to keep your thyroid function normal, and you could wind up with hyperthyroidism. This is particularly the case when multiple autonomous nodules are present as part of a toxic multinodular goiter, which is an enlarged thyroid gland with more than one functioning nodule. When a single autonomous nodule is present, it is sometimes referred to as a solitary toxic adenoma.

Your doctor can see whether a nodule is active during a radioactive thyroid scan, which can show whether cells of the nodule concentrate iodine. Autonomous nodules that cause hyperthyroidism are classified as "hot" because the scan will show that they are very active, concentrating higher amounts of radioactive iodine than normal, while nonfunctioning nodules with minimal activity are classified as "cold." Some autonomous nodules concentrate about as much radioactivity as the normal thyroid tissue that surrounds them. These nodules are sometimes described as "warm" nodules. However, it is important to establish whether they are truly hot, since hot nodules are virtually never malignant, while nodules that are not hot, including those that appear warm, may be malignant. This is established by further testing, which is discussed later in this chapter.

The good news about autonomous nodules is that while many appear to be on a mission to increase your thyroid function, they are virtually never cancerous. Some autonomous nodules are not active enough to make you hyperthyroid. These may be left alone, but your doctor will want to monitor them.

If these nodules are disrupting your thyroid function enough, causing even mild hyperthyroidism, the options for treatment include surgical removal of the nodule or radioactive iodine therapy. Antithyroid medication is only used in certain cases where controlling hyperthyroidism is essential before proceeding with radioactive iodine or surgery.

Surgery may be preferred for a couple of reasons. If the nodule is on the larger side and is pressing against your airway or larynx, surgery is the quickest and most efficient way to remove the obstruction. Radioactive iodine has a high chance of causing an underactive thyroid, even in the setting of an autonomous nodule. Often a substantial portion of the thyroid or even the entire gland gets radiated. Surgery minimizes the chances of subsequent hypothyroidism. For young children, most physicians prefer not to administer radioactive iodine when surgery is a safe option. Their reluctance is based on causing a lifetime of hypothyroidism as well as the possibility that the radiation may be harmful in the young, although little proof of this exists. Radioactive iodine therapy does not confer the same risk for cancer in children as does exposure to radioactive fallout or external head and neck radiation. Also, resolution of the nodule may be incomplete in children treated with radioactive iodine, and therefore a nodule would persist and have to be followed for a lifetime.

## Cystic Nodules

Anywhere from 6 to 25 percent of all nodules are cystic, which means they are mostly filled with fluid or blood. Purely cystic nodules are less likely than solid nodules to be malignant. Occasionally, however, some cystic nodules, particularly those with a solid component, do in fact turn out to be cancerous.

Cystic nodules may hurt. Sometimes there is bleeding into the cyst, which can cause painful enlargement, or the cyst may grow gradually and cause pressure in your neck. Your doctor will be able to determine your nodule's consistency during a simple procedure known as a *fine needle aspiration* that can be done right in the doctor's office. As the name *fine needle* implies, the needle is small, and your doctor will use it to withdraw the cells from your nodule. If a cyst is involved, your doctor will try to get some of the fluid and some solid material for evaluation, but attempts to remove the contents sometimes collapse the nodule. Either way, the cellular contents will be evaluated under a microscope to determine whether the nodule is malignant. Your doctor may decide to leave the cyst alone if the results of its aspiration prove to be benign or if after it collapses it either resolves or stays very small. If it is causing symptoms, it can be surgically removed. No matter what the treatment, it is important that your doctor monitor the cyst on a routine basis. Over time, it may grow back and you'll want to be sure your cyst is not the occasional one that turns out to be cancerous.

## Goiter

A goiter is not a nodule. It is either a partial or a total enlargement of the thyroid gland, but sometimes a doctor cannot tell whether a lump is due to a goiter or a nodule until tests are done. Goiters can be present if you have hypothyroidism or hyperthyroidism, and they may shrink with therapy for these diseases. However, this isn't always the case; for example, if antithyroid drugs are used to treat Graves' disease, the gland may not shrink and may even get bigger. Goiters are virtually always benign and do not have to be evaluated for malignancy if thyroid nodules are not present. Goiters are sometimes removed surgically if they are putting pressure on the surrounding vital structures in your neck, such as your larynx.

## Multinodular Goiter

This is a goiter with more than one nodule. When scanned, the nodules can be autonomous and hot or cold and nonfunctioning. Sometimes the goiter will have a combination of both types. A goiter with nodules that are hot enough to produce an excess amount of thyroid hormone is called a toxic multinodular goiter. These hot nodules produce thyroid hormone independently of one another and are out of control, so much so that hyperthyroidism can be severe. This type of goiter is a common cause of hyperthyroidism in older people and is often easily recognized by a physician who is usually able to feel the bumpy goiter. This condition can also be treated with radioactive iodine, although in some instances surgery is preferred.

## Solid Nonfunctioning Nodules

Some solid nodules do not produce thyroid hormone, or they produce such little amounts that they do not affect thyroid function. These are nonfunctioning, or cold, nodules. Many that turn out to be benign are called *adenomas*. These nodules often appear for no apparent reason. Those that may warrant further evaluation can occur if you have Hashimoto's thyroiditis, but this isn't typical. If you have this condition, what may seem to be a nodule is more often just a prominent region of the thyroid gland. Your doctor may recommend a fine needle aspiration of the nodule as a first step (see "Fine Needle Aspiration [FNA]"). In some cases, a thyroid scan may be done first. If a thyroid scan shows that a nodule is cold, however, your doctor will want to investigate further, since all cancerous nodules are cold; still, the vast majority of cold nodules are not cancerous. If it is not cancerous, there is usually no need for surgery unless it is causing symptoms or putting pressure on any other structures in your neck. You may also want to have it removed for cosmetic reasons.

## How Are Thyroid Nodules Diagnosed?

You may notice or feel a thyroid nodule on your own if it is large or causing any pain, which sometimes occurs. In the case of a particularly large nodule, you might have difficulty swallowing or you might feel a tickle in your throat. In most cases, however, you feel and see nothing, and it is your doctor who stumbles upon it when examining your neck for an unrelated reason. For instance, if you have the flu, your doctor might check for swollen glands and find a nodule, or you may just be in for your annual exam. Your doctor cannot determine whether the nodule is cancerous at this juncture, but he or she may be more suspicious of some nodules than others based on some known characteristics of cancerous nodules. First off, those that are firm and fixed to the touch are more likely to be malignant than those that are soft and mobile.

Upon the discovery of a nodule, your doctor will want to run a series of different tests aimed at ultimately determining whether the nodule is causing problems with your thyroid function or whether it is cancerous. Examining your family history will be part of the process, because your doctor will want to know if anyone in your family has had any thyroid diseases or related diseases or if anyone in your family has had thyroid cancer.

Your doctor will also want to know if you have ever been exposed to radiation. For instance, in the 1940s and 1950s, X-rays were used to treat acne, enlarged tonsils, adenoids, lymph nodes, and enlarged thymus glands. Back then, X-rays were even used in shoe stores to measure foot sizes. This kind of X-ray exposure is no longer used. The kind of routine X-rays you may have today, at the dentist or doctor's office or even in mammograms, involves only a small amount of radiation that in and of itself contributes

# How to Check for Thyroid Lumps

If you have a family history of thyroid cancer or other forms of thyroid disease, you may want to occasionally examine your neck for abnormal lumps. One way to do this involves a handheld mirror and a glass of water. Hold the mirror so that you can see your neck and focus on the area below your Adam's apple, close to your collarbone. Tip your head back and swallow some water. As you swallow, check for any bulges. You might have to repeat the swallowing several times. If you do see something out of the ordinary, be sure to see your physician and ask for a thyroid evaluation.

little, if any, risk to developing cancer. Exposure to radioactive fallout can also cause thyroid cancer.

Nodules that occur in men and children turn out to be cancerous at a higher rate than those found in women. Although thyroid cancer is more prevalent in women, benign nodules on the whole are far less prevalent in men and children, which means the ratio of cancerous to noncancerous nodules is higher in men and children than in women.

## More Tests

To help determine whether your nodule is affecting your thyroid function, you will likely undergo a series of blood tests, including the tests discussed in Chapter 4. You may also have one or more of the imaging tests discussed later in this chapter. But really the only way that the doctor can rule out cancer definitively is with a biopsy that involves surgical excision of the nodule. Another option, fine needle aspiration, is the most reliable alternative to determine whether cancer is present.

***Fine Needle Aspiration (FNA).*** At one time, if you had a nodule, the only way to determine whether it was cancerous was to undergo complete surgical excision of the nodule for biopsy.

Given the number of benign nodules out there, this added up to a lot of unnecessary surgery. The use of fine needle aspiration, which made a comeback in the United States in the late 1970s and early 1980s after years of not being used, has changed all this. Doing this simple procedure as a first diagnostic test has not only limited the number of expensive tests, such as nuclear medicine scans, that were routinely done to evaluate thyroid nodules, but it has also decreased the rate of unnecessary surgery.

The American Association of Endocrinologists recommends FNA any time a nodule is discovered during a physical examination. It is cheap, fast, accurate, and minimally invasive. It requires no preparation or recovery time. You can go home or back to work immediately following the procedure. A needle biopsy feels very similar to having blood withdrawn from your arm, only in this case, the needle must be inserted multiple times so that cells from different sites of the nodule are removed (see Figure 7.1). That is so the doctor is assured of an adequate sample to determine whether cancer is present. Some people complain that the procedure is more painful than expected, while others say it is no big deal. If you are particularly squeamish about needles, your doctor may use a local anesthetic.

After the procedure, you may experience some pain at the site and feel throat discomfort. You may also find that swallowing is a bit painful, but this usually subsides within hours to several days. You will not be left with any scarring, but you may have a bruise afterward.

If the nodule is a cyst, the fluid will be drained, and in some cases, the cyst may collapse. The cells taken from the nodule are then smeared onto slides and examined under a microscope by a pathologist, a physician who interprets cellular changes caused by disease. The pathologist issues a written report, usually within five working days, that can point to any of the following results, also shown in Figure 7.2.

- **A benign nodule.** According to reviews of statistics reported from various medical institutions, the outcome of

## FIGURE 7.1 Fine Needle Aspiration

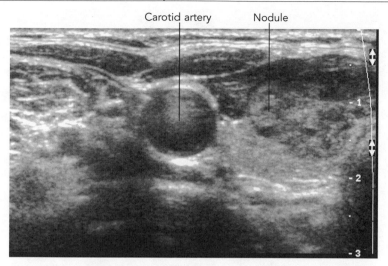

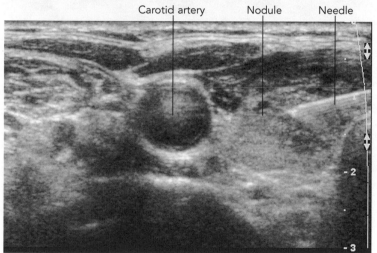

(a) A thyroid nodule and its surrounding structures viewed with ultrasound.

(b) With ultrasound guidance, a needle is inserted into the thyroid nodule and cells from the nodule are removed for examination.

the FNA test is benign in 50 to 75 percent of cases (see Table 7.1 on page 147). This result is almost always accurate, but there can sometimes be false negatives; this typically depends on the experience and skill of the physician who performs the FNA and interprets the results. If you get a

**FIGURE 7.2** Fine Needle Aspiration: Four Possible Results

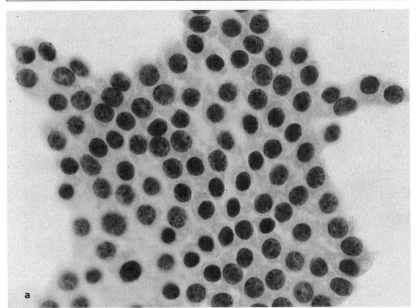

*(a) **Benign:** This result shows some important characteristics of cells that are clearly benign. They are round in shape and normal in size, and they are not stacked or crowded together. They don't overlap in the least bit and have a fairly uniform, even distance between them. They are indistinguishable from normal thyroid cells. Benign aspirates often feature a substantial amount of colloid (not featured in this image), a protein found within clusters of thyroid cells called follicles.*

benign result, your doctor may want to perform another biopsy sometime in the future, particularly if the nodule grows. In some cases, your doctor will prescribe thyroid hormone pills to help shrink the nodule or prevent it from growing, which would prevent it from causing symptoms. If the nodule doesn't grow or shrinks, this is extra assurance that it isn't cancerous.

- **A malignant nodule.** Less than 5 percent of nodules tested by FNA turn out to be malignant. If yours is malignant, your doctor will want to schedule thyroid surgery as soon as possible.
- **An indeterminate result.** An indeterminate outcome occurs in 10 to 30 percent of cases. What it means is that the

**FIGURE 7.2** *continued*

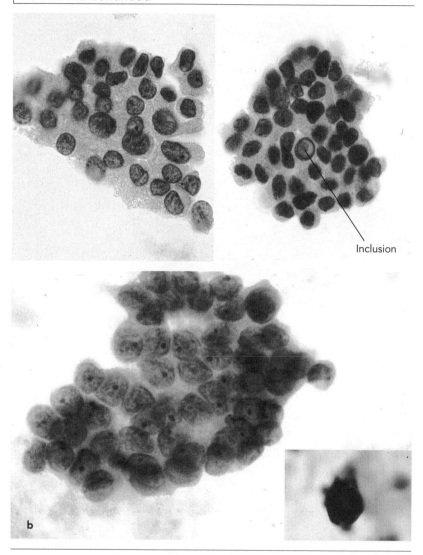

Inclusion

*(b) Thyroid cancer:* These slides show papillary thyroid cancer, the most common type of thyroid cancer. Characteristic features include: big, irregularly shaped cells with large nuclei that are overlapping and stacked together with folds or cleaves across the nuclei that are known as grooves. Cancerous cells are pale in color when compared to benign cells, and some of the cells may have inclusions—small spheres within a cell that show up as nearly clear circles (upper right image). There may be configurations of cells known as psammoma bodies (inset), which are lamellated calcific spherules, or rings of calcium in tiny spheres, that form in the damaged or dying cells of papillary cancer. Finally, in papillary cancer, cells generally configure in the shape of a frond. This is sometimes evident on a cytology specimen, though in the majority of cases it is not.

## FIGURE 7.2 *continued*

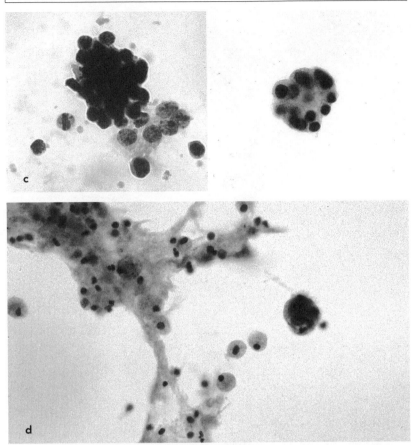

*(c) **Indeterminate result:** Certain benign conditions can sometimes result in some cell configurations that are characteristic of cancer. For instance, cells that appear in overlapping, crowded configurations (left side) can sometimes occur in benign adenomas, Hashimoto's thyroiditis, or a multinodular goiter. Some cells in these configurations may even contain inclusions or grooves. On the other hand, clusters of cells known as macrofollicles (not shown here) may be large enough to make a diagnosis of cancer unlikely, as the bigger the follicle, the less likely it is to be cancer. These configurations of cells are therefore iffy, indicating that cancer is possible. Indeterminate biopsies usually do not have abundant amounts of colloid (see "Benign") and frequently contain a sample of small microfollicles (right side). This result requires complete excision in order to make a definitive diagnosis.*

*(d) **Inadequate result:** Though this slide shows some characteristics of a benign nodule, such as small cells that aren't crowded, there are not enough thyroid cells to make a diagnosis. This often occurs when a cyst collapses upon fine needle aspiration. Although cysts are typically benign, if repeated aspirations yield inadequate results and the cyst does not shrink appreciably, surgical biopsy for further evaluation may be recommended.*

pathologist had a sufficient amount of material for interpretation but was unable to determine whether the nodule was benign or malignant. If this is the case, your doctor may want to order a thyroid scan if you haven't had one to make sure the nodule isn't hot, or to wait and watch your nodule periodically with ultrasound to see if it grows. But often, this result in itself may warrant surgery to remove your thyroid for further testing.

Another option that has sometimes been offered is a trial of thyroid hormone replacement pills. It was thought that if

**TABLE 7.1** Biopsy Results

| FNA Biopsy Result | Chance This Result Occurs* | Chance Nodule Is Malignant | Recommendations | Comments |
|---|---|---|---|---|
| Benign | 50–75% | < 5% (in expert hands, considerably lower) | May need to be repeated to confirm initial result | Thyroid hormone pills may be prescribed to shrink the nodule or to prevent it from growing |
| Cancerous | < 5% | > 95% | Excision of thyroid gland | Depending on the size of the tumor, your doctor may recommend removal of one or both sides of the thyroid, in which case it will probably be followed by radioactive iodine ablation of the remaining thyroid tissue |
| Indeterminate (suspicious) | 10–30% | 15–60% (depending on cell characteristics) | Excision of thyroid gland for further evaluation or sometimes monitor with ultrasound | Your doctor may want to see if thyroid hormone pills shrink the nodule |
| Inadequate | 15–20% | 5–10% | Repeat biopsy | Surgery may be an option, depending on the characteristics and numbers of inadequate FNAs |

*Cited statistic ranges are based on variations among reporting medical institutions and on whether these institutions included inadequate samples in their calculations.

the nodule responds to suppressed TSH levels by shrinking, it isn't cancerous. However, a number of more recent studies indicate that this isn't always so. Thyroid hormone may reduce the size of or prevent growth in up to only 30 percent of nodules thought to be benign, and it may also cause some cancerous nodules to decrease in size. In other words, even if your nodule shrinks, you can't be completely certain that it is harmless. As a result of these findings, this strategy for determining whether a nodule is cancerous isn't generally recommended anymore.

Still, if your nodule is stable or becomes smaller than it was initially—which may be more likely to happen by taking thyroid hormone—and remains so for many years, it does not generally require additional aspirations, at least not on a frequent basis. On the other hand, whenever a nodule grows, even when a previous aspiration was interpreted to be benign, either another FNA or surgery is indicated.

Therefore, while the response to thyroid hormone medication is not definitive, thyroid hormone therapy may prevent surgery and limit the number of repeated aspirations, which can be anxiety provoking because they are always done to rule out cancer. If your test showed an indeterminate result, talk to your doctor about the pros and cons of thyroid hormone suppression therapy and the value of doing a thyroid scan.

- **An inadequate biopsy.** This result means that an insufficient amount of cells was obtained, so a diagnosis cannot be determined. This happens in about 15 to 20 percent of cases. It often happens if you have a cyst, whether or not it collapsed during the procedure. Depending on the situation, you may have the test repeated or may have surgery to remove the nodule for further evaluation.

*Thyroid Scan.* A thyroid scan, discussed in Chapter 4, takes a picture of your thyroid gland, which can show how your thyroid is functioning. Since FNA has become mainstream practice, the scan is used to a lesser degree since it does not definitively determine the presence of cancer. It still is used, however, if results of the FNA are indeterminate (see earlier discussion) in order to establish whether a nodule is taking up radioactive iodine. After you are given a tiny amount of radioactive iodine, usually in the form of a capsule, a special camera takes pictures of your thyroid gland from three different angles. Your doctor will be able to use information from this test to see whether the nodule is cold, warm, or hot.

- **Cold.** If the nodule is cold, this means that it is taking in minimal amounts of radioactive iodine or none at all. As mentioned above, cancerous nodules are almost always cold, so any cold nodules will be referred for a biopsy if you haven't had one yet. If you had a biopsy that was indeterminate, you may be referred for surgery or asked to take a course of thyroid hormone pills to suppress TSH, although this option is falling out of favor.
- **Warm.** A warm nodule is one that behaves just as any normal thyroid tissue does, taking up normal amounts of radioactive iodine. Your doctor will want to be sure to establish whether it is truly warm and not hot. Since hot nodules are virtually never cancerous, all nodules classified as "not hot," including those that are warm and cold, should be biopsied.
- **Hot.** A hot nodule is good news if you are worried about cancer. Although you may have or develop hyperthyroidism, the likelihood of cancer is extremely rare, and you will not need to have a biopsy. However, nowadays more and more physicians are performing a biopsy first so that they can get a definitive answer as to whether cancer is involved without ever determining whether your nodule is hot or not, particularly if your TSH is normal.

**Thyroid Ultrasound.** Ultrasound uses high frequency sound waves to obtain an image of your thyroid gland and identify nodules. The FNA resurgence had diminished the importance of this test as an initial diagnostic procedure to determine whether a nodule is solid or cystic. However, ultrasound technology has become more sensitive and its pictures more detailed. As a result, it can pick up other signs that suggest malignancy. These include whether the nodule has irregular borders; whether it is hypoechoic, meaning that it yields fewer echoes than normal; whether it has calcium deposits, known as calcifications; or whether it has an abnormally high amount of blood flow. In general, however, whether or not your nodule has any of these features, you should still have an FNA biopsy if your nodule is sizeable (> 1 cm) and your TSH is not low, in which case scanning to determine if your nodule is hot or not may be undertaken before the biopsy.

Ultrasound is also sometimes used in conjunction with an FNA biopsy to help your physician determine the exact location of the nodule, which is not always easily felt. It is also useful if your doctor decides to monitor the nodule to see whether it is growing or shrinking naturally over time. A nodule that grows may be more worrisome.

Ultrasound can also be used as a screening tool to see nodules that are too small to be felt. But most doctors agree that screening the general population for nodules using ultrasound would turn up mostly harmless nodules that measure less than 1 cm. Discovery of these tiny nodules, sometimes called *incidentalomas*, raises a management dilemma for doctors over whether to biopsy them. They are even more common than nodules that are both big enough and located in a position where they can be felt, and like larger nodules, only a small percentage of them turn out to be cancerous. The discovery of these small nodules often leads to needless anxiety over further evaluation and sometimes to unnecessary surgery. While ultrasound can lead to early detection of thyroid cancer in a small percentage of cases, some argue that early treatment offers little benefit with respect to thyroid cancer, a slow-growing cancer that 95 percent of the time is detected in time for successful treatment.

Some doctors use ultrasound to check for thyroid nodules if you have some of the risk factors for thyroid cancer, which are outlined in the next chapter. The chances for nodules turning out to be cancerous is much greater if you have these risk factors, particularly exposure to radiation or a family history of thyroid cancer. Be sure to let your doctor know if these risk factors apply to you so that you will be checked for nodules. You may want to perform your own self-exam (see "How to Check for Thyroid Lumps").

## A Suspicious Nodule

Throughout her life, Mary Lou has never had any significant health problems. A very active mother of five and grandmother of twelve, Mary Lou has had her thyroid checked at her annual physical every year for about twenty years or so, ever since her middle daughter was diagnosed with hypothyroidism, a condition known to run in families.

It wasn't until close to her sixty-fifth birthday that her doctor felt nodules on both sides of her thyroid gland. This is Mary Lou's story.

> I've had blood tests to check my thyroid function every year now, and they always came back negative, but last year my neck was swollen and my internist discovered nodules on both sides of my neck. My blood work, for the first time, showed that my cholesterol was high and my TSH test came back high. I told her I wasn't having any symptoms, but now I realize that I was in fact experiencing a very sharp pain that I thought was related to my teeth. I thought that I needed to have a root canal and didn't at all connect the pain to the nodules. I had put off going to the dentist because I dreaded another root canal.
>
> My internist referred me to my endocrinologist, and he did a biopsy. The results came back that there were suspi-

cious cells, so he had me come in for a second biopsy, which he did under ultrasound this time.* Again, the results were inconclusive. After a third biopsy failed to rule out cancer, my doctor recommended that I have my entire thyroid gland removed. This was the only way he could be sure there was no cancer.

For me, the decision to have surgery wasn't difficult. This was something I had to do to rule out cancer, and I just did it. My internist is wonderful and really helped me find a surgeon that I was very happy with. She went on the computer and did all the research for me and gave me two names. I have a friend who works at the hospital where I had my surgery, who helped me choose between the two. Both were highly qualified, but my friend who knew them both made a choice based on the personality that would best suit me.

Going into surgery, I wasn't nervous. The surgeon made a very small incision in the front of my neck and I had to stay overnight. Afterward I had a sore throat, but I have not had any problems with my voice or damage to my parathyroid glands. And best of all, it wasn't cancerous.

I was started on the lowest dose of thyroid hormone replacement soon after, and I went for blood tests every month. After each visit, my dose was gradually increased and now I am on 125 micrograms of Levoxyl. I have been on this dose for about five months now, and I feel good. That sharp pain that I thought was related to my teeth also went away. That's when I realized that the nodules were causing the pain.

I will continue to go for annual physicals and I'm thankful that everything turned out the way it did.

---

* Medical editor's note: If an initial FNA result proves to be suspicious, it is not standard practice to repeat the test, since even a more reassuring result the next time should not discount a more worrisome reading the first time. Usually, either the nodule is surgically removed for further evaluation, a thyroid scan is done, or it may be monitored to see whether it grows.

## Treatment Options

If your nodule is benign, your doctor may want to observe it over a period of time to see whether it grows or naturally diminishes. Unless it is causing problems with surrounding structures in your neck, an autonomous nodule may be treated with surgery or radioactive iodine therapy. Otherwise, nodules may be treated in any of the following ways.

### Thyroid Hormone Suppression Therapy

Thyroid hormone medication is typically used by patients with hypothyroidism to supplement insufficient levels of thyroid hormone in the bloodstream. It can also be used to treat nodules or a multinodular goiter, as long as the nodules involved are not autonomous and are unresponsive to changes in TSH levels. The extra thyroid hormone in your system suppresses production of thyroid-stimulating hormone (TSH), which normally promotes thyroid activity. Shutting this hormone down can cause a nodule to shrink, but this doesn't always happen. If it doesn't, surgery may be an option, particularly if the nodule grows.

### Lobectomy or Thyroidectomy

An operation involving surgical removal of part of your thyroid, called a *lobectomy* or a *subtotal thyroidectomy*, may be recommended in some circumstances. For instance, if the nodule is causing any pain or pressure on your neck or is causing breathing problems, it will likely be removed. If the FNA biopsy was indeterminate, your doctor may want to remove the nodule for further evaluation. And if the nodule affects your appearance, you may want to have surgery.

The surgical procedure is performed under general anesthesia (for more information, see "Preparing for Surgery" in Chapter 8). An incision measuring about 4 to 8 cm is made at the base of your neck. Once the nodule is removed, it is sent to a pathologist for examination. If it is cancerous, you will be scheduled to have the remainder of your thyroid gland removed as soon as possible.

(Treatment for thyroid cancer is discussed in the next chapter.) For most thyroid surgery, you'll probably be hospitalized anywhere from one to three days, depending on how complex the surgery is.

## Thyroid Surgery Risks

As with any medical procedure, there are risks with thyroid surgery. Overall, these complications occur in less than 50 out of 1,000 operations, but these odds can vary depending on where you are having your surgery and the experience of your surgeon. It's always a good idea to find out how many thyroid operations your surgeon has performed and how often those operations have resulted in complications. Before consenting to surgery, you should be aware of the risks and talk about these risks with your doctor.

Most people have four parathyroid glands, which regulate the level of calcium in your bloodstream. These glands sit behind the lobes of your thyroid gland. Damage can occur to these glands when a section of the thyroid is being removed, and this can cause temporary low blood calcium. A small percentage of people will need to take calcium and substantial amounts of vitamin D supplements permanently if all four parathyroid glands have been damaged. This only happens when both sides of the thyroid gland are operated on. Damage to the vocal cords, which sit in close proximity to the thyroid, can also occur when the nerves controlling their function are damaged. This can lead to permanent hoarseness or, if severe enough, loss of voice.

Other complications that are far less common include infection in the wound, which would require antibiotics; bleeding during the operation, which would require a blood transfusion; and the risks of anesthesia.

If your entire thyroid is removed, and in some cases, when only part of the thyroid is removed, you will become dependent on thyroid hormone replacement for life.

CHAPTER 8

# Thyroid Cancer

There aren't many words dreaded nearly as much as the word *cancer* when it comes to your diagnosis. If you're like most people, you may be flooded with feelings of fear or disbelief upon its mention. With thyroid cancer, the news may come as a surprise since you may have read or were told that the odds that your nodule is cancerous are extremely low.

While no one wants to hear that they have cancer, keep in mind that with thyroid cancer, there is often a silver lining. Thyroid cancer is often called a "good cancer," if there is such a thing, because it is typically slow growing, rarely causes pain or disability, is easily treated, and may be cured with surgery alone. Most people with thyroid cancer are also treated with radioactive iodine to be sure all of the cancerous cells are destroyed. Chemotherapy is used rarely, when the cancer has spread to other organs.

Once you are treated, the long-term survival rates are excellent. According to the National Cancer Institute (NCI), about 95 percent of people who are diagnosed with thyroid cancer survive the disease for at least five years, and about 92 percent survive the disease for at least twenty years. Even more encouraging, the NCI reports that only 5 percent of thyroid cancers eventually result in death; a large percentage of those deaths are attributed to a rare form of aggressive thyroid cancer, called anaplastic thyroid cancer, which is discussed later in this chapter.

Thyroid cancer makes up less than 1 percent of all malignancies. Still, it is twice as common as Hodgkin's disease and equal in incidence to myeloma, a bone cancer, and cervical cancer. Population studies show, however, that it is on the rise.

Although the incidence of the most common form of thyroid cancer, papillary thyroid cancer, is growing faster than the population is growing, the odds of dying from thyroid cancer are falling. Studies have shown that exposure to nuclear fallout and other forms of radiation have contributed to this increase.

## Why Me?

If you've been diagnosed with thyroid cancer, one of the foremost questions you probably have is, "Why me?" In most cases, this is the most difficult question for doctors to answer conclusively, if at all. Some forms of thyroid cancer are known to run in families, but more common forms usually appear sporadically, although researchers are discovering that even a small percentage of sporadic types can sometimes run in families.

While the causes of most cancers are a mystery, scientists believe that a combination of factors, including genetic predisposition, environment, and lifestyle, together play a role. Some risk factors known to make you more susceptible to thyroid cancer have been identified. To better understand how these risk factors contribute to cancer, it helps to understand how cells function normally and how they can turn cancerous.

### The Biology of Cancer

Cells are the building blocks of the human body. You began life as a single cell. That cell, a fertilized egg, divided in two, then four, and so on. As your cells grew more and more numerous, they began to differentiate, forming specific tissues and organs, such as your brain, lungs, heart, and thyroid. Even after birth, human beings are, in some respects, constantly being "reborn." Your cells continue dividing—duplicating their genetic code, a process known as replication. As new cells emerge, the older ones die out. In this way, your body remains healthy. Orchestrating this process are the genes contained in each cell's nucleus. These genes consist of strands of DNA (deoxyribonucleic acid), which function like detailed molecular blueprints, providing instructions on everything from your hair color to your metabolism. They also produce protein cells that provide the "stop" and "go" signals for the process of growth, development, and renewal.

Your cells are actually programmed to die after a certain time so that healthy new cells can replace them. When an old cell dies, nearby cells come in to clean up the debris. This process of orderly and planned cell death is called *apoptosis*. When it works well, apoptosis helps your body maintain a delicate balance between old and new cells. As old cells die, new ones take their place.

Cancer is a perversion of these normal processes. What was once orderly becomes chaotic and unmanageable. Normal cells replicate at a steady pace; cancerous cells replicate uncontrollably. Normal cells maintain a balance between old and new. Cancerous cells never die, and eventually so many of them accumulate that a tumor forms. Normal cells respect boundaries and stay put. Cancerous cells migrate elsewhere in a process known as *metastasis*. Since cancerous tumors, or nodules, of the thyroid are slow growing, they are often caught before they metastasize to vital structures, such as the lungs or bone.

## How Cells Are Damaged

For years, researchers have wondered why normal cells turn cancerous. Why does the precisely choreographed dance of cellular life disintegrate into a free-for-all? In recent years, thanks to a host of discoveries, researchers have begun to understand cancer as a multistep process that takes place over several years or even decades. Seldom does one factor, such as heredity, result in cancer. More often, the disease develops because of the complex interaction between the genes inside your cells and external factors, such as diet and exposure to toxins, which can damage those genes.

The first step in this long process is known as initiation, which occurs when DNA, the genetic material contained within a normal cell, suffers some type of permanent change or mutation. Once the gene has mutated, the instructions it provides to the cell also change. Genetic mutation is responsible for initiating a series of events that—unimpeded—can lead to cancer.

Genetic mutations can occur in a number of ways. You may inherit a damaged gene, for example, or a gene may inadvertently mutate or change during normal cell replication. It's often a matter of chance—every million divisions or so, a mistake happens. More often, genes mutate because they are exposed to some type of initiator, a broad range of substances that includes well-known carcinogens, such as tobacco smoke, to substances you may never have heard of. In the case of thyroid cancer, researchers have discovered that exposure to I-131 (see Chapter 11) and to certain kinds of X-ray therapies can act as an initiator and damage thyroid cells, causing genes to mutate. Although mechanisms of damage vary, all initiators inflict some permanent change in a cell's DNA.

## Who's at Risk for Thyroid Cancer?

The following are risk factors researchers have identified as potentially triggering the kinds of cell damage that can lead to thyroid cancer. But remember that cellular damage is the result of the interplay of multiple factors, many of which are unknown. You may find that you have thyroid cancer but don't identify with any risk factors. As with many folks with cancer, you may never know what caused yours to occur.

### Exposure to Radiation During Childhood

During the 1940s and 1950s, it was very common for children to receive X-ray treatments to the head and neck for enlarged tonsils and adenoids, an enlarged thymus gland, acne, and ringworm. Studies have shown that certain levels of this kind of exposure to radiation during childhood results in a seven- to eightfold increased risk for thyroid cancer later in life, particularly in children who were exposed under the age of ten. An adult thyroid gland appears to be more resistant to the effects of radiation.

Exposure to radiation as a result of nuclear fallout also increases your risk for thyroid cancer if you were exposed during childhood. This knowledge comes from numerous recent studies on the highly publicized accident that occurred at the Chernobyl nuclear reactor in Ukraine in 1986 as well as studies on fallout from atomic bomb tests done in the United States during the 1950s.

## Heredity

Many people with thyroid cancer can find someone in their extended family who has had some kind of thyroid disease, cancerous or noncancerous. Others have no family history of problems with the thyroid whatsoever. For years, only one type of thyroid cancer was conclusively linked to a mutated gene passed down in families. That type, medullary thyroid cancer, occurs in 3 to 4 percent of all thyroid cancers and is sometimes caused by a defect in a gene identified as the RET protooncogene. A blood test to check for the presence of a defect in this gene, which can be inherited, is available. More recently, population studies have shown that there in an increased risk of thyroid cancer in relatives of people with papillary thyroid cancer.

## Age and Gender

Thyroid cancer is much more common in women than in men at all ages. In the United States, women are two to three times more likely than men to develop thyroid cancer. The incidence per million per year is highest in women by the age of forty.

## How Doctors Diagnose Thyroid Cancer

If you have a nodule and your doctor suspects cancer, you will likely undergo blood tests and a series of imaging tests (these are discussed in Chapter 7, which outlines how doctors determine whether a nodule is cancerous). A biopsy, either through fine needle aspiration (FNA) or surgical removal of the nodule, is the only way to definitively determine whether cancer is present. Doctors can use FNA to classify which type of thyroid cancer you have, information that is vital in determining the best course of treatment and the long-term outlook on your cancer. Your thyroid cancer will be classified as any of the following types. A summary of these types of cancer is found in Table 8.1.

## Papillary Thyroid Cancer

About 75 to 80 percent of people diagnosed with thyroid cancer have papillary thyroid cancer, making it by far the most common type, affecting more than fifteen thousand people each year. It is primarily responsible for thyroid cancer's reputation as a "good" cancer, as generally speaking, it happens to be the easiest to treat. It's slow growing and most of the time the outlook for a cure is excellent. It gets its name from how it looks under a microscope. A papilla is a small nipplelike projection. Papillary cancers have multiple projections, which give them a fernlike appearance.

This kind of cancer is an example of what is known as a *differentiated* thyroid cancer. This means that the cells in this cancer are not primitive but are similar to thyroid cells, called follicular cells—so similar that they behave like thyroid cells, make Tg, may make small amounts of thyroid hormone, and typically grow slowly. As a result, differentiated cancers generally have a better outlook than the undifferentiated sort because they are less prone to reproduce and spread.

Still, papillary cancer may spread through the body's lymphatic system to lymph nodes in the neck, but even then the prognosis remains comparable to those tumors confined to the thyroid. A very small number of cases can become more challenging. Typically, these challenging cases involve variants of papillary thyroid cancer, including tall and columnar cell variants.

At the time of diagnosis, your doctor will be able to determine your prognosis by looking at several features of your disease. The best-case scenario is a tumor confined to your thyroid. The outlook worsens when the tumor has spread to tissues in your neck outside of the lymph nodes. Thyroid cancer can eventually spread through the bloodstream to the lungs and bones. Fortunately, this only happens in a small minority of cases. You may be more at risk

TABLE 8.1 Comparison of Thyroid Cancer Classifications

| Type | Percent of Thyroid Cancer Cases | Method(s) of Diagnosis | Treatment | Prognosis* | Comments |
|---|---|---|---|---|---|
| Papillary thyroid cancer | 75–80% | FNA | Surgery and radioactive iodine | Excellent | |
| Follicular thyroid cancer | 10% | FNA result is usually indeterminant. Tumor usually requires total excision for diagnosis. | Surgery and radioactive iodine | Very good to good | Differentiated thyroid cancer that occurs primarily in people over 50 |
| Hurthle cell thyroid cancer | 3% | FNA result is usually indeterminant. Tumor usually requires total excision for diagnosis. | Surgery and radioactive iodine | Good to fair | Considered by most to be an aggressive variant of follicular thyroid cancer |
| Medullary thyroid cancer | 3–4% | FNA and blood test that measures calcitonin | Surgery | Good to poor | Undifferentiated thyroid cancer that is often inherited |
| Anaplastic thyroid cancer | < 2% | FNA plus biopsy | Surgery to the extent possible, chemotherapy, and external radiation | Poor | Most aggressive form of thyroid cancer, made up of purely undifferentiated cells |
| Thyroid lymphoma | < 2% | Biopsy and special lymphocyte studies | Chemotherapy and external radiation | Good to poor | Arises in the setting of preexisting Hashimoto's thyroiditis |

*Prognosis applies to most cases.

for this kind of metastasis if you are older than forty-five or if your tumor is more than 4 cm in diameter.

## Follicular Thyroid Cancer

About 10 percent of thyroid cancers are follicular. Malignant follicular tumors occur primarily in people over fifty years old. Under a microscope, their cells resemble the normal follicular cells of the thyroid. (The thyroid is made up almost entirely of follicular cells, but it also contains parafollicular cells, which are discussed in the next section.) Therefore, the appearance of the follicular cells alone generally does not distinguish whether a nodule composed of predominantly follicular appearing cells is benign or malignant. Rather, it is only by demonstrating the invasion of follicular cells into the capsule or vessels surrounding the tumor that a diagnosis of a follicular thyroid cancer is made. This requires the total removal of the tumor so that a pathologist can thoroughly examine the tissue surrounding the tumor.

This kind of thyroid cancer is also differentiated, but it tends to grow faster than the papillary type and is more likely to spread to blood vessels. One variant in particular, called Hurthle cell thyroid cancer, is an aggressive variant of follicular thyroid cancer. However, if follicular thyroid cancer is caught after it has spread to only a small number of blood vessels, the outlook is still good. The prognosis is not as good if the cancer has spread to a substantial number of blood vessels, since it is then more likely to spread to lungs and bones, but this occurs in a small minority of cases. Generally speaking, the prognosis for this cancer tends to be better for younger people than for those over forty-five years old.

## Medullary Thyroid Cancer

Medullary thyroid cancer occurs in the parafollicular, or C, cells of the thyroid. Normally, C cells help your thyroid perform its secondary job, which is producing a hormone called *calcitonin* that helps regulate calcium levels in your bloodstream. Medullary thyroid cancer, which accounts for 3 to 4 percent of all thyroid cancers, is made up of functioning thyroid C cells, which form a tumor that sometimes occurs on both sides of the thyroid. These cells are somewhat primitive in nature, however, making this an *undifferentiated* thyroid cancer. That means that it generally is more aggressive than papillary and follicular cancers, but not as aggressive as anaplastic. In some people, the tumor is quite tame; even in its more aggressive forms, the outlook is generally positive.

Malignant C cells produce excessive amounts of calcitonin. So one telltale sign that this kind of cancer is present is elevated levels of calcitonin, which can be measured through a blood test. This kind of blood test is not routinely used, but in cases where a fine needle aspiration biopsy of the nodule leads the pathologist to suspect this kind of cancer, calcitonin levels are checked.

About 20 percent of the time, medullary thyroid cancer is inherited. If you have the familial form, that means that your child has a 50/50 chance of inheriting the defective RET protooncogene. Research shows that almost everyone who inherits the altered gene develops the cancer. A blood test can check for the presence of the defective gene, so if the abnormal gene is found in a person with medullary thyroid cancer, your doctor will want to test your first-degree family members, including your parents, children, and siblings. If any of these family members are found to carry the altered RET gene, the doctor may recommend frequent lab tests or surgery to remove the thyroid before cancer develops. There are three different kinds of inherited medullary thyroid cancer. Two of the three typically also involve problems with other endocrine glands.

## Anaplastic Thyroid Cancer

Anaplastic thyroid cancer has the worst prognosis of thyroid cancers. Luckily, it is one of the most rare forms. Affecting less than 2 percent of people diagnosed with thyroid cancer, this cancer emerges as a rapidly growing tumor that is the most likely of all the thyroid cancers to spread to distant sites throughout the body. It is a purely undifferentiated cancer, made up entirely of primitive cells, and unlike differentiated cancerous thyroid cells that behave like normal thyroid cells, these cells are focused solely on reproducing. Your doctor may be able to diagnose this kind of cancer with a FNA biopsy. Treatment for this cancer is far more complex than treatment for differentiated thyroid cancer, and the prognosis is generally not good. However, it is sometimes treated successfully.

It is hoped that a new class of drugs under investigation will improve the chances for success in treatment for those with anaplastic thyroid cancer. These drugs work against angiogenesis, a process by which cancer cells form blood vessels and connect to blood supplies for oxygen and nutrients as they fix to a tissue and form a tumor. Antiangiogenesis drugs attack and destroy these vessels by triggering a change that blocks the flow of blood to a tumor, depriving it of what it needs to survive. They have been shown to work against the growth of human thyroid cancer cells both in cell cultures and in animal models.

Early results from clinical trials with one agent in this class of drugs, called combretastatin (CA 4P), shows promise without causing low blood counts or hair loss, which are two common side effects of chemotherapy. Numerous Phase I and Phase II clinical trials are under way for this drug at different sites around the country. (In Phase I trials, researchers evaluate the safety of the drug, watch for side effects, and establish dosing. In addition to safety, Phase II trials are focused on how effective the drug is at treating a disease.) For more information on clinical trials, contact the National Cancer Institute (see the Additional Resources).

## Thyroid Lymphoma

Lymphoma is a cancer that originates in the white blood cells of a lymph node, which occurs with Hodgkin's disease and non-Hodgkin's lymphoma. On rare occasions, lymphoma originates in the thyroid gland, where white blood cells, called lymphocytes, are sometimes present. Most people who develop thyroid lymphoma have Hashimoto's thyroiditis, an autoimmune condition that attracts wayward lymphocytes that attack the thyroid. However, Hashimoto's thyroiditis is an extremely common condition and thyroid lymphoma is rare. So if you have the former, it is unlikely that you will develop the latter. Thyroid lymphoma doesn't involve thyroid cells, so it is treated differently than other thyroid cancers, typically with chemotherapy and external radiation. The outlook for this cancer varies, but it often is treated successfully, particularly if it is confined to the thyroid.

## Treating Thyroid Cancer

Most of the time, thyroid cancer is treated with surgical removal of all or most of the thyroid gland and any affected lymph nodes, followed by radioactive iodine therapy. Radioactive iodine, which is sometimes used to treat hyperthyroidism, is different from the external radiation that is typically used in most cancer treatments, although external radiation is sometimes used in more aggressive cases of thyroid cancer. Radioactive iodine therapy works internally and involves swallowing a capsule or fluid that contains enough of the substance to destroy any remaining thyroid cells the surgeon may have missed. Chemotherapy and external radiation are seldom used to treat thyroid cancer, unless the cancer is unusually aggressive and has spread to vital structures.

### Thyroid Surgery

Surgery is, without a doubt, the first and foremost—and sometimes only—treatment required for thyroid cancer. There has, however, been a lot of debate over how much of the thyroid should be removed in best-case scenarios—instances where the tumor is small and slow growing and the chances for recurrence are minimal.

The argument for lobectomy, or removal of only the side of the thyroid that contains the cancerous nodule, is that you are left with some healthy thyroid tissue, perhaps enough to avoid reliance on hormone replacement therapy. It also diminishes the risk that your surgeon will nick the parathyroid glands or laryngeal nerves on both sides of your neck, which is more problematic than when it happens on only one side of your neck. Most patients with the kind of "good" tumor that is at the heart of the debate have an encouraging prognosis with lobectomy as long as no residual cancer cells are left behind.

The argument for total thyroidectomy, even in cases where the cancerous nodule is contained, is that with no thyroid tissue left, the chances of recurrence are even smaller. Total resection of the thyroid gland offers more of a guarantee that no residual cancer cells are left behind. Even though survival rates from this kind of tumor are excellent, the recurrence rate for all but the smallest tumors is sufficiently high (about 15 percent or more over twenty years). Many experts advocate total removal of the thyroid to reduce the chance of recurrence.

Studies have shown that the risk of damaging surrounding structures is 2 percent or less when an experienced thyroid surgeon is at the helm. The risk increases when less-experienced surgeons are operating, which is why choosing a surgeon, discussed in Chapter 10, is important.

Many people, when faced with the prospect of cancer, have no problem with losing their entire thyroid gland. Some say they never even knew they had a thyroid before a nodule was discovered. After switching to thyroid hormone replacement, the gland they never knew most likely won't be missed. Lifetime dependence on thyroid hormone medication, with virtually no side effects when given the appropriate dose, is viewed by many as a small price to pay for the peace of mind that comes with being cured of cancer with certainty.

If your thyroid tumor is large or has spread to the lymph nodes or beyond or if you're considered at higher risk for recurrence due to your age, total or near-total thyroidectomy is almost always recommended. If your doctor decides on less than a near-total or complete thyroidectomy, it may be because the size and nature of your tumor makes removing the entire gland more complicated. It may be more efficient to let radioactive iodine therapy take care of what is left behind after surgery.

**Preparing for Surgery.** Prior to surgery, your job is to learn as much as you can about the procedure and what to expect so that you are comfortable with your decision to consent to it. You will meet with your surgeon, who will explain what is done during your operation and what it will accomplish. If you have questions about your treatment, this is a good time to get them answered. Do not leave this meeting until you fully understand why you need the operation, what the alternatives are, and how much of your thyroid will be removed and why, along with any risks you might face during surgery. You should also ask about how long your hospital stay will be and how you can expect to feel afterward. You may also want to ask about the scar left behind from the incision, which will be made at the base of your neck near your collarbone.

At some point before your surgery, you will be asked to sign an informed consent form, which is required in every state. By signing this form, you are acknowledging that you received an explanation of the procedure, understand its risks and benefits, and agree to the proposed care.

After you meet with your surgeon, you will be scheduled for a preoperative evaluation to make sure that your body is able to tolerate surgery and anesthesia. The evaluation should include a thorough medical history and physical examination. You will also have blood tests to assess your blood counts and your risk of infection. If you are over forty-five or have any history of heart problems or symptoms, including high blood pressure, your doctor will order an EKG and a chest X-ray before your surgery. Your doctor will also want to check your vocal cords if you have had any voice changes due to your condition. You will also have a blood test to determine whether you have a bleeding disorder.

Since your surgery will involve general anesthesia, you'll probably meet with your anesthesiologist—the doctor who will administer the anesthesia. This doctor will also examine you, ask you a series of questions related to your medical history, and answer any of your questions. General anesthesia uses drugs that both relieve pain and produce unconsciousness. It is commonly started by having you breath into a face mask or injecting a drug into a vein in your arm. Once you are asleep, an endotracheal (ET) tube is placed in your throat so that medicine can be continually administered. The tube also allows your doctor to monitor your breathing rate. A doctor or nurse who specializes in giving anesthesia watches you throughout the procedure and monitors your heart rate and blood pressure until you wake up.

You will be asked not to have anything to eat or drink after midnight the night before your surgery. It is important that your digestive tract be empty because vomiting under anesthesia can cause an infection in your lungs.

*After Surgery.* The operation usually takes anywhere between two to three hours. Afterward, you will be moved to a recovery room where you will be monitored until the effects of the anesthesia wear off, which may take several hours. When you wake up, everything will seem a bit hazy. This dreamlike state may last the whole day. Your throat may feel sore from the breathing tube, and you may notice a surgical tube, called a drain, coming from the incision in your neck. This tube drains excess fluid that collects at the site of the surgery. It will be removed the morning after your surgery.

Once you are awake, you will probably be moved to a hospital room from between one to three days. Once you are in your hospital room, there are usually no restrictions on eating and drinking, although you may not feel hungry.

## Radioactive Iodine Therapy

Radioactive iodine therapy is often used as an extra precaution. It helps ensure that no thyroid cells remain in your body. Even if your cancer has metastasized, radioactive iodine acts like a guided missile, searching out and destroying cancerous thyroid cells, no matter where they are, with little or no damage to the surrounding tissue. When used after surgery, this procedure is known as radioactive iodine remnant ablation (RRA).

It may also be used in cases where your surgeon decides to remove only the cancerous side of the thyroid because the size and nature of the tumor would complicate removing the entire thyroid. Radioactive iodine is used to destroy the remaining thyroid tissue. In 25 percent of cases, differentiated thyroid cancer does not pick up radioactive iodine. When this happens and there is residual disease or metastasis, radioactive iodine does not work and is of no benefit.

Radioactive iodine isn't used to treat medullary thyroid cancer because parafollicular cells that are involved in this form of cancer do not concentrate it. It also isn't used to treat anaplastic thyroid cancer or thyroid lymphoma because these cancers don't pick up radioactive iodine either.

The same type of radioactive isotope that is used to treat hyperthyroidism, I-131, is used to treat thyroid cancer. The difference lies in the dosing. For treatment of hyperthyroidism, a person may receive a dose of anywhere between 5–30 mCi. In many centers the standard dose for destroying thyroid tissue after surgery is between 75–150 mCi, depending on the amount of remaining thyroid tissue. (This does not apply to metastases.) In recent years, some hospitals in the United States have adopted lower-dose regimens of 25–29.9 mCi to treat thyroid cancer, particularly in cases where the amount of thyroid tissue remaining is small. Still, more difficult cases sometimes require more than 150 mCi. If your dose is on the higher end, you will probably need to stay at the hospital for 24 to 48 hours in complete isolation. However, newer guidelines from the Nuclear Regulatory Commission have led some states to permit the outpatient administration of higher doses that previously required hospitalization.

Radioactive iodine therapy does not cause any pain. Sometimes, if your dose is on the high end, you may feel some soreness in your neck. Your mouth might feel dry afterward or you might experience a metallic taste, because salivary glands are sometimes disrupted during the treatment. These glands may also become inflamed and tender. These symptoms usually go away in a few days. Mild nausea or vomiting may occur during the first few days after treatment. Some men may experience slightly lower sperm counts after treatment, but this returns to normal. Potential long-term impact of this treatment can include the possibility of permanent salivary gland damage and diminished saliva production. There is also a small risk of developing a malignancy, including leukemia.

Doctors will want to rule out pregnancy before treatment because radioactive iodine has been known to cause serious birth defects, even when used six months before conception. It can also lead to congenital hypothyroidism in babies (see Chapter 9). As a result, doctors recommend waiting a full year after treatment before trying to conceive. That way, you can safely undergo follow-up tests and any follow-up treatment that may be required.

***Special Preparations for Radioactive Iodine Therapy.*** Cancerous thyroid cells do not take up radioactive iodine as well as non-cancerous cells. However, TSH can stimulate thyroid cancer cells to take up significant amounts of iodine, so one way to encourage them to do so is to have high levels of TSH in your blood. That is why it will be necessary for you to discontinue your thyroid hormone medicine before being treated with radioactive iodine. You'll need to do this anywhere between two to six weeks before treatment. The time frame varies depending on whether you stop your medicine cold turkey or gradually reduce it.

Once your TSH level is high enough, a whole-body iodine scan is done. This is like a thyroid scan, which you may have already had. As with the thyroid scan, your doctor will administer a small dose of radioactive iodine, except this time pictures of the whole body are taken to detect any remaining thyroid cells, including those that may have migrated to areas outside of your neck. This also helps your doctor calculate how much radioactive iodine you'll need.

About seven days prior to receiving the radioactive iodine, you will need to go on a low-iodine diet, which will enhance the uptake of radioactive iodine even further because, without dietary iodine, any remaining thyroid cells in your body will be hungry for iodine when you receive the treatment. You may also be given a diuretic to help deplete your body of its natural stores of iodine or lithium in order to increase the amount of radioactive iodine that your body retains. Both increase the effect of the radioactive iodine.

When you stop your medicine—or if you never started it after your thyroid was removed—your pituitary gland will sense that you need thyroid hormone and will start producing high levels of TSH, stimulating the cancerous thyroid cells to take sufficient amounts of radioactive iodine.

Unfortunately for you, discontinuing or never starting your thyroid hormone medication after surgery makes you deficient in thyroid hormone and produces sudden, sometimes drastic, symptoms of hypothyroidism. Among other symptoms, you may feel fatigued, constipated, and puffy. You may also feel cold or experience muscle cramps or a pins-and-needles sensation in your hands. Some people feel depressed or have difficulty concentrating. This can be a very difficult period, but try to keep in mind that it will be short-lived and that once you begin or resume your thyroid hormone replacement two to five days after your radioactive iodine treatment, you will feel much better. To help offset these symptoms, your doctor may prescribe T3 (Cytomel) to take while you are hypothyroid. The T3 may help you feel better and will not significantly delay the rise in TSH levels.

*Low-Iodine Diet Guidelines.* Avoiding iodine isn't easy. Iodine is used in animal feed and in food processing. It's found in most salt and dairy products, grains and cereals, white bread, fish, processed meats, pudding mixes, jams, candies, frozen dinners, and some fast foods. But remember, you don't have to follow a no-iodine diet, just a low-iodine one. General guidelines that will help you steer clear of foods high in iodine are found in Table 8.2. You may also want to visit the Thyroid Cancer Survivors' Association website (thyca.org). ThyCa has an online cookbook containing low-iodine recipes that you can download for free. If you don't have access to a computer, you can find ThyCa's contact information in the Additional Resources at the back of this book.

**TABLE 8.2** Low-Iodine Diet Guidelines

| Food Group | Foods Allowed | Foods to Avoid |
|---|---|---|
| Dairy | Avoid all dairy foods | Cheese, evaporated milk, eggnog, ice cream, milk, pudding, sour cream, yogurt |
| Fish | Avoid all fish | Canned tuna, fish, kelp, shellfish, sardines, seaweed |
| Fruits | All fresh fruit and fresh fruit juices (not canned) | Canned fruits, canned fruit juices, powered juice drinks |
| Grain/starches | Fresh potatoes, homemade rice | Breads (except at breakfast), cereal, packaged rice, pasta, pastry |
| Meat (protein) | Small portions of fresh chicken, turkey, beef, or pork | Lunch meats, bacon, sausage, hot dogs |
| Vegetables | All fresh vegetables except spinach | Canned or frozen vegetables with sauce, pickles, sauerkraut, olives |
| Snack foods | Popcorn popped with vegetable oils and noniodized salt | Pretzels, corn chips, crackers |
| Miscellaneous | Butter, garlic powder, honey, onion powder, vegetable oils, vinegar | Candy, canned soups, cocoa mix, granola bars, power bars, powdered instant breakfast meals |

Since a low-iodine diet also is very low in calcium, doctors recommend taking supplements that contain 1,000–1,200 mg of pure calcium. However, calcium supplements aren't always practical because they can be constipating. Therefore, some physicians don't recommend taking them while you are becoming hypothyroid. But if you also have *hypoparathyroidism*, a condition that can occur if your parathyroid glands were damaged in surgery, you will be required to take supplements so that your serum calcium levels remain in the proper range.

You can usually resume a normal diet two days after treatment.

***Your Hospital Stay.*** With so much going on—surgery, followed by what for some is an intense period of hypothyroidism that leaves you feeling lousy—the last thing you think about preparing for is being separated from your support system. But if your radioactive iodine dose requires hospitalization, you will be in an isolated room anywhere from twenty-four to forty-eight hours. That means no visitors. You will be physically separated from everyone, including the medical staff, who will have limited contact with you but can communicate with you through intercom or phone. This lasts while the radioactive iodine that isn't stored in your thyroid is eliminated through your urine, stool, and, to a lesser extent, through your saliva and sweat. The idea behind your isolation is to miminize unnecessary radiation exposure to others that cumulatively, over a lifetime, adds to their cancer risk. Even though exposure to small amounts carries little risk in the short run, it is of no benefit to anyone and should be avoided. Risks of radiation exposure are even greater for children or fetuses, thus pregnant women and children must avoid contact with you until the radioactive iodine has cleared your system.

The best way to prepare for your hospital stay is to bring items with you—books, magazines, crossword puzzles, and the like— that will help you pass the time. Keep in mind that you may have to dispose items that you bring with you. So while you may want to leave your knitting at home, don't let that stop you from bringing in a good book. One patient interviewed said she didn't bring her book in because she didn't want to throw it out if she didn't finish it, but she soon realized, as the time dragged, that having her book would have been worth buying another copy. The same patient was very pleased when her husband asked close friends and family members to call her. She didn't anticipate wanting to talk to anyone, but after a few hours of being isolated, she felt the need to stay connected.

Another patient brought in her own small refrigerator, and her friends prepared home-cooked, low-iodine meals, which gave her something to look forward to. She also brought in audio books to help her relax.

**Going Home.** Once you are home, there may still be some radioactivity from the treatment remaining in your body. The following precautions are recommended.

For the first two days (especially if you are not hospitalized and go directly home after treatment):

- Minimize the time you spend close to people. Try to maintain a distance greater than three or more feet from others.
- Drink plenty of fluids.
- Avoid preparing food for others.
- Avoid sharing cigarettes or toothbrushes or kissing anyone.
- Avoid pregnant women and young children (continue with this precaution for a week).

## Thyroid Hormone Pills with a Dual Purpose

If you've had your thyroid removed or ablated through radioactive iodine therapy, you will need to take thyroid hormone pills (levothyroxine sodium) for the rest of your life. This not only replaces the hormone that your thyroid normally produces, but it also acts as a suppressive therapy for most types of thyroid cancer. As a form of cancer treatment, your thyroid hormone pills serve to suppress your TSH levels to abnormally low ranges, a form of therapy known as "TSH suppression." TSH is known to encourage growth of follicular-based cancer cells, so if you were treated for thyroid cancer of follicular-cell origin, your doctor will prescribe higher doses of levothyroxine sodium than he or she would for a patient who was hypothyroid for reasons unrelated to thyroid cancer treatment. There is debate among clinicians over how low TSH levels should be in thyroid cancer patients, because the combination of abnormally high T4 levels and abnormally low TSH levels can leave you hyperthyroid. As discussed in Chapter 3, hyperthyroidism can have long-term adverse affects on your bones and heart, leading to osteoporosis and atrial fibrillation.

A normal TSH level is within the range of .45 and 4.5 mU/L. It was once thought that in all cancer patients, complete TSH suppression to practically undetectable levels of less than .01 to 0.1 mU/L provided the best chance that cancer wouldn't recur. However, prospective studies have not established that there is any extra benefit for the majority of cancer patients who are at a lower risk for recurrence.

The American Association of Clinical Endocrinologists, in its thyroid cancer treatment guidelines published in 2001, states that the goal for most thyroid cancer patients should be a TSH level in the range of 0.1 to 0.4 mU/L. Long-term complete TSH suppression in the ranges less than .01 to 0.1 mU/L should be reserved for those with persistent cancer or those at a high risk for recurrence and death.

When you start taking your thyroid hormone pills will depend on your treatment schedule. You might begin right after you've had surgery, but if radioactive iodine therapy is scheduled soon after your surgery, you'll need to keep your TSH levels up, so your doctor will hold off until after that therapy.

## Beating Thyroid Cancer

Two years after successfully overcoming a rare tumor of the pituitary gland, forty-nine-year-old Terry learned that he faced another battle, this time with papillary thyroid cancer. This is his story.

After my first experience with a tumor, I found myself starting to respect my annual checkup. During one visit, my doctor felt lumps in my neck. I told him that I have always had swollen glands, but he told me that it felt like my thyroid. I was leaving for vacation in Florida in a couple of days, but he insisted, because of my history, that I have an ultrasound and a biopsy before I leave.

The doctor doing the fine needle biopsy told me that he doubted it was cancer. He said something like, "Besides you're a guy and you're only forty-nine." So the next day I went to Florida. I didn't hear anything at first and assumed that no news is good news. But then, as I'm sitting on my exercise bike, the phone rings and the doctor left a message saying, "I got your results back, call back immediately." So I go upstairs and I call him. This is a moment that haunts me until this day. It was around four in the afternoon. My kids were at the pool and I was about to join them. On the phone, my doctor tells me it's thyroid cancer—papillary stage 1—a particularly slow-growing kind of cancer. But I didn't hear any of that. All I heard was the word *cancer* and that's a dreaded disease no matter what cancer it is. All I could think of was, "What have I done to deserve this? Why is my body going to war with itself?"

I flew home immediately and consulted with a group of specialists I had come to know because of my previous bout with a tumor. I wanted to know how it could be that I had a pituitary adenoma and now thyroid cancer. No one in the entire circle of doctors had ever heard of both kinds of tumors occurring in one person. It was just a random coincidence. I was told that it could be much worse—I could have liver cancer.

Once I was able to swallow all of this, I had to consider my options. I did some homework. That's where the Internet came in handy. I got the basic information and then I interviewed surgeons and research guys. I learned everything about my three options. I could either do nothing for a while, have half the gland taken out and wait to see what happens, or have the entire gland removed followed by ablation with radioactive iodine.

I initially decided on the second option. The odds for recurrence seemed small. And I was concerned about potentially harming my vocal cords since I do a bit of TV commentary. Not to mention that I'd like to hold on to my organs and glands as long as possible. But everyone I talked to thought that was a bad choice. The attitude was that you don't mess around with cancer. What I was hearing was get the whole gland and get an aggressive dose of radioactive iodine to be sure every thyroid cell is gone. The surgeons I talked to who had once advised patients to go with partial thyroidectomy told me they were seeing people they treated ten years ago coming back with cancer that spread into the neck. I was told, "You don't want to come back in ten years." So I decided to heed the advice.

When the day of surgery came along, I told myself that there was nothing I can do at this point but just hope for the best. The last thing I remember is the anesthesiologist talking to me before I succumbed to the anesthesia. It turned out that the surgery was smooth with no unexpected turns or complications.

What I did not expect is that the hardest part of my treatment plan was the two weeks spent preparing for radioactive iodine therapy. Nobody tells you this, but the preparation makes you insane. Let's just say that after having little or none of your thyroid gland and no thyroid medication for a week, you really respect what the gland does for you. You just feel awful while at the same time, you're just in a nasty mood the whole time.

Then I had to be isolated for a couple of days for the actual treatment. All I could think of is how I just wanted to deal with something I used to think was a problem like getting my car repaired. This whole experience just puts your life in perspective.

The treatment worked. A complete body scan showed that the radiation whacked what was left of my thyroid and I am cancer free. That was two months ago. My thyroid hormone medication is still being adjusted, and actually, I feel good. I stopped smoking and I'm eating better than I ever did. I now realize that people walk around every day taking their health for granted and that's a huge error. The problem is, you don't know that until something like this happens. I'm also grateful for great doctors. People dump on the American health-care system all the time, but it has occurred to me that there is nothing like it in the world.

## Follow-Up

With all of these disruptions in hormone levels, it may take months before you feel right again. Everyone has his or her own timetable for healing and adjusting, so if months have gone by and you can't bring yourself to return to the gym, do not fret. Your body has been through a lot. You may feel exhausted or just plain out-of-sorts for weeks or months. Everyone is different.

In the aftermath of your treatment, periodic follow-up exams are crucial, in the short term and over the long haul, because thyroid cancer can recur, sometimes decades later.

Periodic follow-up exams can include physical examinations, blood tests, and various imaging procedures, such as chest X-rays, radioactive iodine scans, ultrasound, computerized tomography (CT)—also known as computerized axial tomography (CAT)—or magnetic resonance imaging (MRI). These studies may be used to determine if there is any cancer in your neck or anywhere else in your body. Less often, in the minority of aggressive cancers that have not been cured, positive emission tomography (PET) scans may be done, usually if a thyroglobulin blood test result is high but no disease is detected on a whole-body iodine scan.

## Blood Tests

A blood test will measure your TSH to be sure that it is in the right range, which in most cases would be below normal. Your free T4 will be measured or estimated to make sure that you are not receiving excessive amounts of thyroid hormone.

Unless you had only part of your thyroid removed, a blood test will also measure a protein called thyroglobulin (also known as Tg). Tg is produced by both normal thyroid cells and most types of cancerous thyroid cells. So if you have no thyroid cells, you should have no detectable amount of Tg in your blood. Therefore, doctors can use Tg as a tumor marker if your thyroid has been completely removed and ablated. Normal cells won't grow back, but cancerous cells can. If you have a Tg test following your treatments, a positive result may only indicate that some normal thyroid cells remain. Your doctor then may want to give you another dose of radioactive iodine to rid you of the normal cells, just so that this test can be used to detect a cancerous growth.

A Tg test isn't reliable for everyone. About 15 to 20 percent of thyroid cancer patients have antibodies to Tg, called TgAb, which interfere with Tg measurement. Your doctor can test to see if TgAb antibodies are present in your bloodstream.

If you had medullary thyroid cancer, you will have periodic blood tests to check for calcitonin, the substance produced by cancerous C cells.

## Scans

Anywhere from six months to a year after your treatment, your doctor may want to perform another whole-body iodine scan to be sure that all thyroid remnants were destroyed and that there is no uptake of radioactive iodine in or outside the thyroid bed. This means you may again have to stop your thyroid medication anywhere from two to six weeks beforehand, in preparation for the scan, so that your TSH levels go up and promote uptake in any thyroid cells that still exist. Again, you may experience the effects of hypothyroidism. For some, this is a nuisance; for others, it can lead to severe symptoms; and for people with heart disease, the rapid fluctuation in thyroid hormone can be dangerous.

## Recombinant Human Thyrotropin (rhTSH)

A relatively new drug that became available in 1998 offers a way around becoming hypothyroid before your scan. This drug, rhTSH, is a synthetic version of human TSH. It works by replacing your otherwise naturally produced TSH while you continue to take your thyroid hormone pills. The drug, which is sold under the brand name Thyrogen, is injected in the doctor's office or hospital for two days preceding your iodine scan.

So far, most studies on this new drug have shown that scans following Thyrogen injections are as efficient in picking up recurring thyroid cancer as scans that follow withdrawal from thyroid hormone in the majority of cases. But sometimes, the old way works better.

One study, published in the *New England Journal of Medicine* in 1997, concluded that synthetic TSH effectively stimulates uptake of radioactive iodine for scanning in patients with thyroid cancer, but that scanning after Thyrogen is not as sensitive as scanning done after the withdrawal of thyroid hormone. Another study, published in the *Journal of Clinical Endocrinology & Metabolism* in 1999, had similar results. However, the latter study also found that accurate detection of any remnant thyroid tissue improved significantly when researchers combined results of both Tg blood tests and a body scan after Thyrogen is given. Both studies found that patients receiving synthetic TSH experienced no hypothyroid symptoms, but the drug can have some side effects, including headaches, vomiting, dizziness, chills, and fever.

If you need to have a scan, talk to your doctor about whether Thyrogen is appropriate for you. It seems to be a good alternative if you have heart problems or if you suffer debilitating hypothyroid symptoms. If you are considered at higher risk for recurrence and can withstand the symptoms that come with withdrawal from thyroid hormone, you should probably stick to the traditional method of testing. If further treatment with radiaoctive iodine is intended, the withdrawal method is recommended.

However, researchers are looking at whether Thyrogen can be used prior to radioactive iodine therapy without diminishing the effectiveness of the treatment. Preliminary studies are promising. One that followed up on two groups of patients with similar types of thyroid cancer seemed to show that Thyrogen was a slightly better preparation method for treatment with radioactive iodine than the withdrawal method. In 84 percent of patients in a group that prepared for treatment with Thyrogen injections, radioactive iodine uptake could no longer be demonstrated, signifying the elimination of either normal thyroid tissue or cancerous tissue that was capable of concentrating radioactive iodine. Among the group that prepared for treatment by withdrawing from thyroid hormone, 81 percent of the patients showed complete disappearance of radioactive iodine uptake. More research needs to be completed on Thyrogen before it is recommended before treatment.

## Coping with Cancer

In its most common forms, thyroid cancer is typically easier to treat and cure than many other types of cancer. While this comes as reassuring news to most, it does not diminish the wide range of emotions you may experience. Cancer, with its distressing stigma, can stir up fear, anxiety, anger, sadness, and depression, even when the odds are in your favor. The following tips can help you manage these feelings.

- **Find a positive support system.** No one should have to cope with cancer alone. Some people find they need just one person to share their feelings with, someone who will acknowledge their fears yet help them stay focused on the positive. Others find that support groups are very helpful because they offer personal insights from people who have gone through treatments you may face. Support groups provide a forum for you to express yourself to people who understand best. An excellent resource for support groups is the Thyroid Cancer Survivors' Association (ThyCa) (see the Additional Resources). This organization maintains local support groups in every state, e-mail support groups, and a network of cancer survivor volunteers who are available to share their experiences and coping strategies.
- **Become informed.** If you are like many people, you may find that you are better off emotionally when you are an active participant in your treatment decisions. One way to become informed is to read this book, but you can also obtain information from the sources outlined in the

Additional Resources. These resources provide a good foundation, but you should always talk to your doctor about any concerns you have.

- **Choose a good surgeon.** Knowing you are in good hands provides peace of mind. Follow the tips on choosing a surgeon outlined in Chapter 10.

- **Try relaxation.** One way to take the edge off of your anxious feelings is to incorporate relaxation time into your day. This can involve meditation, yoga, exercise, or participating in activities you enjoy.

## Staying Positive and Informed

Carmen, age thirty-eight, a hospital administrator, was diagnosed and treated for thyroid cancer in 1995. Now happy and pregnant with her second child, she recalls the loneliness that comes with having cancer and the value of staying positive.

I was sitting in a meeting and just kind of feeling my neck when I discovered the lump. I saw my doctor, and he told me that I needed to have a thyroid scan done. During the scan, the technician seemed concerned. He sent for the radiologist, who came in and looked at the scan and then said to me, "Well, if you're going to have cancer, this is the best one to have." This was the first time I heard the word *cancer*, and I was just kind of stunned. Up until that point, I hadn't really considered cancer a possibility. When you hear the word *cancer*, you think of death. It didn't matter what kind of cancer it was. Now looking back, I know he was right, but back then, it was hard not to focus on what having cancer could mean.

I was then referred to a surgeon who did a fine needle biopsy. At the time, the surgeon kind of waved off what the radiologist said and told me not to worry about it. He said I was young and the chances were very small that the nodule would be cancerous. But the results of the biopsy confirmed what the radiologist suspected. When delivering the bad news, the surgeon tried to reassure me by telling me that there is a 95 percent chance for recovery and cure. Still, I was afraid and confused. Everyone seemed to be downplaying my diagnosis, and yet I had cancer.

Telling my husband and my parents was incredibly difficult. I knew I had to be strong for everyone else, so I continued to downplay my disease and kept my worst fears to myself. In the end, all of this downplaying that I did to reassure everyone else left me feeling completely alone.

I didn't go out and buy books or learn all I could about the illness. I was outwardly treating it like it was no big deal, in a sense so no one in my family would worry. As a result, I didn't know as much as I should have and didn't feel in control of the situation. I felt as though I was blindly following directions.

Since I work in health care, I instinctively know the value of choosing a good surgeon and endocrinologist, and that's what I focused on, and, lucky for me, that turned out to be time well spent. In the end, I had no complications from treatment and I have remained cancer free. So throughout my ordeal, I did know I was in good hands. I just wish I had been more prepared for surgery and for my seclusion following radioactive iodine therapy.

When I woke up from surgery, I was vomiting due to the anesthesia and felt very sick throughout my recovery. The seclusion compounded my loneliness. To this day, if I pass by the hospital where I was treated, all kinds of bad feelings creep up.

On the flip side, my husband's determination to keep me positive really prevented me from wallowing in my loneliness both before and after my treatment. He convinced me that we had to continue living as we always had as best we could. That meant continuing with planned trips and doing the things that we normally do. For me, this was critical. If I had to give one single piece of advice to someone going through this, it would be to surround yourself with positive, supportive people. Do not allow yourself to be around people who pity you or have a negative attitude. In my opinion, your fate is in the hands of modern medicine and God, and being focused on the worst that can happen is not going to help at all. It's very easy to slip into this kind of thinking if you are not with people who are helping you stay focused.

I was very fortunate to be around people who kept my spirits up. I do wish I had not downplayed the disease so much that I didn't feel comfortable sharing my fears. You can still be positive in the end. The people who love and support you will also be good listeners.

# CHAPTER 9

# Childhood
# Thyroid Diseases

Thyroid problems are much less common in children than adults, but when they strike, they can be more worrisome because of their potential effect on children's growth and developing brains.

In adults, treatment usually reverses the effects of thyroid diseases, even when they go undetected for years. Yet in early childhood, hypothyroidism can lead to permanent mental deficiencies and short stature if it is not treated promptly. Hyperthyroidism can lead to accelerated growth in children, and when it affects infants, it can be fatal.

Thanks to screening programs that test all newborns for hypothyroidism, the immutable effects of that disease are prevented in numerous children. Each year, in North America alone, more than five million newborns are screened annually, and hypothyroidism is detected and treated in fourteen hundred of these infants.

A child may be born with a thyroid condition or may develop one sometime during childhood. Diagnosing thyroid diseases that aren't detected through screening programs can be especially tricky, since it is up to the parent to recognize when something is wrong. This certainly isn't easy when you are dealing with young children who aren't talking yet or with older children who may not be able to describe what they feel—or even know that what they are feeling isn't normal.

If you or someone in your family has a thyroid condition, your child may be at a higher risk for developing a thyroid disorder. This chapter outlines the most common types of thyroid diseases that occur in children. It is meant to help parents recognize symptoms of these diseases and to offer guidance on the latest treatment options. Although this chapter is written for mothers and fathers, in some cases you'll notice that "you" addresses mothers when referring to pregnancy.

## Hypothyroidism in Children

Childhood thyroid diseases are sometimes referred to as *congenital* or *acquired*. A congenital condition is a condition that is present at birth. It may be inherited, occur in the womb, and be noted during delivery. An acquired condition is one that was not present at birth. It too can be inherited but not develop until sometime after birth.

### Congenital Hypothyroidism

Nowadays, in the United States and in many other countries, nearly every baby born in a hospital has a special blood test for a number of rare genetic, metabolic, or hormone-related conditions that, if left untreated, can cause mental or physical impairment or even death. In the United States, conditions that your baby is tested for vary depending on what state you live in. Yet in all fifty states, all newborns are tested for congenital hypothyroidism (CH), a leading cause of preventable mental retardation. Babies with hypothyroidism are deficient in thyroid hormone, which is critical to the development of their central nervous system during early childhood. If CH is left untreated, it can lead to significant mental retardation and stunted growth.

Newborn screening for CH has single-handedly changed the poor outlook for children born with this disease. Before this testing was instituted in the mid-1970s, it was virtually impossible to detect hypothyroidism in newborns because most appear completely normal for the first six to twelve weeks of life. This is probably because placental transfer of maternal thyroid hormone protects the fetus. Now, infants who are born with hypothyroidism worldwide—accounting for 1 of each 4,000 births—are immediately placed on levothyroxine sodium and can look forward to a normal healthy life with little or no ill effects of the disease. CH is twice as common in girls than boys, is least common in African-Americans (1 of 20,000 births), and is most common in Hispanics and Native Americans (1 of 2,000 births).

**Causes.** CH often results from the abnormal development of a baby's thyroid gland during fetal growth. Some babies are born with no thyroid tissue whatsoever, known as *thyroid aplasia*; others may be born with some tissue, called *thyroid hypoplasia*; while others have all of their thyroid gland outside its normal position in the neck, known as an *ectopic thyroid*. Sometimes the thyroid tissue is located close to the tongue, called a *lingual thyroid*; in these cases, the thyroid may provide adequate amounts of thyroid hormone for many years or may fail during early childhood. A child affected with a lingual thyroid sometimes comes to clinical attention because of a growing mass at the base of the tongue or, in the case of other causes of ectopic thyroid, in the midline of the neck, in which case, surgical removal may be required and the child would then have to take thyroid hormone replacement. In some babies, the thyroid appears normal or slightly enlarged, and the defect lies in any of the mechanisms that synthesize thyroid hormone, a condition known as *dyshormonogenesis*.

These kinds of developmental defects sometimes run in families, but often they don't. One thing is for certain: there is no correlation between parental lifestyle during pregnancy and CH if you live in the United States or in other countries where severe iodine deficiency is not a problem.

In developing countries where maternal iodine deficiency is prevalent, CH is most often due to severe maternal hypothyroidism. The most severe form of this kind of hypothyroidism

187

caused by iodine deficiency is cretinism, where severe neurological damage begins in the womb and leads to severe mental retardation, short stature, deaf mutism, and spasticity. Unfortunately for these children, much of the irreversible damage is done before they are born. In areas where salt is iodized and iodine deficiency is rare, cretinism is unheard of. Babies born with CH who have mothers with healthy thyroids are protected during fetal development by maternal thyroid hormone, so these babies do fine so long as the condition is caught promptly.

Some forms of CH are short-lived and resolve on their own, but your baby may still need to be treated. This can occur when a fetus is exposed to antithyroid drugs or iodides. If you took antithyroid drugs for hyperthyroidism while you were pregnant, be sure that your baby's doctor knows so that your baby's thyroid hormone levels can be properly interpreted when they are checked. Doctors typically prescribe a minimal dosage of antithyroid drugs in pregnant women to help safeguard against the development of hypothyroidism in their babies. Sometimes topical antiseptics containing iodides used in nurseries can lead to temporary hypothyroidism, especially in low birth weight infants.

Temporary CH can also result when maternal antithyroid antibodies cross the placenta and inhibit TSH binding to its receptor in the newborn. However, this form of hypothyroidism in newborns is rare.

**What Happens During Newborn Screening?** Newborn screening involves a simple procedure. Sometime after you deliver your baby, hospital personnel will take a blood sample by pricking your baby's heel. This single blood sample is used to determine whether your baby has any number of genetic, metabolic, or hormonal disorders that your state tests for, including CH. The blood sample will then be sent to a laboratory for analysis.

To determine if CH is present, most programs in North America use a blood test that measures total T4, followed by a TSH test only when the T4 result is below normal. Japan, Europe, and a few states in the United States use a TSH test as a primary screening tool and follow up with a T4 test if the first result is abnormal. Both methods have advantages and drawbacks. (See "Advantages and Drawbacks of Two Screening Methods" later in this chapter.) The T4-only method misses conditions character-ized by an abnormal TSH and a normal T4. The TSH-only method misses conditions characterized by normal TSH and abnormal T4 readings. As a result, both tests miss anywhere from 5 to 10 percent of newborns with CH.

No matter which method is used, if there is an abnormal result, you probably won't know about it until after you are dis-charged. Your baby's doctor will notify you and will ask you to come to the doctor's office to have the test repeated to be sure the test result was not a false positive. If the second result is abnormal, your baby will be referred to a pediatric endocrinologist, and treatment will begin immediately.

**Recognizing Signs and Symptoms.** Even though every newborn is tested for hypothyroidism, testing methods aren't perfect and laboratory errors are possible, which means that some babies with hypothyroidism are missed. So it is important to be aware of the signs and symptoms in babies for whom prompt treatment is most important.

Hints of CH usually begin to emerge somewhere between six and twelve weeks after birth, but it can be delayed for months. This usually depends on how severe the condition is. A more severe condition is generally noticeable earlier than a more mild condition, and if serious enough, it can sometimes be recognized as early as the first few weeks. Adding to the difficulty in recog-nizing this disease, the symptoms emerge gradually. But by three to six months, symptoms are usually obvious (see Figure 9.1).

As a general rule, trust your parental instincts. If something seems wrong with your baby or appears abnormal, even if it might seem trivial, always call to let your baby's doctor know. Any of the following common signs and symptoms in infants certainly war-

FIGURE 9.1 Six-Month-Old Hypothyroid Girl Versus
Normal-Appearing Six-Month-Old

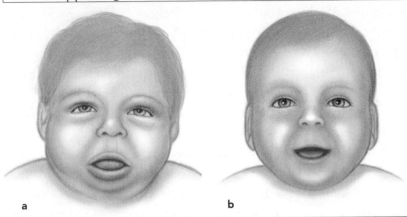

a                                        b

*By the time an infant with hypothyroidism is six months of age (a), she may have a
puffy face, a dull expression, no social smile, a short neck, and very little head control.
Her enlarged tongue may fill her mouth so that she cannot close her lips. Her hair
may be thin and coarse, yet her hairline may be low on her forehead. By contrast, a
healthy infant (b) has a well-developed social smile, can hold her head upright, and
appears alert.*

rant a visit to the doctor's office. Although they are grouped by
the typical age of onset, you may notice these symptoms in your
infant at any age.

### Signs and Symptoms Tending to Occur in the First Few Weeks

- **Feeding difficulties.** This can include poor appetite,
  sluggishness, and choking spells during nursing due to
  difficulty swallowing.
- **Jaundice.** This is a yellowing of the skin and whites of the
  eyes that is quite common in newborns. It is caused by a
  buildup of bilirubin, a by-product of the body's normal
  breakdown of red blood cells. Prolonged jaundice of more
  than three days may be a sign of hypothyroidism.
- **Enlarged thyroid gland.** Some babies are born with a
  goiter, which in the case of hypothyroidism is usually the
  result of maternal antithyroid drugs or iodides taken during

pregnancy. It can also indicate dyshormonogenesis, an inborn error in how thyroid hormone is synthesized.

- **Wide soft spots.** Your baby's soft spots on his or her head, called fontanels, may be wider than normal. Doctors check these during physical examinations.

### Signs and Symptoms Tending to Occur During the First Month

- **Breathing difficulties.** These include episodes of apnea, or cessation in breathing; noisy breathing; and in some cases, rapid shallow breathing. Sometimes, breathing problems are due to an enlarged tongue.
- **Slow pulse.** Your baby's doctor will monitor your baby's pulse during regular checkups. If your baby's pulse is slower than normal, the doctor will want to see if any other symptoms are present. A normal newborn's heart rate can range anywhere from 70 to 190 beats per minute.
- **Enlarged tongue.** You may notice a thick tongue that may appear slightly enlarged or so large it fills your baby's mouth so that your baby can't entirely close his or her lips.
- **Failure to gain weight.** Your baby may not be gaining as much weight as he or she should.
- **Decreased stool frequency.** Your baby may not yet be constipated but could have bowel movements less frequently than normal.
- **Lethargic behavior.** Your baby may seem to sleep constantly, may be generally sluggish, and may cry very little.
- **Skin changes.** Your baby may develop scaly, mottled skin that may be grayish in appearance.

### Signs and Symptoms Emerging Anytime During the First Three Months and Beyond (May Occur with Symptoms Previously Mentioned)

- **Dull and puffy facial appearance.** Your baby may appear to have a droopy, drowsy, or dull-looking appearance; a puffy face; and swollen eyelids. The bridge of your baby's nose may look depressed.

# Advantages and Drawbacks of Two Screening Methods

Most hospitals in North America use a total T4 blood test to screen newborns for CT, while some states and other countries use a TSH test as the primary screening tool. The following are the pros and cons of each screening method.

Hospitals that use a total T4 test identify newborns with the following conditions.

- **Primary hypothyroidism.** This indicates an underactive thyroid. Test results show a low total T4 result, followed by a high TSH result.
- **Secondary hypothyroidism.** Secondary hypothyroidism indicates a pituitary or hypothalamic problem. Test results show a low total T4 result, followed by a normal TSH test. This condition is rare, however, and occurs in only 1 out of 50,000 children.
- **Thyroxine-binding globulin (TBG) deficiency.** This is a deficiency of a protein that binds most of the thyroid hormone circulating in the blood. TBG deficiency accounts for a low total T4. However, the serum TSH is normal because the amount of free T4 is normal. The combination of a low total T4 and a normal TSH prompts a TBG measurement. When it is low, it is not always reported because it does not have any direct clinical impact. Still, many programs do report this result to a newborn's doctor because the information may be useful if hypothyroidism is suspected in the future.

On the other hand, programs that use T4 as a primary screening tool may miss children with the following conditions.

- **Mild hypothyroidism.** In this case, test results show a normal T4, but TSH is elevated. These children are at risk for developing overt hypothyroidism in the future.
- **Ectopic thyroid.** The baby's thyroid gland is located outside its normal position. This is a type of mild hypothyroidism sometimes seen with a normal total T4 and an elevated TSH. Your baby would have to have a thyroid scan for this result to be confirmed.

Programs that use TSH as a primary screening tool can flag cases of the following conditions.

- **Primary hypothyroidism.** Test results show an elevated TSH followed up by a low T4.
- **Mild disease.** Tests show an elevated TSH and a normal T4.

However, this test will miss the following conditions.

- **Secondary hypothyroidism.** Tests show a normal TSH test result but a low T4. Secondary hypothyroidism is rare.
- **TBG deficiency.** Tests show a normal TSH, but a low total T4.

Another disadvantage of the TSH method is a potential for excessive false positive results. A normal newborn's TSH level is often elevated during the first days of life, which is when the test is administered.

- **Hoarse cry.** Some babies develop a gruff-sounding cry, which may be due to swelling of the vocal cords.
- **Wide-set eyes.** In addition to a dull appearance, your baby's eyes may seem widely spaced apart.
- **Slow growth.** In addition to gaining weight poorly, your baby may not be growing enough lengthwise as well. Slow growth may be difficult to notice, but your baby's doctor will monitor his or her growth during regular checkups, plotting length and weight measurements on a growth chart. This is one of the reasons why these early visits to the doctor are so important. Poor growth alone should raise a red flag and prompt your baby's doctor to order blood tests, including thyroid function tests.
- **Constipation.** You may notice that your baby has abnormally infrequent bowel movements, hard and dry stools, or difficulty passing stools.
- **Enlarged abdomen.** Even though your baby is growing poorly, you may notice a distended abdomen.
- **Umbilical hernia.** This appears as a soft lump or bulge in your baby's naval area.

*Diagnosis and Treatment.* If your baby is showing any signs or symptoms of hypothyroidism, if you took antithyroid drugs during pregnancy, or, in some cases, if you have a family history of the disease, your doctor will want to do a complete series of blood tests measuring T4, TSH, and sometimes thyroid antibodies.

If blood work shows that your baby is hypothyroid, treatment will be prescribed immediately. The doctor may also want to do an X-ray to see if there is any delay in bone growth. To determine what's causing the hypothyroidism, a radioactive iodine uptake test and/or thyroid scan and possibly an ultrasound may be done. These tests will show how well your baby's thyroid is taking up iodine, whether your baby has a partially developed thyroid or no thyroid, or whether the thyroid is in an abnormal location. For the scan, the baby is given a small dosage of radioactive iodine

## Fast Fact: Giving Thyroid Hormone Medication to Children

Liquid suspension forms of levothyroxine sodium are not available, so, for a baby or young child, you'll need to crush the thyroid hormone pill and mix it with a couple of teaspoons of water and feed it to your child in a bottle, dropper, or teaspoon according to the package instructions. Once it is dissolved, it cannot be stored because it quickly loses potency. Be sure not to mix it with soybean-based formula, which could interfere with its absorption.

(I-123) orally or an injection of another radioactive substance called technetium.

If your baby has permanent hypothyroidism, he or she should be immediately started on an aggressive dose of thyroid hormone replacement. New recommendations call for a dosage high enough to put your child's T4 test result in the upper half of the normal range for the first three years of life. This is the best assurance for optimal development. The average starting dose is 10–15 mcg/kg of weight. The dose will need to be continually adjusted as your baby grows.

There is clear evidence that infants with low T4 levels during the first year of life have lower IQ values than those whose T4 levels were held constant at higher concentrations. Children kept within a high normal range who are routinely monitored so that they stay within this range grow normally and do not have compromised IQs. A number of studies coming out of Canada in the early years of newborn screening suggested that even babies with CH who were caught through screening and treated right away faced some slowed bone growth and lower IQs than children without CH. Nowadays, it is understood that these problems resulted because the dosages were not high enough to maintain steady upper normal levels of thyroid hormone in the bloodstream.

Some babies are born with *congenital goiter*, which results from antithyroid drugs or drugs containing high levels of iodine that you may have taken during pregnancy. This kind of goiter is rarely permanent and it can be treated with thyroid hormone, which will help shrink it and manage any symptoms of hypothyroidism. Medicine can usually be discontinued once the condition is resolved. In the occasional instance that the goiter is large enough to cause respiratory obstruction, your baby may need surgery to remove part of the thyroid gland.

**Follow-Up.** Routine visits to the doctor that involve thyroid function blood tests are crucial for children with hypothyroidism. Your child's dose of thyroid medication will be continually adjusted as your child grows to ensure his or her optimal growth. The American Academy of Pediatrics recommends blood tests that measure T4 and TSH at the following intervals:

- two and four weeks after treatment begins
- every one to two months during the first year of life
- every two to three months between one and three years of age
- every three to twelve months thereafter until growth is completed
- at more frequent intervals when abnormal values are obtained or compliance is questioned

## Acquired Hypothyroidism

Some children are born with normal thyroid glands but develop hypothyroidism as they get older. As with hypothyroidism that affects most adults, the most common cause for acquired hypothyroidism in children is Hashimoto's thyroiditis (see Chapter 5). Disorders of the pituitary gland or treatment for hyperthyroidism or thyroid cancer may also be to blame. Hashimoto's thyroiditis most often develops among children from eleven to fourteen years of age, but it can occur as early as the first year of life. When the disease occurs later in childhood, the long-term problems seen with CH, such as mental retardation or stunted growth, do not occur. If the problem goes untreated, however, growth may be slowed and puberty may be delayed.

**Signs and Symptoms.** The signs and symptoms of acquired hypothyroidism are similar to those that adults experience (see Chapter 2). In addition, your child may exhibit an inability to concentrate, cold intolerance, or delayed puberty. Some children have headaches, vision problems, precocious puberty, or a spontaneous flow of milk from the nipple, called galactorrhea. These latter symptoms may also indicate a problem with the pituitary gland.

**Diagnosis and Treatment.** In addition to a physical exam, the same tests used to identify hypothyroidism in adults and infants may be used to diagnose hypothyroidism in older children. With steady treatment, the symptoms of acquired hypothyroidism disappear. During the first year of treatment, however, as your child is adjusting to the medication, you may notice some not-so-favorable changes in personality. Some children have trouble sleeping, develop a short attention span, and become very active. Keep in mind that this will subside once your child's body becomes accustomed to the increase in thyroid hormone.

## Trusting Parental Instincts

Signs and symptoms of hypothyroidism can be even more difficult to detect in children than adults. Claire believes that if she didn't have hypothyroidism, she may have never recognized the problem in her twelve-year-old daughter Tracy. This is her story.

> The first thing I noticed was that every day when Tracy came home after school, she would lie down. I would go into her room to check on her and she would be sound asleep. I thought that was really strange. Normally when she came home from school, she would either do her homework or play on the street with her friends, but now

she just seemed tired and listless all the time. Even if she went up to do her homework, she'd fall asleep on her book.

At the time, she was always freezing. We'd be inside and she'd be shivering. At first, I thought that she's got to have some kind of a bug. For a week or two you think it's a bug, but after that, you know it's not a bug anymore. So I put this together with a few other unusual things I noticed that had been going on. First of all, her hair never grew. She never needed a haircut. Her nails never needed to be trimmed. She also had been gaining weight. We had learned at her last checkup that her cholesterol was sky high. I assumed it was because high cholesterol runs in our family. Even though I have hypothyroidism, it didn't really click right away, but as everything came together, I realized it had to be her thyroid.

We went to her pediatrician, and I told him that I thought she needed a TSH test. He told me she was fine and that there was nothing wrong with her thyroid. He told me that her reflexes were fine, and he said, "I have seen hypothyroidism in children, and this is not it." But I pushed for the test. I know my own daughter and I know when something isn't right. I said, "It's my dime and this is what I want."

He wound up calling me at work, and he said, "I owe you an apology. Your daughter is very hypothyroid. Her TSH is very high, and she must get to an endocrinologist as soon as possible." He told me that I must have recognized it before it started showing in her reflexes. I got her to a pediatric endocrinologist, who turned out to be great. Her symptoms resolved soon after she began taking her medication, her cholesterol came down, and she became herself again.

## Hyperthyroidism in Children

Hyperthyroidism is much less common than hypothyroidism in children. Newborns are not specifically screened for this problem because congenital hyperthyroidism is virtually unheard of unless the baby is born to a mother with a history of Graves' disease—and only 2 percent or less of these babies have the disease. In these instances, transfer of a significant amount of maternal antithyroid antibodies causes the disease. However, it is sometimes diagnosed through the hypothyroid screening program, particularly if the mother has not been treated with antithyroid drugs, which can normalize thyroid hormone levels or make the baby hypothyroid.

Graves' disease is the most common cause of acquired hyperthyroidism, and it typically emerges during adolescence, although about 5 percent of patients are under the age of fifteen. As with adults, solitary toxic adenoma and a toxic multinodular goiter can also cause hyperthyroidism in children, but these causes are rare.

## Congenital Hyperthyroidism

Hyperthyroidism in newborns is very serious and can be fatal if left untreated. Fortunately, it rarely occurs. It can often be detected prenatally through ultrasound, which may show a fetal goiter or an abnormally high heartbeat, called *fetal tachycardia*. A rapid heartbeat may also be detected through the Doppler device your obstetrician uses during your prenatal visits to measure your baby's heartbeat. If you have an overactive thyroid due to Graves' disease, your obstetrician will generally monitor your baby for evidence of hyperthyroidism during gestation and check his or her umbilical cord blood for elevated thyroid hormone levels at delivery. If you are hypothyroid as a result of radioactive iodine treatment or surgery for Graves' disease, your obstetrician or endocrinologist will monitor your thyroid receptor antibodies. Monitoring usually starts around midpregnancy, the point at which antibodies start to cross the placenta and are capable of producing hyperthyroidism in your baby.

Even if hyperthyroidism is present at birth, it may not be noticeable for several days or sometimes weeks. Sometimes congenital hyperthyroidism resolves on its own after six to twelve weeks, but sometimes it persists for longer periods of time. This usually depends on the level of antibodies your baby inherited through placental transfer.

*Signs and Symptoms.* Hyperthyroidism in newborns requires prompt medical attention, so if you notice any of the following signs and symptoms, be sure to let your baby's doctor know immediately.

These features can be quite variable, usually depending on the presence of antithyroid drugs that you may have taken, which can take a few days to clear your baby's system. They are also influenced by the combination of thyroid receptor antibodies that you have transmitted across your placenta to your baby. These antibodies are a combination of stimulators and blockers. (For more on these antibodies, see "Autoimmune Thyroid Disease" in Chapter 5). If there is a significant amount of the blocking antibody in addition to the stimulating antibody, hyperthyroidism may not be evident for weeks. This occurs when the blocking antibody has disappeared but the stimulating antibody lingers.

- **Goiter.** A goiter may emerge after your newborn is discharged from the hospital. However, even then it may not be noticed visually.
- **Failure to gain weight despite high caloric intake.** This typically occurs in babies who are severely affected.
- **Eye changes.** Your baby's eyes may seem to be protruding or look as though they are staring.
- **Cardiovascular problems.** Your baby may have a rapid heartbeat or hypertension.
- **Abnormal behavior.** All newborn babies cry. But a baby with hyperthyroidism may be extremely irritable and cry inconsolably or may appear anxious or wired. With babies, it is sometimes difficult to distinguish between normal and abnormal behavior, so when in doubt call your baby's doctor.
- **Fever.** Your baby's temperature may be elevated.

- **Jaundice.** You may notice a yellowing of your baby's skin and the whites of his or her eyes.
- **Rapid breathing.** Your baby may seem to be breathing too fast.

*Diagnosis and Treatment.* Your baby's doctor will perform a physical examination and order thyroid function blood tests along with tests that measure antibodies. The severity of the condition is often predicted by the amount of thyroid receptor antibodies (TRAb) present. The higher the concentration of these antibodies, the more severe the disease is.

Since the disease can be serious and often fatal in newborns, these babies are treated aggressively with a combination of iodine solution drops and PTU (see "Antithyroid Drugs" in Chapter 3). The iodine drops, which work like antithyroid drugs, work faster than PTU. If your baby is severely thyrotoxic, he or she will need to be hospitalized for several days until his or her condition stabilizes. Once stable, PTU is given for several months until his or her condition remits.

## Graves' Disease (Acquired Hyperthyroidism)

Graves' disease more commonly occurs during childhood than it does in babyhood.

*Signs and Symptoms.* When Graves' disease occurs in older children, typically adolescents, its clinical course is similar to the typical adult experience, but the signs and symptoms may not be as evident as they are in adults. The features are either less pronounced or attributed to emotional or behavioral factors. Still, a child with Graves' disease may experience any of the signs and symptoms of hyperthyroidism listed in Chapter 3. The symptoms usually emerge gradually, over the course of six months to a year. The biggest difference in a child's experience is the disease's effect on growth. Your child may grow faster than usual and may seem tall for his or her age; this may be your first clue that your child is having a problem. If you don't notice the accelerated growth, your pediatrician may when measuring your child's height during a regular checkup. Another sign that parents tend to notice involves behavior. Children with Graves' disease become irritable and excitable and cry easily. Your child may have considerable trouble sleeping and have a short attention span. These behavioral problems may poorly affect your child's school performance, and your child's teacher may be the one who recognizes that something is wrong.

***Diagnosis and Treatment.*** As with babies, your child will undergo a physical examination, blood tests, a radioactive iodine uptake test, and a scan.

Your child has the same treatment options as adults with Graves' disease. However, most pediatric endocrinologists recommend antithyroid medication over thyroid surgery or radioactive iodine. Antithyroid drugs, however, aren't always reliable when it comes to the younger set. While they may provide a temporary solution, only 20 to 30 percent of children treated during puberty and 15 percent of children who are treated before puberty experience long-term remission.

Surgery, due to its risks, is usually a last resort, even with adults, unless there is an obstructive goiter or nodule. The radioactive iodine used to destroy thyroid tissue, I-131, is theoretically riskier in children than adults. It is widely known that children are more vulnerable than adults to thyroid cancer after exposure to I-131 through radioactive fallout. Yet I-131 was first introduced as a treatment for children more than fifty years ago. Since then, follow-up studies on more than one thousand children on whom this therapy has been used reveals no increase in risk for thyroid cancer among these children or genetic abnormalities in their offspring. Studies have also shown that long-term risks of thyroid cancer are lower when the thyroid gland is substantially ablated rather than partially ablated, when residual thyroid tissue remains. However, it is widely believed that larger population studies are needed to definitively rule out the risk that this therapy may pose to children.

When considering a treatment plan, be sure to listen carefully to the doctor's recommendation, yet be sure to discuss the pros and cons of each option with him or her before making a decision. If you opt for radioactive iodine, you will want your child to receive a dose that is high enough to result in hypothyroidism so that the chance of recurrent hyperthyroidism is virtually eliminated. Persistent residual thyroid abnormalities are less likely after larger doses are administered, thereby simplifying follow-up and minimizing concern about the nature of any persistent findings, such as nodules. Dosages vary depending on the size of your child's thyroid gland.

## Nodules and Cancer

While thyroid nodules are common in adults, they are uncommon in children. In a survey of children and adolescents in the southwestern United States, 1.8 percent had palpable nodules. Most nodules in children turn out to be benign, yet anywhere from 15 to 20 percent turn out to be malignant. This means that a child with a nodule is statistically more at risk for cancer than an adult with a nodule, which generally has a 10 percent or so chance of being malignant. This is why nodules in children tend to be treated more aggressively than in adults. Your child's doctor may be inclined toward thyroid surgery unless the nodule is clearly benign.

# Negotiating Life with Thyroid Disease

This chapter outlines your role in overcoming thyroid problems. When it comes to managing your thyroid condition, the most important steps you can take are to find a good doctor who you visit regularly, be thorough in explaining your symptoms, and follow a healthy lifestyle.

## You and Your Doctor

If you suspect that you have thyroid disease or if you aren't feeling right but you don't know what's wrong, it is important to talk with your doctor. But before you do, prepare for your visit by taking some steps that will enable you to take full advantage of the doctor-patient relationship.

### Your Primary Care Doctor

Your primary care doctor is on the front lines. This is the first, and sometimes only, doctor you'll see. Two of the most common complaints that primary care doctors hear are "I'm always tired" and "I'm feeling depressed." This is not much to go on, considering that fatigue can indicate a wide variety of problems or simply that your life is busy, you've been under a lot of stress, and you're not getting enough sleep.

Before you go to your doctor's office, take a good look at what's going on in your life and note anything that strikes you as unusual, as minor as it seems. Remember, with thyroid disease, even symptoms that may sound insignificant, such as excessive thirst or feeling cold all the time, may suggest a thyroid problem.

Here are some other tips that will help you foster a good doctor-patient partnership.

- Be thorough about your family's medical history. Even if you think you know it, you may have some family members that you're unsure of. It may be helpful to make a family tree, list all of the medical conditions your family members have had, and take it to your doctor.
- Before your visit, prepare a list of questions and write down symptoms you may forget to mention.
- If you are diagnosed with thyroid disease, become informed. Ask your doctor for literature on your condition. Read this book and check the Additional Resources at the back of this book to find organizations that can supply information, referrals, and support. After reading about your condition, write down any questions you have and be sure to discuss any concerns with your doctor. Also write down important information your doctor gives you so that you won't forget it after you leave the doctor's office.

## Your Thyroid Specialist

Depending on your condition, you may see several different kinds of specialists over the course of your treatment. But initially, you may be referred to either an endocrinologist or a thyroidologist. A thyroidologist specializes in thyroid disease, but not all endocrinologists do. Many endocrinologists treat mostly people who have diabetes or other disorders of the endocrine system.

Therefore, it may be wise to do a bit of your own homework to find a doctor who specializes in thyroid patients or who sees a significant caseload of thyroid patients. You will want to choose your doctor carefully because thyroid disease requires continual follow-up, so this could be the beginning of a long-term relationship.

For references, start with your primary doctor or with the organizations listed in the Additional Resources at the back of this book to get the names of thyroid specialists in your area. A friend or relative with a thyroid problem may also be a good source.

Once you have some names, call those doctors' offices to verify that the doctor accepts your health insurance. Ask if the endocrinologist is board certified, which indicates that he or she has fulfilled the requirements of the American Board of Internal Medicine to be designated a specialist in the field of endocrinology and metabolism. Find out how many thyroid patients the doctor sees each year versus the number of diabetes patients. If thyroid patients are few, you may want to go elsewhere. You can also get other practical information from this phone call. For instance, if you have a preference about hospitals, be sure to see if this doctor has admitting privileges at that hospital. You could also ask how long it normally takes to get an appointment, what the office hours are, and how long you typically would have to wait to see the doctor.

Once you've settled on a doctor, ask your health insurance company about whether you need a referral. When you visit the specialist, be sure that you fully understand the tests and procedures that the specialist recommends for you. Request literature on the procedures and write down any questions you may have or concerns that you have about them. The more you know, the more active a participant you can be in deciding which therapy is right for you. If, after your questions are answered, you are not convinced that the treatment your doctor recommends is right for you, you can seek a second opinion.

## Your Other Specialists

Your endocrinologist or thyroidologist may recommend that you see one or more of the following specialists.

* **Cardiologist.** If your thyroid disease is causing any problems with your heart, such as abnormal heart rhythms, you may be referred to a cardiologist, a doctor who specializes in treating people with heart problems. A cardiologist may be very involved in your treatment if you are being treated for hyperthyroidism and have a preexisting heart condition or are at risk for heart disease.
* **Ophthalmologist.** An ophthalmologist specializes in eyes; you may be referred to one if you have Graves' eye disease.
* **Nuclear medicine specialist.** If you are being tested with radioactive iodine, you will likely encounter a doctor who specializes in nuclear medicine. This specialist typically administers the radioactive iodine uptake test or radioactive thyroid scan. If you are being treated with radioactive iodine, your endocrinologist will usually administer your treatment, although sometimes a nuclear medicine doctor will handle this treatment.
* **Pediatric endocrinologist.** If your child has a thyroid problem, he or she will be referred to a pediatric endocrinologist, who treats children for a range of endocrine problems.

## Your Surgeon

If you are having a partial or total thyroidectomy, you will need to see a surgeon. Choosing a surgeon carefully is extremely important. Your risk for complications, such as damage to your parathyroid glands or laryngeal nerve, depends on the competency and experience of your surgeon. Choosing an experienced surgeon who specializes in endocrine surgery can significantly improve your odds against these problems.

First off, you'll want to find a surgeon who performs thyroid operations more than occasionally. That means that you'll need to find either a general surgeon who specializes in endocrine surgery or a head and neck surgeon, also known as an otolaryngologist or an ears, nose, and throat (ENT) surgeon, who has special expertise in endocrine surgery. If your child needs surgery, you should look for an endocrine surgeon, a pediatric surgeon, or an ENT surgeon with experience in the surgical management of childhood thyroid disorders.

Your endocrinologist is a good place to start your search, since he or she is likely to recommend someone who meets the criteria outlined below. You may want to ask for more than one name. Another source is the professional organizations listed in the Additional Resources section at the end of this book. Once you have a couple of names, you can call and get some basic information about the doctor over the phone, including the information in the first two bullet points below. At your first appointment with the surgeon, be sure to ask the following.

- **Find out if the surgeon is board certified.** This means that the surgeon has passed rigorous examinations prepared by leaders in their field of expertise. General surgeons are certified by the American Board of Surgery. Otolaryngologists are certified by the American Board of Otolaryngology.
- **Find out how many thyroid operations the surgeon performs each year.** You'll want to be sure the surgeon performs at least twenty-five thyroid or parathyroid operations each year. In addition, you'll want to know what the surgeon's complication rate is—it should be less than 2 percent. Many top-notch, experienced surgeons have a complication rate well under 2 percent. To figure out this rate, ask the surgeon how many procedures he or she has performed in total and how many complications in total have resulted.

- **Talk to the surgeon about the surgical procedure.** Discuss the specifics about what the procedure involves, the risks, why it is recommended, and what your alternatives are. Ask any questions you might have. The surgeon should be willing to answer all of your questions.

- **If you are seeing a general surgeon, ask if he or she is a member of the American Association of Endocrine Surgeons.** A general surgeon must perform a substantial number of thyroid operations each year with excellent outcomes to become a member of this professional organization. While you needn't discount a surgeon because he or she isn't a member, learning that the surgeon is a member is extra assurance that you are in experienced hands.

If you have any concerns about the qualifications of a surgeon, if you are not satisfied with the treatment plan, or if the surgeon seems unwilling to answer your questions, seek a second opinion.

## Taking Care of Yourself

The most important thing to know about living with thyroid disease is that in most cases, you will probably need to take thyroid hormone replacement for the rest of your life. Whether you developed hypothyroidism or were treated for hyperthyroidism or thyroid cancer and became hypothyroid, you'll need to stay on a regimen of daily medication and regular thyroid tests. The good news is that once medication puts your thyroid hormone levels within normal ranges—or your TSH level slightly suppressed if you had thyroid cancer—you are in a sense cured and can go on with your normal life, so long as you continue your medication. You'll also need to guard against any substances that can decrease the effectiveness of your thyroid hormone pills (see Table 2.2). There are also a few other measures you must keep in mind to ensure your optimal health.

## Regular Checkups

If you are taking thyroid hormone medication, you need to have your levels of thyroid hormone checked every month or so in the beginning, until your doctor is satisfied that you are getting the precise dosage of hormone that your body requires. Once your symptoms improve, schedule a visit with your doctor every six to twelve months as your requirements for thyroid hormone might change over time.

If your thyroid hormone medication was recently increased, be sure to tell your doctor if you are experiencing any side effects that may result from too much thyroid hormone, particularly if you feel your heart race or experience any cardiovascular symptoms. Even if you were treated for thyroid cancer or are being treated for a nodule and the goal of your treatment is to suppress your TSH level, your medication needs adjustment if you have any symptoms of hyperthyroidism.

You should also honor regular doctor visits if you have a mild condition that does not require medication, if you have a benign nodule that your endocrinologist wants to watch, or if you are one of the few people who have been successfully treated for an overactive thyroid without becoming hypothyroid. Some people in the latter group do eventually become hypothyroid many years down the road, so it is important to schedule checkups at least once a year.

If you are taking antithyroid drugs and develop any type of infection or even signs of infection, such as a sore throat or fever, stop taking your medicine and tell your endocrinologist, who will want to be sure that your white blood cell count is within the appropriate range.

When you're feeling good and leading a busy life, it's easy to put these checkups low on your list of concerns. But keep in mind that a number of factors can affect your thyroid hormone levels: stress, increasing age, changes in your diet, or pregnancy. You may periodically need an adjustment in your medication.

If you've been treated for thyroid cancer, follow-up tests may include blood tests to measure thyroglobulin in addition to thyroid function tests and various types of imaging procedures.

## Healthy Eating and Exercise

There is no special diet you must follow while you are on thyroid hormone medication, with a couple of exceptions. Avoid foods high in soy protein, which can interfere with the absorption of thyroid hormone. If you are taking antithyroid drugs, your thyroid was not removed or destroyed, and you still have a substantial portion of your thyroid, avoid excessive amounts of iodine, either in medications or supplements, as this could trigger more problems with your thyroid. Most iodine-rich foods, such as iodized products or fish, are acceptable, but you should avoid kelp and other thyroid supplements.

If you were treated for thyroid cancer, you may at times have to "go hypo" in preparation for a follow-up radioactive iodine scan. This means that in addition to following a low-iodine diet, you may have to go off your thyroid medication for several weeks, unless rhTSH is recommended. (See "Recombinant Human Thyrotropin [rhTSH]" in Chapter 8.) If you go off of your medication, you can expect to experience intense symptoms of hypothyroidism, so plan to take it easy. Let your family and friends know what you'll be going through so they can help you with work or home responsibilities during this time.

Aside from the above-mentioned dietary restrictions, you are free to eat whatever you want, but as always, adopting a healthy diet that includes lots of fruits, vegetables, and whole grains is an important part of healthy living.

Eating a nutritious diet not only contributes to the renewed good feeling you experience once your thyroid levels are normal, but it helps your digestive system function smoothly and your heart pump efficiently—both of which support a healthy metabolism. If you still aren't feeling good despite your medication, improving your diet and beginning an exercise program may help. If you were treated for thyroid cancer or hyperthyroidism recently, remember that everyone has a different time frame for feeling better. For instance, some people treated with radioactive iodine feel worse before feeling better. It may be several months before you feel right. It may be even longer before the right dosage of thyroid hormone medication is achieved. If you were treated for thyroid cancer, keep in mind that it can take an entire year before your energy is restored to what it was before you were diagnosed.

The following are some additional tips for healthy living.

- **Eat nutritious foods.** Soft drinks, potato chips, candy, crackers, and other junk foods that are high in calories and low in nutrition have become a mainstay of the American diet. If you normally eat a lot of these foods, minimizing them or cutting them out altogether and replacing them with a variety of fruits, vegetables, and whole-grain foods could make a difference in your overall health.

- **Cut down on "bad" fats.** Certain dietary fats contribute to heart disease and some forms of cancer. The Food and Nutrition Board of the National Academy of Sciences has recommended eating a range of 20 to 35 percent of daily calories from fat of all kinds and reducing saturated fats and trans fats in your diet to a minimum. Saturated fats, which come mainly from animal products, and trans fats, which take the form of hydrogenated oils in manufactured food products, should both be minimized because they raise levels of LDL cholesterol. LDL cholesterol, otherwise known as "bad" cholesterol, can build up in the inner walls of your arteries and form plaque that can clog your arteries.

  Most processed foods and snacks contain trans fats, so you may be consuming them without realizing it. Instead, choose fats that help reduce LDL cholesterol. These include monounsaturated and polyunsaturated fats from vegetable oils and omega-3 fats, which are found in certain kinds of fish. Fats from seeds, nuts, and legumes are also healthy choices.

Carbohydrates, a source of great debate these days, should fall in the range of 45 to 65 percent of your daily calories. Stick with complex carbohydrates, which are found in multigrain foods, fruits, and vegetables, and avoid relying on white starches and sugars. Protein should make up about 10 to 35 percent of your diet. Most people in developed countries get plenty of protein in their diets.

- **Cut down cholesterol.** The American Heart Association recommends limiting dietary cholesterol to no more than 300 mg per day. If your cholesterol levels are high, try to consume no more than 200 mg per day. Sources high in cholesterol include animal fat, eggs, and full-fat dairy products.
- **Increase dietary fiber.** Dietary fiber helps improve digestion. Eating whole-grain foods and a variety of vegetables and fruits helps ensure that you have an ample supply of dietary fiber. The Food and Nutrition Board recommends that men ages fifty years old and younger get 38 grams daily; men over fifty, 30 grams daily; women ages fifty and younger, 25 grams; and women over fifty, 21 grams.
- **Exercise.** People who exercise tend to live longer because exercise increases the heart's pumping ability and the body's oxygen use, which provides extra energy and stamina. It also burns calories and can help keep your weight down. Just walking thirty minutes a day on most days can help prevent heart disease and stroke and promotes general good health.

Putting your health first may seem overwhelming, especially if you have many other responsibilities—such as children to care for, a demanding job, and so on. But most people find that making time to pay attention to their health, preparing healthy meals, and adopting an exercise program is neither as difficult nor as time-consuming as it seems. Maintaining this way of life goes a long way in helping you feel good, even energized, when managing life's daily challenges.

# CHAPTER 11

# Your Thyroid and Nuclear Radiation

As a diagnostic tool and as a treatment for hyperthyroidism and thyroid cancer, radioactive iodine has helped countless people recover from thyroid diseases. Yet, despite its glowing role in modern medicine, exposure to this powerful substance can surreptitiously lead to thyroid cancer. Knowledge of this comes from studies of populations exposed to the isotope I-131 from the accident at the Chernobyl nuclear power plant in the Ukraine during the 1980s and from atomic bomb tests carried out in the United States during the 1950s and 1960s.

In the aftermath of the September 11 terrorist attack on the World Trade Center and the Pentagon, there has been a renewed effort toward disaster planning in the United States. As a result, many states have incorporated the distribution of potassium iodide pills into their plans to respond to any incident involving nuclear power plants within their borders. When taken at the appropriate time, potassium iodide pills can block the radioactive iodine in your system so that it will not enter your thyroid gland.

This chapter explains how radioactive iodine can put healthy thyroid glands in danger and how you can protect yours in the case of a nuclear accident or terrorist attack that releases radioactive iodine into the environment.

## Lessons from Nuclear Disasters

Medical science has learned a good deal about the harmful effects of radioactive iodine by studying nuclear disasters. Here is what is known about populations exposed to its release into the atmosphere.

### The Chernobyl Accident

Radioactive iodine is a by-product of the fission of uranium atoms. One way it is made is through the fission of the uranium that is used to fuel nuclear reactors.

Nuclear reactors are used to produce power or the radioisotopes used in medical diagnosis and treatment. Under normal circumstances, when a reactor is operating, minimal radioactive iodine is released. But in 1986, when an accident at the Chernobyl nuclear power plant led to an explosion, a six-mile-high plume—a radioactive cloud—carried many millions of curies of radioactive iodine into the atmosphere. Shifting winds enabled the material to travel far distances before settling over the earth's surface in surrounding parts of the world as fallout.

Much of what is known about the link between radioactive iodine and thyroid cancer comes from studies of populations following this disaster, considered the worst nuclear accident in history. Although it had long been suspected that radioactive iodine exposure has its worst effect on children, whose developing thyroid cells divide more frequently than those of adults, by the 1990s there was indisputable proof of this.

In 1992, hospitals in the hardest-hit countries—the Ukraine, Belarus, and Russia—were reporting that the incidence of childhood thyroid cancer, an extremely rare cancer in children, was at least ten times higher than normal. According to a U.S. government report, childhood thyroid cancer rates went from .5–3 per million per year to 30–90 per million per year in 1992 in countries where the worst impact was felt. By 2000, about two thousand cases of thyroid cancer were directly attributed to the Chernobyl incident. It is believed that eight to ten thousand more cases will develop within the next ten years among people who were exposed as children.

Researchers believe that most people were exposed through contaminated food and drink, particularly from milk from cows that were contaminated through grazing. When it is consumed, radioactive iodine enters the bloodstream through the digestive process, and it is concentrated in the thyroid gland.

The Chernobyl accident also made it clear that the risk for thyroid cancer decreases with increasing age at the time of exposure and that there is almost no risk to those who were over the age of forty when exposed. The accident also demonstrated that exposure to fallout increases the risk for benign thyroid diseases, including benign nodules and hypothyroidism. Among children, higher TSH levels were found in the geographic areas where there was the highest exposure to fallout; however, the total incidence of hypothyroidism that resulted from such exposure is unknown. Theoretically, hypothyroidism can result from receiving radiation doses high enough to destroy part of the thyroid. Less often, fallout exposure is believed to induce autoimmune thyroid disease by sensitizing lymphocytes to thyroid cells. This can result in hypothyroidism and, very rarely, hyperthyroidism.

## Atomic Bomb Tests

Radioactive iodine is produced when a nuclear weapon is detonated. If you were the target of a nuclear attack and you managed to survive the huge explosion and the direct exposure to radiation, thyroid cancer would be one of many cancers you would be at risk to develop. Studies of populations that survived the atomic bomb attacks in Japan at Hiroshima and Nagasaki during World War II found two- to threefold increases in thyroid and a variety of other cancers. These studies concluded that most cancers, even thyroid cancers, resulted from direct external radiation exposure rather than exposure through ingested radioactive iodine. Studies have also shown that in addition to thyroid cancer, there was a significant increase in solid nodules and autoimmune thyroid diseases among survivors.

In the United States, atomic bomb tests were carried out in secluded, uninhabited areas. Most people who were exposed to radioactive materials were exposed through fallout in contaminated food. Studies have found that tests carried out on the Marshall Islands in the Pacific Ocean and tests in Nevada caused increased exposure to radioactive iodine and increased cancer rates. One test that was more powerful than anticipated at the Marshall Islands caused some inhabitants of the islands to suffer from direct external radiation exposure.

In 1997, the National Cancer Institute (NCI) issued a congressionally mandated report that documents how much I-131 Americans were exposed to from the Nevada tests. According to the report, ninety tests carried out in 1952, 1953, 1955, and 1957 released about 150 million curies of I-131 into the atmosphere. Winds deposited some of this fallout everywhere in the United States. The overall average thyroid dose to 160 million people living in the United States during this time frame was 2 rads—a rad is the amount of radiation absorbed per gram. To compare, the average person in the United States receives an I-131 dose that is the equivalent of 0.1 rad of I-131 each year due to exposure to naturally occurring radioactivity.

The highest exposures to I-131 were documented in parts of Colorado, Idaho, Montana, South Dakota, and Utah. People living in these areas were exposed to anywhere from 9–16 rads. The report states that children, particularly those between the ages of three months and five years, absorbed the highest dose because their thyroid glands were the tiniest; surveys also found that young children were the biggest consumers of milk—the chief source of exposure. The full report, with a breakdown of how much I-131 people were exposed to based on where they lived and their age, is available online. The National Cancer Institute website has an interactive "I-131 Dose/Risk Calculator" that enables you to calculate your risk for thyroid cancer if you believe you were exposed. Contact information for the NCI is listed in the Additional Resources section at the back of this book.

If you worry that you may be at risk for thyroid cancer due to this kind of radiation exposure, keep in mind that just because you were exposed does not mean that you will develop cancer. Even among those exposed to I-131, most do not develop thyroid cancer as a result. Exposure does, however, elevate your risk, and certain other risk factors increase your odds further, including your age at the time of exposure and how many times your thyroid has been exposed to radiation. For instance, as a young child in the 1940s and 1950s, you may have also been exposed to high-dose X-rays, which were commonly used in those days to treat enlarged tonsils, acne, and other problems affecting the head and neck. These treatments were discontinued after doctors began to notice increases in thyroid cancer rates.

If you believe that you were exposed either through fallout or X-ray treatments, be sure to tell your doctor so that he or she will periodically check your thyroid gland.

## Protecting Your Thyroid Gland with Potassium Iodide

Potassium iodide, which goes by the chemical symbol KI, is a salt, similar to table salt. In fact, it is the ingredient added to table salt to make it "iodized." KI is also available in pill form and can protect your thyroid from exposure to I-131 in the event of a nuclear accident.

The way it works is this. You swallow the pill before or within the first few hours after exposure to I-131. KI enters your bloodstream and iodine is concentrated in your thyroid gland. With the appropriate dose, your thyroid is essentially flooded with "safe" iodine. As a result, the harmful radioactive iodine you might inhale or ingest is not taken into your thyroid but rather excreted because your thyroid gland has no room for it. In addition, for some time after taking KI, the safe iodine circulating in your system becomes very high. This markedly reduces the percentage of iodine that may be radioactive. Since your thyroid does not dis-

## Reconciling the Helpful and Harmful Effects of Radioactive Iodine

It may sound more than a bit ironic that a single isotope that is used to cure thyroid cancer can also cause it. But it is believed that most of the radiation exposure involved in both the Chernobyl incident and the atomic bomb tests was due to the iodine isotope I-131, the same isotope sometimes used to treat thyroid cancer and hyperthyroidism.

I-131 is the chief culprit due to its relatively lengthy half-life of eight days. As a result, it was not until at least two weeks after the Chernobyl accident that enough radioactivity either decayed or dispersed to reduce atmospheric radioactive fallout to levels that are considered safe. Other iodine isotopes are also released in nuclear disasters, but they are believed to pose minimal danger because they have significantly shorter half-lives.

Yet in treatment, I-131 effectively destroys overactive or cancerous thyroid cells with minimal risk. This irony hasn't been lost on scientists, particularly with respect to treating hyperthyroidism, which does not result in complete destruction of the thyroid gland, as treatment for thyroid cancer does. You might expect that the

tinguish between safe and radioactive iodine, the small amount of iodine that your thyroid is still able to pick up will be virtually all safe iodine.

In the immediate aftermath of the Chernobyl incident, this strategy apparently worked in Poland, which sits next to Belarus and Ukraine, both countries that have struggled with increased thyroid cancer rates. In Poland, plain iodine in the form of drops or KI pills were administered and apparently protected this population. Follow-up studies showed no increases in thyroid cancer rates. In contrast, populations with high thyroid cancer rates happened to be iodine deficient, which made their exposure even remaining thyroid tissue is vulnerable. Numerous population studies have followed up on patients many years after being treated for hyperthyroidism, and there seems to be no increased risk for thyroid cancer from I-131 treatment. It is believed that the doses used in treatment, which are high enough to cause the destruction and death of thyroid cells, leave only a small population of vulnerable thyroid cells, which do not seem to be at risk for the kind of damage that leads to thyroid cancer.

When used in treatment for thyroid cancer, dosages of I-131 are high enough to cause complete destruction of the thyroid gland. Destroyed cells cannot mutate and divide.

If you are exposed to radiation during an accident, you are not exposed to levels high enough to destroy your thyroid cells, but you may be exposed enough that the DNA in some of your thyroid cells are damaged. The main expected consequence of this kind of radiation exposure is an increased risk for thyroid tumors or hypothyroidism.

riskier. This is because the thyroid glands of those who live in iodine-deficient areas have higher radioactive iodine uptakes than the thyroid glands of those from areas with sufficient iodine intake. As a result, those from iodine-deficient areas pick up more radiaoctive iodine from radioactive fallout when exposed than those populations with sufficient iodine intake (see "Radioactive Iodine Uptake [RAIU] Test" in Chapter 4).

## Who Should Have KI Pills on Hand?

If you live anywhere near a nuclear power plant, it is a good idea to have KI pills available. Depending on how far you live from a power plant, taking the pill is part of an emergency response plan that includes other protective measures such as evacuation, sheltering, and the avoidance of contaminated food and drink.

In the United States, officials from many states that have nuclear reactors within their borders have incorporated the distribution of KI pills in their emergency plans. States have different ways of distributing the pills. Some states predistribute the pills, while others have them on hand at fixed locations, such as schools and other local public centers, to be distributed in the event of an incident at the plant. Most states with KI distribution plans cover everyone who lives within twenty miles of a nuclear plant. The U.S. Nuclear Regulatory Commission (NRC) offers states that have included KI distribution in their response plans free stockpiles of potassium iodine, enough to provide those who live within this distance two pills each.

The issue of distance has become somewhat controversial. The NRC has stressed that evacuation is the most effective protective measure in the event of a nuclear accident or attack, because it protects people's whole bodies, not just their thyroid glands, from the effects of radiation exposure. It cautions against a false sense of security that KI pills may bring. The NRC also says that administering potassium iodide is a reasonable, prudent, and inexpensive supplement to both evacuation and sheltering.

In its literature, the American Thyroid Association points out that thyroid cancer is the only cancer that results from exposure to fallout. It recommends that in addition to evacuation, sheltering, and other response precautions, KI pills be made available to everyone who lives within a 200-mile radius of a plant. The organization is pushing for federal legislation that favors broadening stockpiling.

If you live within a 200-mile radius of a nuclear power plant, and your state doesn't cover you, you may want to consider purchasing KI pills on your own. There are three FDA approved brands of available over-the-counter KI pills. They are IOSAT and Thyro-Block, both available in full adult doses of 130 mg, and Thyrosafe, available in 65-mg strength. See Table 11.1 for dosing

TABLE 11.1 Recommended Dosage of KI for Different Age Groups

| Age group | KI Dosage (mg) | No. of 130 mg KI Tablets | No. of 65 mg KI Tablets | No. of 32 mg KI Tablets |
|---|---|---|---|---|
| Adolescents and adults 12–40 years old* | 130 | 1 | 2 | 4 |
| Pregnant and lactating women | 130 | 1 | 2 | 4 |
| Children 3–11 years old | 65 | ½ | 1 | 2 |
| Infants 1 month to 3 years old | 32 | ¼ | ½ | 1 |
| Newborns (birth to 1 month old) | 16 | ⅛ | ¼ | ½ |

*KI pills are only recommended for those forty years old and younger.
Source: Adapted from National Research Council, "Distribution and Administration of Potassium Iodide in the Event of a Nuclear Accident," National Academy of Sciences, 2004.

information. Your pharmacist may not have KI pills in stock but can probably order them, and they can also be purchased over the Internet. With proper packaging, KI pills have a shelf life of at least five years and possibly as long as eleven years.

## How and When Do I Take KI Pills?

Not every incident at a nuclear plant requires you to take KI, so it should be used under the guidance of local authorities, who can determine whether radioactive iodine isotopes are released during a nuclear event. Only radioactive iodine is harmful to your thyroid, and these pills only protect your thyroid. If radioactive iodine is released, you will be warned by local authorities, who will tell you when to take your first KI pill and how long to keep taking it.

Your first dose should be taken six to twelve hours before exposure to radioactive iodine at the doses suggested in Table 11.1. It can also be taken within the first few hours after exposure. You need only one dose per day. Check with your local authorities to see how many days you should take the pill. Childhood doses vary depending on age. Because there is no liquid suspension form of KI, you may have to crush the pill into liquid, depending on your child's age. The FDA dosage guidelines suggest mixing KI pills with water, low–fat milk (white or chocolate), infant formula, orange juice, or flat sodas.

If you have been exposed to radioactive iodine through fallout, X-ray treatments during the 1940s or 1950s for benign conditions in the region of your head and neck, or external radiation treatment for head and neck cancers, remember that you won't necessarily develop thyroid cancer, but there is a risk of doing so. Be sure to see your doctor annually for a physical exam that includes checking your neck for abnormalities. If a thyroid nodule is discovered, it should be followed up with a fine needle aspiration and a thyroid scan, as outlined in Chapter 7.

As with all thyroid problems, and most health problems in general, paying attention to your health and learning all you can about it can aid in early diagnosis and treatment, which improves your odds for overcoming any thyroid problems you may encounter.

# Glossary

**Acquired.** Describes any disease that was not present at birth.

**Acropachy.** A condition characterized by elevation of the nail beds, swelling in the hands and feet, and sometimes a bulbous enlargement of the fingertips (clubbing).

**Adenoma.** A common benign nodule.

**Anaplastic thyroid cancer.** A rare aggressive form of thyroid cancer.

**Antibodies.** Substances naturally produced in your body that protect it from harmful viruses and bacteria. Antibodies are made by white blood cells called B cells.

**Antigen.** A molecule that causes an immune response.

**Antithyroglobulin (anti–Tg).** Antibodies that attack thyroglobulin and that may contribute to thyroiditis.

**Antithyroid drugs.** A class of drugs that are sometimes prescribed to block the thyroid gland's ability to make thyroid hormone, thus reducing the level of thyroid hormone in the body.

**Antithyroid peroxidase (anti–TPO).** Antibodies most frequently found in people with autoimmune thyroiditis. They work against the enzyme known as thyroid peroxidase.

**Apoptosis.** The body's natural process of orderly and planned cell death to make room for new healthy cells.

**Atherosclerosis.** A condition characterized by narrowed, hardened arteries, which is a precursor to heart disease and stroke.

**Atrial fibrillation.** An unusually rapid, disorganized heart rhythm originating in the heart's upper chambers. It is sometimes a sign of hyperthyroidism, particularly in older people.

**Autoimmune disease.** A disease that occurs when the body's immune system attacks its own tissues, mistakenly perceiving them as foreign.

**Autonomous nodule.** A thyroid nodule that contains active thyroid cells that independently produce thyroid hormone.

**B cells.** A type of lymphocyte, which is a white blood cell that is involved in the body's immune responses. See *Lymphocytes*.

**Beta-blockers.** Drugs used primarily to treat hypertension, angina, and coronary artery disease, but also to relieve heart-related symptoms in patients with hyperthyroidism. Also known as beta adrenergic blocking agents.

**Calcitonin.** A hormone secreted by the thyroid's parafollicular, or C, cells that are separate from the cells that produce thyroid hormone. Although it may act on bones and influence the way kidneys handle calcium, under normal circumstances it has a negligible effect on calcium balance.

**CAT scan.** See *CT (computerized tomography) scan*.

**CT (computerized tomography) scan.** A test that sometimes involves injection of a contrast agent. Afterward, X-rays are sent through the body at different angles to produce computer-generated pictures, showing a cross section of an organ or anatomical area. For patients with thyroid cancer, it is usually used to obtain images of the chest and neck. It should be avoided around the time that radioactive iodine imaging or therapy is being considered or in process because it is often done with contrast material, which contains a substantial amount of iodine that makes imaging and therapy ineffective.

**Clonal expansion.** The rapid duplication of B and T cells upon recognition of their specific antigens; this process generates the voluminous fighting forces of the immune system. See *B cells*, *T cells*.

**Cold nodule.** A nodule that on a thyroid scan concentrates minimal or no radioactive iodine or technetium.

**Congenital.** Describes a condition that is present at birth.

**Congestive heart failure.** A condition that results from decreased blood flow to muscle tissues and organs throughout the body. This ineffective pumping also causes blood to back up into the veins that return blood to the heart. Blood backs up into the lungs, which causes them to become congested with fluid. Hyperthyroidism can precipitate this condition, while hypothyroidism may contribute to it.

**Curie.** A unit of radioactivity. One millicurie is one thousandth of a curie. The term *curie* is being replaced by *becquerel* (1 disintegration per second).

**Cystic nodule.** A nodule that is entirely or mostly filled with fluid.

**Desiccated thyroid pills.** A formula of animal thyroid gland that has been dried and powdered. To *desiccate* means "to dry out."

**Euthyroid.** A term used to describe normal thyroid status.

**Exophthalmos.** Protrusion of the eyeball due to swelling of tissues behind the eyes. This is often seen in Graves' eye disease. See *Proptosis*.

**Fallout.** Radioactive particles that fall from the atmosphere after a nuclear explosion.

**Follicular thyroid cancer.** A common form of thyroid cancer that can be aggressive but is usually slow growing.

**Goiter.** An enlarged thyroid gland that creates a lump protruding from the neck. It is commonly found when the thyroid produces too much or too little thyroid hormone.

**Half-life.** A medical term used to describe the time required for half the amount of a substance to be eliminated. It can be secreted, decayed, or even, in the case of fallout, blown away.

**Hashimoto's thyroiditis.** An autoimmune condition that is the leading cause of hypothyroidism in the United States. Two types of antibodies, antithyroid peroxidase (anti-TPO) and antithyroglobulin (anti-Tg), promote the destruction of thyroid cells, making them unable to produce adequate amounts of thyroid hormone. See *Antithyroid peroxidase* and *Antithyroglobulin*.

**Hot nodule.** An autonomous thyroid nodule that concentrates higher amounts of radioactive iodine on a thyroid scan than normal and that may contribute to or cause hyperthyroidism.

**Hyperthyroidism.** A disease that occurs when the thyroid produces more thyroid hormone than the body needs, thereby abnormally speeding up metabolism.

**Hypoparathyroidism.** A condition that results when the parathyroid glands produce too little parathyroid hormone, which normally regulates calcium levels in the blood. It is sometimes the result of parathyroid gland damage or removal during surgery.

**Hypothalamus.** A section of the brain that releases thyrotropin-releasing hormone (TRH), which stimulates the pituitary gland to produce thyroid-stimulating hormone. This network of communication between the hypothalamus, pituitary, and thyroid glands is referred to as the hypothalamic-pituitary-thyroid axis (HPT axis).

**Hypothyroidism.** A disease that occurs when the thyroid fails to produce enough thyroid hormone to meet the body's needs, thereby slowing metabolism.

**Iodine.** A dietary element found in iodized table salt, seafood, bread, and milk. Your thyroid uses iodine to synthesize thyroid hormone.

**Iodine–123 (I-123).** A weak radioactive isotope of iodine with a mass number 123. It is used as a tracer in radioactive iodine tests. See *Isotope, Radioactive iodine.*

**Iodine–131 (I-131).** A strong radioactive isotope of iodine that has the mass number 131 and a half-life of eight days. It is used to treat hyperthyroidism and thyroid cancer. See *Isotope, Radioactive iodine.*

**Iodize.** To treat with iodine or iodide, which is a kind of salt used to enrich table salt and other food products with iodine.

**Isotope.** One of a number of forms of a single element that are chemically identical that may or may not be radioactive.

**Levothyroxine sodium.** The active ingredient in synthetic thyroxine (T4) pills.

**Liothyronine sodium.** The active ingredient in synthetic triiodothyronine (T3) pills.

**Lymphocytes.** White blood cells that can recognize antigens. The two main classes of lymphocytes are B lymphocytes (B cells) and T lymphocytes (T cells).

**Macrophages.** White blood cells that are members of the phagocyte family. Also known as "big gobblers." See *Phagocytes.*

**Magnetic resonance imaging (MRI).** A procedure in which a patient lies inside a hollow magnetic cylinder while bursts of a magnetic field create superior-quality images of body organs and structures without exposing the patient to radiation. In patients with thyroid cancer, this test is sometimes ordered to image the neck, chest, spine, or other regions where cancer is suspected.

**Major histocompatibility complex (MHC) molecule.** There are two classes of MHC molecules on the surface of each cell. While every cell in the body has one, only dendritic cells have a second one, which is instrumental in signaling danger and stimulating an immune response.

**Medullary thyroid cancer.** A type of thyroid cancer that can be inherited and that occurs in the thyroid's parafollicular cells, which make calcitonin.

**Multinodular goiter.** A goiter that contains more than one lump or nodule. This type of goiter can cause hyperthyroidism if the nodules are actively producing thyroid hormone.

**Myxedema.** A term used to describe clinically severe hypothyroidism or the firm tissue swelling associated with it. It is not to be confused with pretibial myxedema, a skin finding in some patients with Graves' disease. See *Pretibial myxedema.*

**Neonatal.** Of or related to a newborn during the first month of life.

**Nodule.** A lump on the thyroid gland that sometimes contains active thyroid cells that produce thyroid hormone. Most nodules take up less iodine than normal thyroid tissue and make little, if any, thyroid hormone. Therefore 90 percent of thyroid nodules appear "cold," or demonstrate less than normal function, on scans that employ radioactive materials to delineate the thyroid.

**Painless thyroiditis.** A temporary condition that causes the thyroid to leak thyroid hormone into the bloodstream, causing thyrotoxicosis. This is usually followed by a period of hypothyroidism until the condition resolves itself, although the hypothyroidism sometimes becomes permanent. Also known as resolving thyroiditis.

**Papillary thyroid cancer.** The most common type of thyroid cancer, which usually grows slowly.

**Parathyroid glands.** The glands responsible for controlling calcium and influencing bone metabolism. There are usually four glands located behind the thyroid.

**Pathogen.** A disease-causing microbe.

**Peroxidase.** A thyroid enzyme instrumental in synthesizing thyroid hormone.

**Phagocytes.** Cells that can ingest other cells, bacteria, and foreign particles; hence their nickname of "gobblers."

**Pituitary gland.** The "master gland," located at the base of the brain, that controls and regulates the thyroid and other glands throughout the endocrine system.

**Plasma cells.** Cells that result from the clonal expansion of B cells after they have met their specific antigens. See also *B cells*.

**Positive emission tomography (PET) scan.** An imaging test that uses radioactivity to search for cancer metastasis. The scan can show tumors with a high level of metabolic activity. It is used in the diagnosis and management of more aggressive forms of thyroid cancer, typically when thyroglobulin (Tg) blood tests are high but no cancer can be found with a whole-body scan using radioactive iodine. See *Thyroglobulin*.

**Postpartum thyroiditis.** The most common type of resolving thyroiditis, which occurs during the months following pregnancy. It causes the thyroid to leak thyroid hormone, causing thyrotoxicosis. This is usually followed by a period of hypothyroidism until the condition resolves itself, although in some instances the hypothyroidism becomes permanent.

**Potassium iodide (KI).** A salt similar to table salt that is available in pill form and that can protect your thyroid from exposure to nuclear radiation.

**Prenatal.** Before birth.

**Pretibial myxedema.** A thickening of the skin that can occur with Graves' disease but that involves a separate autoimmune attack against the skin, usually around the shins. Also known as Graves' dermopathy.

**Proptosis.** Protrusion of the eyeball due to swelling of tissues behind the eyes. See *Exophthalmos*.

**Rad.** The amount of radiation absorbed per gram of tissue.

**Radioactive iodine.** A radioactive isotope that can be used as a tracer during a radioactive iodine uptake test or a radioactive scan. Much larger amounts are used to treat hyperthyroidism and thyroid cancer. See *Iodine-123, Iodine-131, Isotope*.

**Resolving thyroiditis.** See *Painless thyroiditis, Postpartum thyroiditis*.

**Rheumatoid arthritis.** An inflammatory autoimmune disease that typically attacks the connective tissue of the joints.

**Solitary toxic adenoma.** A single thyroid nodule that is overproducing thyroid hormone, thereby producing hyperthyroidism.

**Subacute thyroiditis.** This viral thyroiditis causes symptoms that may mimic the flu, including fever, muscle aches and pains, and a painful swollen thyroid gland. Also known as de Quervain's thyroiditis. See *Thyroiditis*.

**Subclinical hyperthyroidism.** A condition characterized by a mildly overactive thyroid that may or may not produce symptoms.

**Subclinical hypothyroidism.** A condition characterized by a mildly underactive thyroid that may or may not produce symptoms.

**Tachycardia.** An abnormally fast heart rate that tops 100 beats per minute. It can be a sign of hyperthyroidism.

**T cells.** A family of lymphocytes. Some T cells are part of the first line of defense against pathogens. Memory T cells, for example, sit out the first battle but retain a memory of the pathogen as insurance against future attacks. See *Lymphocytes, Pathogen*.

**Thyroglobulin.** A thyroid protein that stores thyroid hormone.

**Thyroidectomy.** A surgical procedure to remove all or part of the thyroid.

**Thyroiditis.** Inflammation of the thyroid. Types of thyroiditis include Hashimoto's thyroiditis, subacute thyroiditis, and postpartum or painless thyroiditis. See *Hashimoto's thyroiditis, Subacute thyroiditis*.

**Thyrotropin receptor antibodies (TRAb).** Antibodies that attach themselves to the TSH receptor and either stimulate overproduction of or block production of thyroid hormone. These are most frequently seen in Graves' disease.

**Thyroid-stimulating hormone (TSH).** A hormone secreted into the bloodstream by the pituitary gland that stimulates the thyroid gland. The amount of hormone produced by the thyroid gland depends on how much TSH is in the blood. Doctors measure levels of TSH to determine whether a person's thyroid hormone levels are normal. Also called thyrotropin.

**Thyrotoxicosis.** The presence of too much thyroid hormone in the body. This may be caused by an overproductive thyroid, by inflammation of the thyroid, or by taking too much thyroid hormone. This term is often used interchangeably with hyperthyroidism.

**Thyrotropin.** See *Thyroid-stimulating hormone.*

**Thyrotropin receptor (TSH receptor).** A protein complex located on the surface of thyroid cells that receives TSH signals from the pituitary gland.

**Thyroxine (T4).** One of two types of major thyroid hormone manufactured by the thyroid gland. It contains four iodine atoms.

**Thyroxine-binding globulin (TBG).** The principal thyroid hormone-binding protein. When bound to this protein, thyroid hormone is not available for use by your cells.

**Toxic multinodular goiter.** An enlarged thyroid gland with nodules that produce excess thyroid hormone and that causes hyperthyroidism. This type of goiter is to blame for hyperthyroidism in many people over sixty.

**Triiodothyronine (T3).** One of two types of major thyroid hormone manufactured by the thyroid gland. Outside the thyroid gland, the liver and other organs convert T4 to T3. See *Thyroxine.*

# Additional Resources

## Organizations

American Association of Clinical Endocrinologists (AACE)
1000 Riverside Avenue, Suite 205
Jacksonville, FL 32204
Phone: 904-353-7878
Fax: 904-353-8185
E-mail: info@aace.com

AACE is a professional medical organization devoted to enhancing clinical endocrinology and improving medical care for patients. Part of its mission is to educate patients about endocrine disorders such as thyroid diseases, and it offers referral services for finding specialists.

American Association of Endocrine Surgeons
University of Calgary, Foothills Medical Center
Department of Surgery
1403 29 Street NW
Room 1014, North Tower
Calgary, AB T2N 2T9
Canada
Phone: 403-944-2491
Fax: 403-283-4130
Website: endocrinesurgery.org

American Thyroid Association
6066 Leesburg Pike, Suite 650
Falls Church, VA 22041
Phone: 800-THYROID (800-849-7643, toll-free)
E-mail: admin@thyroid.org
Website: thyroid.org

This professional society includes nine hundred U.S. and international physicians and scientists who specialize in the research and treatment of thyroid diseases. The group promotes research, patient care, and the education of patients, the public, and the medical and scientific communities. It operates a referral service, and its website offers extensive patient information.

Endocrine Society
8401 Connecticut Avenue, Suite 900
Chevy Chase, MD 20815
Phone: 301-941-0200
E-mail: endostaff@endo-society.org
Website: endo-society.org

This professional organization of endocrinologists promotes research and clinical advancements in endocrinology and metabolism. The society provides names of specialists and information for patients.

National Cancer Institute (NCI)
NCI Public Inquiries Office
6116 Executive Boulevard, Room 3036A
Bethesda, MD 20892-8322
Phone: 1-800-4-CANCER
Website: cancer.gov or cancer.gov/I131

The NCI is part of the U.S. National Institutes of Health. It funds cancer research and serves as an information clearinghouse for cancer patients. Its website has many pages devoted to thyroid cancer along with detailed information and resources for Americans exposed to radioactive iodine through fallout from above-ground nuclear testing.

Thyroid Cancer Survivors' Association (ThyCa)
P.O. Box 1545
New York, NY 10159-1545
Phone: 877-588-7904 (toll-free)
Fax: 630-604-6078
E-mail: thyca@thyca.org
Website: thyca.org

ThyCa is an all-volunteer, nonprofit organization of thyroid cancer survivors, family members, and health-care professionals. The group maintains current information about thyroid cancer and offers support services available to people at any stage of testing, treatment, or lifelong monitoring for thyroid cancer. On its website, the group offers a free low-iodine cookbook.

Thyroid Foundation of America
1 Longfellow Place, Suite 1518
Boston, MA 02114
Phone: 800-832-8321 (toll-free)
E-mail: info@allthyroid.org
Website: allthyroid.org

The foundation provides patients with information on thyroid illnesses through its website, e-mail update service, newsletters, and a free telephone service for patients.

## Recommended Books

Rubenfeld, Sheldon. *Could It Be My Thyroid?* New York: M. Evans, 2004.
Van Nostrand, Douglass, Gary Bloom, and Leonard Wartofsky. *Thyroid Cancer: A Guide for Patients.* Baltimore, MD: Keystone Press, 2004.

Wood, Lawrence C., David S. Cooper, and E. Chester Ridgeway. *Your Thyroid: A Home Reference.* New York: Ballantine, 1995.

## Recommended Medical Text

Braverman, Lewis E., and Robert D. Utiger. *Werner and Ingbar's The Thyroid: A Fundamental and Clinical Text.* 8th ed. Philadelphia: Lippincott Williams & Wilkins, 2000.

# Index

237

Diet
healthy eating, 212–14
low-iodine, 171–72
as risk factor, 14–16
Doctors
cardiologist, 208
endocrinologist, 32–33, 35, 60–61, 206
nuclear medicine specialist, 208
ophthalmologist, 103, 208
pathologist, 142
pediatric endocrinologist, 189, 198, 202, 208
primary care, 32, 60, 205–6
surgeon, 208–10
thyroid specialist, 33, 206–7
Drug interactions, 44
Drugs. See Medications
Dry skin, 26, 51, 125

Ectopic thyroid, 187, 193
Elderly people
Graves' disease in, 99
hyperthyroidism in, 52–53, 56–57
hypothyroidism in, 27–29
Endocrinologists, 32–33, 35, 60–61, 206
Estrogen, 10–11, 56
Estrogen therapy, 38, 44, 48
Ethnicity, 12
Euthyroid, 63
Euthyroid Graves' (eye) disease, 99
Exercise, 48, 49, 214
Exophthalmos, 101, 102
Eye disease, thyroid
description of, 9, 99–102
smoking and, 18, 98
symptoms of, 55, 102–3
treatment for, 103–4

Family history
doctor visit and, 206
Florence's story, 112–15
as risk factor, 13–14, 83–84
Fatigue/exhaustion, 21, 25, 54
Fetal tachycardia, 199
Fine needle aspiration (FNA)
description of, 134, 138, 139, 141–48
for thyroid cancer diagnosis, 159–60, 161
Fingernails, brittle, 26
Fingertips, enlarged, 105
Follicular thyroid cancer, 161–62
Food, Drug and Cosmetic Act of 1938, 39
Free T4 (FT4) test, 75–76. See also Thyroid tests

Free T3 (FT3) test, 75, 76
Free T3 index, 75, 77

Gender
Hashimoto's thyroiditis and, 93–94
as risk factor, 10–11
thyroid cancer and, 141, 159
Generic thyroid drugs, 41–42
Gestational transient thyrotoxicosis (GTT), 129–30
Goiter Belt, 15
Goiters
defined, 5, 8, 26
iodine deficiency and, 14–15
in newborns, 200
pregnancy and, 134, 196
thyroid disorders and, 6
Goitrogens, 15
Graves, Robert, 58
Graves' dermopathy, 100, 104–5
Graves' disease
age and, 52
antithyroid drugs for, 66–68
as autoimmune disease, 97–99
in children, 201–3
defined, 6, 9, 58
estrogen and, 11
eye problems, 65–66, 99–104, 105
Jerry's story, 69–72
pernicious anemia and, 111
pregnancy and, 129–34
skin problems, 100, 104–5
smoking and, 18, 98
Graves' eye disease
description of, 9, 99–102
smoking and, 18, 98
symptoms of, 55, 102–3
treatment for, 103–4

Hair loss, 26, 33
Hand tremors, 55, 56, 132
Hashimoto, Hakaru, 93
Hashimoto's thyroiditis
age and, 11
as autoimmune disease, 90
in children, 196–97
description of, 5–7, 92–94
estrogen and, 11, 94
family history of, 13–14
goiter from, 37, 94
iodine and, 16
pernicious anemia and, 111
pregnancy and, 123
thyroid lymphoma and, 164–65
treatment for, 94